THE CLINIC OF DISABILITY

D1695860

THE CLINIC OF DISABILITY

Psychoanalytical Approaches

edited by

*Simone Korff Sausse and
Régine Scelles*

First published in 2017 by
Karnac Books Ltd
118 Finchley Road, London NW3 5HT

British Library Cataloguing in Publication Data

A C.I.P. for this book is available from the British Library

ISBN 978 1 78220 445 9

Edited, designed and produced by The Studio Publishing Services Ltd
www.publishingservicesuk.co.uk
email: studio@publishingservicesuk.co.uk

Printed in Great Britain

www.karnacbooks.com

CONTENTS

ABOUT THE EDITORS AND CONTRIBUTORS

Pierre Ancet is a graduate of the Ecole Normale Supérieure de Fontenay Saint-Cloud and Doctor of Philosophy (ethics and philosophy of sciences). He taught philosophy and psychology at the University of Toulouse-Jean Jaurès for six years before becoming lecturer in philosophy at the University of Burgundy in 2006 and researcher at the Centre Georges Chevrier (CNRS – University of Burgundy Joint Research Centre). He also acts as Director of the University for All, Burgundy, and is Vice-President Delegate for Cultural Policies at that University. He has published many works, either alone or in collaboration, on philosophical and disability related themes, especially in situations of caring between disabled adults and professionals.

Albert Ciccone is a psychologist, psychoanalyst, and Professor of Psychopathology and Clinical Psychology at the University Lumière-Lyon 2. He is founder and President of ALPACE (Association Lyonnaise pour une Psychanalyse À partir de la Clinique de l'Enfant). He is a trainer member of CPGF (Collège de Psychanalyse Groupale et Familiale) and FFPPEA (Fédération Française de Psychothérapie Psychanalytique pour l'Enfant et l'Adolescent), a member of the EFPP (European Federation for Psychoanalytic Psychotherapy), and the

AIPCF (Association Internationale de Psychanalyse de Couple et de Famille). He is a founding member of SIICHLA.

Charles Gardou is an anthropologist, professor at the University Lumière Lyon 2, and lecturer at the Institut de Sciences Politiques in Paris. Charles Gardou conducts research into human diversity and vulnerability, and their multiple expressions. He has published twenty works with Editions Érès, where he created and directed the "Knowledge of Diversity" Collection including the titles *La société inclusive, parlons-en*, *Fragments sur le handicap et la vulnérabilité*, and *Pascal, Frida Kahlo et les autres*, as also *Quand la vulnérabilité devient force*, and a trilogy sub-titled *Variations anthropologiques*.

Marcela Gargiulo, PhD, is a clinical psychologist and lecturer and researcher at the Clinical Psychology, Psychopathology and Psycho-analysis Research Laboratory (EA 4056), Paris Descartes University. Since 1992, she has worked at the Institute of Myology and the Genetics Department of the Pitié-Salpêtrière Hospital, where she is head of the psychology team, providing psychological consultation to patients suffering from genetic diseases. Her main research interests lie at the crossroads between clinical psychology, psychoanalysis, and ethics. She is a founding member of SIICHLA.

Simone Korff Sausse is a psychologist–psychoanalyst, member of the Société Psychanalytique de Paris and Emeritus Lecturer at the Psychoanalytical Studies Faculty at the University Denis Diderot, Paris 7. She has conducted studies into the psychoanalytical approach in care for disabled children and their families, then into the creative process in artists. She is a founding member of SIICHLA (Séminaire Universitaire International sur la Clinique du Handicap).

Sylvain Missonnier has university training in philosophy, psychol-ogy and psychoanalysis. He is especially interested in early preven-tion and has worked in maternity units, with very young children in paediatrics, and in medical and psychological centres. He is Professor of Clinical Psychology at the University Paris Descartes, attached to the Clinical Psychology, Psychopathology and Psycho-analysis Research Laboratory (PCPP EA 4056). He is a psychoanalyst and a full member of the Société Psychanalytique de Paris, Co-President of IVSO (Institut du Virtuel Seine Ouest) and former

President of the French group of the World Association for Infant Mental Health www.psynem.org/Hebergement/Waimh_France (WAIMH France). He is also a founding member of the scientific committee and editorial board of the monthly review *Le Carnet Psy* and webmaster of its website. He is a founding member of SIICHLA.

Roger Salbreux is a child psychiatrist in Paris. He has worked in the field of disability, mainly on the topic of those with intellectual deficiencies, and the psychopathology of children suffering from epilepsy and cerebral palsy. He was behind the creation of research associations in these fields and directed the first large-scale epidemiological survey on early childhood disabilities. Having observed that detection of such situations was occurring too late, he contributed significantly to the creation of early medico-social action centres (CAMSP). He is a member of the National Disability Consultation Council and of the editorial committee of the review *Contraste*. He has written many articles on prevention in the field of disability and is a founding member of SIICHLA.

George Saulus is a psychiatrist having followed a postgraduate course in philosophy. For many years, he has worked as a physician and psychiatrist with severely disabled children, adolescents, and adults, their families, and teams of professionals. He specialises in questions relating to the epistemology of psychopathology. He also works on institutional dynamics and has published many articles on the ethics relating to situations of severe disability.

Régine Scelles is Professor of Clinical Psychology and Psychopathology at the University of Paris West Nanterre la Défense. She works in a department providing early help to disabled children and has considerable experience working in disabled people's own domestic environments. She has conducted research into the family and, more specifically, siblings, adolescents, and adults facing disability. She has published works on the family and multiple disabilities and is a founding member of SIICHLA.

Henri-Jacques Stiker is Director of Research (historical anthropology of infirmity) at the Identités, Cultures, Territoires Laboratory, University Denis Diderot, Paris VII. He was guest lecturer for three years at EHESS (École des Hautes Études en Sciences Sociales) for three years (1996–1999) and also taught disability studies in the USA for three years (1999–2001). He is senior editor of the review *ALTER*, the *European Journal of Disability Research* (published by Elsevier-Masson). He has many publications to his name on the history of disability, art and disability, and fundamental works on anthropology and disability.

Denis Vaginay is a Doctor of Clinical Psychology and works both in specialised institutions and in private practice as a clinician and trainer. He has conducted and published research works on mental disability, especially on psycho-affective development and sexuality and also on interactions between social groups and the intellectually deficient subject when identity and sexuality come into play.

Introduction

Valerie Sinason

Over the past fifty years, there has been an international transformation in the understanding of intellectual disability. Children and adults deemed ineducable, unworthy of democratic life and experiences, confined to appalling modern-day "oubliettes", hidden away in hospitals, silos and isolated rural areas have slowly regained and expressed their personhood and started to enter community life and consciousness. This progress is slow, uneasy, and fraught with discomfort. It can be set back at any moment due to war, economic problems, or fears of national and personal identity. The meaning of difference and human identity exercises every country and there is a deep reluctance to include all facets of the human condition as well as fear. However, the increased awareness of social handicapping processes, stigma, abuse, and poverty has aided this slow but inspiring development.

Psychoanalysts have played a significant direct part in this as well as through the applications other professions have made of psychoanalytic thinking. In the past quarter century, Dr Johan de Groef (1999), a Belgian psychoanalyst and former medical director of Zonnelied, a residential centre for adults with an intellectual disability, took the lead in gathering European colleagues together. At different times, Dietmut

Niedecken, Evelyn Heinemann, and Christian Gaedt (1995, 2001) came from Germany, Brett Kahr, Judith Usiskin, and I came from the UK, Johan de Groef and Joost Demuynck came from Belgium, and Claude Boukobza, Colette M. Assouly-Piquet, Cecile Herrou, Claire Morelle, Monique Schneider, Regine Scelles, and Simone Korff Sausse came from France. Through these connections came links with South Africa (Professor Leslie Swartz) and America (Richard Ruth).

What we all shared was a passionate commitment to this work and a realisation that there should be access to psychotherapy for children and adults with a disability. We all accepted that disability involved processing chronic loss, trauma, and mourning (Frankish, 1989a,b; Hollins, 2000; Korff Sausse, 1996; Sinason, 1994) that, despite improved conditions, was an internal and external hurdle to be dealt with. We agreed that mortality, loss, sexuality, and dependency became key issues in negotiating disability (Blackman, 2003; Hollins & Sinason, 2001; Korff Sausse, 1996; Niedecken, 2003) We also all agreed, and continue to agree, that children and adults with disabilities could make use of psychoanalytic treatments (Beail et al., 2005; Corbett et al., 1996; Frankish, 1989a,b; Gaedt, 1995). In my own work, I examined the way the concrete organic impairment was dealt with defensively by the creation of a secondary handicap in which there was an exacerbation of symptoms in order to hide the shame of feeling different (Sinason, 1994).

In gathering together psychoanalysts and psychologists across Europe and holding regular shared meetings, it became apparent that there was a far larger number of interested French colleagues than from other countries. We all found this hard to make sense of initially.

Was there a generational transmission of the principles of the French revolution? Could it be that the rights of the disabled to *egalité* were more intellectually and emotionally ingrained? Did this fuse with the brilliance of Maud Mannoni, who died at the age of seventy-five in Paris (15 March 1998) and brought concerns of disability to Lacan and the French psychoanalytic movement?

Maude Mannoni was born in Belgium, spent some of her childhood in Ceylon, studied criminology, but then became a psychoanalyst, the first to be appointed by the Belgian Society. One of her training cases was a child with an intellectual disability, a topic usually excluded from analytic thinking. Her important link to France came first from her significant encounters with the "French

Winnicott", François Dolto, and then her psychoanalyst, Jacques Lacan. Her famous book, *L'enfant arriéré et sa mère* (The Backward Child and His Mother) (1964), was praised by Lacan in his lectures (1994, p. 238) and meant that the significant interest in Lacan and his thinking in France was expanded intellectually and philosophically to include thinking about intellectual disability, even if it did not include treatment.

In 1996, when de Groef brought us all together for a three-day conference, we were all thrilled to be told he had a message from Mannoni, which was published in his book. Her question (de Groef, 1999, p. 6) was "about their claim for the right to be *different*. How can we give them the means to live without requiring that they be socially rehabilitated?" Mannoni would have loved British author Jeanette Winterson's seminal autobiography with its magnificent title, *Why Be Happy When You Could Be Normal?* (Winterson, 2012)

Mannoni was profoundly affected by her multi-cultural experiences and the way she gained or lost languages according to what was expected her. This capacity to understand the meaning of words and communications from her own lived experience fitted with Lacan's interest in language and the meaning of speech for the disempowered.

However, within the last two decades, the French beacon for theory and practice has come from the wonderful collaboration between two women professors, Simone Korff Sausse and Regine Scelles. Korff Sausse is a psychoanalyst and doctor of clinical psychology who has been a professor at the University of Paris VII, and Scelles is a professor at Rouen University, and a director of dialogue. She is a founder member of the Seminaire Inter-universitaire International sur la Clinique du Handicap (SILCHA), and the remarkable spread of disability research and interest in French universities comes from this.

As an English psychoanalyst who has been working in this field for over three decades, I have been amazed at the level of interest in, and the depth of knowledge held within, SILCHA. To see hundreds of psychology, psychotherapy, philosophy, anthropology students and professionals attend SILCHA meetings when the theme is disability and psychoanalysis or applied psychoanalysis is truly to experience a cultural difference. It is the owning of this subject within the university system that is so remarkably different. While there have been universities in the UK that developed a significant expertise because of the influence of key figures (Professors Joan Bicknell and Sheila Hollins at St Georges, Professor Nigel Beaill at Leeds), SILCHA represents a major inter-university powerhouse of thought and research.

Language is not only a crucial issue in working with the disempowered; it links to the politics of publishing. Whose voice is communicated where? It is only recently that I have been able to read the work of Dolto, for example. English audiences are largely monolingual as we have the luxury of knowing that, partly because of America and Australia and the history of the Commonwealth, our language is spoken in many countries. Scandinavian professionals know they have to publish in English to gain an international reputation, as few English speakers are proficient in their languages. Although French is popular as a second language in UK schools, it is rarely of a level that enables access to academic books. Therefore, we have to be grateful to our French colleagues for translating their work themselves, and to Karnac for deciding to provide access to this thinking.

English readers accessing this book are gaining many privileges. It not only allows us to be educated in major advances in this field by the writers of this book, but it is also a chance to appreciate the intellectual, philosophical, and psychoanalytical thinking that can happen when a culture has been established which welcomes such thought.

While there have been individual edited books published in the UK by psychoanalytic psychotherapists (e.g., Simpson & Miller, 2004), they have needed to educate a therapeutic audience unused to dealing with loss, trauma, abuse, and delinquency when combined with case material derived from children and adults with intellectual disabilities. Owing to the lack of emotional understanding on this subject, most have needed to include a psychoeducational role, focusing our analytic or applied analytic thinking on key points in order to establish baselines. Corbett (2015) might be pointing to the UK future in that, in writing for an already specialised forensic audience, he is able to let his thinking soar.

This, therefore, is a book I would like to have written, which now I do not have to write!

I do not mean this in an imitative way. Not being philosophically trained or brought up in French intellectual and clinical culture, I found issues in this book that were a feast to me and a source of further inspiration and curiosity which I have not, and would not have, written about or thought about before. What I mean is that this book takes certain concepts for granted and can, therefore, proudly and profoundly activate or sustain a high level of thinking. For example, I and others in the UK have written briefly about the way parents who have a child with a disability can feel injured over their procreative process and feel that their masculinity or femaleness is damaged in some way. Here, such a theme is taken further and expanded by useful questions that invite dialogue.

For example, Pierre Ancet, lecturer in philosophy at Dijon University, starts the first chapter, "Virility, masculine identity, and disability" with the question "What exactly is masculinity, when not equated with virility?" Instead of a few lines, a substantial chapter unpacks this painful and crucial subject, helpfully accompanied by something reminiscent of a Socratic dialogue.

And so it continues. There are eleven chapters written by key influential thinkers and practitioners.

Dr Albert Ciccone, psychoanalyst at Lumiere-Lyon University, looks at the bond and psychic transmission created by disability. Dr Charles Gardou, anthropologist from Lyon University, looks at the cultural interpretations of disability. Dr Marcela Gargiulo, lecturer in the Laboratory of Clinical Psychology and Psychopathology, Paris Descartes University, examines genetic science and the impact of testing and diagnosis. Professor Korff Sausse provides a detailed psychoanalytic approach to disability. Dr Roger Salbreux, a child psychiatrist, looks at the normality of the abnormal and interrogates that paradox. Professor Régine Scelles focuses on the theme of talking about disability to children and aiding children to talk about it. She looks at the emotional hurdles that have to be overcome in dealing with this. Jacques Henri Sticker, from Diderot University's department of Identity, Culture and Territory, provides a historical account of major periods in the history of disability. Dr Sylvain Missonnier, from the University of Paris Descartes, looks at prenatal diagnosis, and legal and professional issues. Dr Georges Saulus, psychiatrist and philosopher, raises the ethical issues connected to severe disability—"Your child is a vegetable"—while Denis Vaginay concludes with an examination of adolescence and disability.

Each chapter has a significant amount of useful references, many of which will be new to a UK/English-speaking readership. There might be some initial narcissistic twinges that some ideas that have been accepted in the UK are not referenced and that the main UK-known references are the major psychoanalysts (Freud, Klein, Winnicott), rather than disability therapists. However, the politics of translation go both ways. Our work has not been translated into French and SILCHA's work has not been translated into English. Korff Sausse is one of the few French thinkers on this subject, outside of Mannoni, whose work has been published in English. However, there then comes the pleasure in consensus, in realising that thinkers from another culture working with similar populations have come to the same conclusions. Moreover, even when there are shared ideas, the ways of expressing them are different and the theories used are different, even if overlapping.

In reading this book, I also experienced an unexpected pleasure in thinking about the English language. There were English words I read which I did not recognise and, on looking them up in a dictionary, found they were correct. In trying to find appropriate words for French words that are unique the translators have enlarged our knowledge of language.

So, instead of *"le miroir brisé"*, or the small national mirror, we find a whole mirror of our French twin, who, with commitment, passion, and rigour, actively reflects back, validating our impressions and appearance and enlarging our perspective. This is a seminal piece of work that is essential for all the multi-disciplinary groups working with disability.

References

Beail, N., Warden, S., Morsley, K., & Newman, D. (2005). Naturalistic evaluation of the effectiveness of psychodynamic psychotherapy with adults with intellectual disabilities. *Journal of Applied Research in Intellectual Disabilities, 18*(3): 245–251.

Blackman, N. (2003). *Loss and People with Learning Disabilities*. London: Jessica Kingsley.

Corbett, A. (2015). *Disabling Perversions*. London: Karnac.

Corbett, A., Cottis, T., & Morris, S. (1996). *Witnessing, Nurturing, Protesting: Therapeutic Responses to Sexual Abuse of People with Learning Disabilities*. London: David Fulton.

De Groef, J. (1999). *Psychoanalysis and Mental Handicap*. London: Karnac.

Frankish, P. (1989a). Childhood repeated. In: D. Brandon (Ed.), *Mutual Respect: Therapeutic Approaches in Working with People who have Learning Difficulties* (pp. 65–75). Surbiton: Good Impressions.

Frankish, P. (1989b). Meeting the emotional needs of handicapped people: a psychodynamic approach. *Journal of Mental Deficiency Research, 33*: 407–414.

Gaedt, C. (1995). Psychotherapeutic approaches in the treatment of mental illness and behavioural disorders in mentally retarded people: the significance of a psychoanalytic perspective. *Journal of Intellectual Disabilities Research, 30*: 233–239.

Gaedt, C. (2001). Psychodynamically oriented psychotherapy in mentally retarded children. In: A. Došen & K. Day (Eds.), *Treating Mental Illness and Behaviour Disorders in Children and Adults with Mental Retardation* (pp. 401–414). Washington, DC: American Psychiatric Press.

Hollins, S. (2000). Developmental psychiatry, insights from learning disability. *British Journal of Psychiatry, 177*(3): 201–206.

Hollins, S., & Sinason, V. (2001). Psychotherapy, learning disabilities and trauma: new perspectives. *British Journal of Psychiatry, 176*: 32–36.

Korff Sausse, S. (1996). *Le miroir brisé: l'enfant handicapé, sa famille et le psychanalyste*. Paris: Calmann-Lévy.

Lacan, J. (1994). *The Four Fundamental Concepts of Psycho-analysis*. London: Penguin.

Mannoni, M. (1964). *L'enfant arriéré et sa mère*. Paris: Seuil.

Niedecken, D. (2003). *Nameless. Understanding Learning Disability*. London: Brunner-Routledge.

Simpson, D., & Miller, D. (2004). *Unexpected Gains: Psychotherapy with People with Learning Disabilities*. London: Karnac.

Sinason, V. (1994). *Mental Handicap and the Human Condition*. London: Free Association.

Winterson, J. (2012). *Why Be Happy When You Could Be Normal?* London: Vintage.

CHAPTER ONE

Virility, masculine identity, and disability

Pierre Ancet

Introduction: virility and masculinity

What exactly is masculinity, when not confused with virility? Can one be manly without being virile, or should the very image of virility be revised in order to integrate it within new forms of masculinity? These questions are not anodyne, since they relate to sexual identity, a part of identity that is socially constructed in a deployment of sexuality. Masculinity–virility intervenes therein not in the sense of sex, as a descriptive concept ("a male individual"), but in the sense of gender ("a real man"), which is an evaluative and prescriptive notion: "being a man" means having to show muscle power, strength, daring, or even aggressiveness. These characteristics, to which must be added genital potency, are traditionally attributed to the male. Virility places individual masculine identity within the dimension of social gender and its attributes. This issue can thus be seen to affect all men, not just physically disabled man, supposedly devoid of virility. Many men would like to correspond to the virile heterosexual ideal of the dominant male, but many of them must content themselves with being merely male individuals. Each man will probably admit that he possesses only some of the

1

characteristics of virility. How then could such relative virility be denied to men with disabilities? Is it not possible to play a masculine role (e.g., sexually or in the workplace) without having the stereotypical attributes of virility? Are not modern-day fathers themselves far removed from the traditional image of the father (Korff Sausse, 2009), in a masculine role that is, therefore, also accessible to a disabled man?

Virility, rivalry, and seduction

It would be easier to put virile values into perspective if they were not so strongly associated with domination: domination over a female partner, but, above all, supremacy over male competitors. Virility is created in and by rivalry, for which the mere love of a woman (whether mother or lover) cannot compensate. The feeling of being virile is largely linked to self-confidence, as a man among men. The foils of virility, such as "doddering old man", "the disabled man", or "the gay man/the queer" can never be seen as competition, but each in a different way. Their only link is to be perceived as being beneath any conceivable form of rivalry. Such individuals are attributed the position of neutered males, not as asexual beings, but, rather, as emasculated by their supposed weakness.

The fact still remains that heterosexual virility can also be tested through female desire, and that such desire may focus on someone theoretically excluded from male rivalry. The disabled man can prove himself there, *just as any other man may*, by such qualities as steadfastness, temperance, the ability to listen, and might perhaps succeed *even better than many men*, in terms of being attentive to his partner.

When questioned about representations of virility, Zig Blanquer, a consultant and trainer with a degenerative illness that has slowly caused him to become quadriplegic, remarked that most disabled men whose muscular capacity is impaired do not have deep voices,

> but rather a quiet, almost inaudible, even reedy, voice. Because of this, we tend to focus more on the eyes, on visual communication, which is not generally a male strong point (the male gaze is more circular, more sweeping, whereas the female gaze is more settled, more focused).

> Similarly, the male body must be fully present, with a presence which resolutely occupies space, whether through posture or gesture. A man

will often sit on a sofa and spread out his arms and legs, thus occupying more space. We lack the opportunity to occupy space in this way, confined as we are to our wheelchairs. It seems to me that this particular spatial concentration of disabled men, their way of not "gesticulating" in space allows them to acquire instead an acute consciousness of space, paying great attention to others. (Personal interview)

The perception *of* space and the perception of others *in* space become particularly acute. The motionless body fills this space with intensity, through the face and the eyes. The gaze can be a way of touching other people, a form of contact in its own right for someone who can neither caress with his own hand nor draw nearer with his own body. Many men with disabilities have developed this capacity to caress with their eyes and with their smile, a quality that is often overlooked in masculine seduction, yet is essential to it.[1] The discussions I have had on this subject with Marcel Nuss are extremely revealing: his considerable disability (quadriplegia related to infantile spinal muscular atrophy) does not undermine his potential for seduction, or women's perception of his virility.[2] Indeed, the strength of character, the determination, courage, and certainty of creating desire and giving pleasure that fall within the definition of manhood may very well exist in the *absence* of muscle power. Virility also involves assertiveness, which is not only the fact of imposing oneself on others: regarding sexuality, says Marcel Nuss,

> everything depends on your attentiveness, your way of being present and open with your partner, not on your way of doing things. No physical ability is required in order to give and receive, rather than merely take and wait. And such giving and receiving can be completely successful, whatever the disability. Whatever the circumstances, everything is a matter of attention and intention, not of what passes for performance. (Ancet & Nuss, 2012, p. 74, translated for this edition)

The "feminine"[3] perception of virility must, therefore, involve greater attention to the qualities of presence, commitment, and sensitivity than a "masculine" viewpoint could foresee, even in the domain of seduction, where norms function to the highest extent. This does not prevent men from seeking to establish their identity through a stereotyped virility, which presents the normative advantage of anchoring the individual in the group.

Learning to be virile

The virility of the "male" is perceived as that by which it is possible to measure up to each other "man to man". Whoever refuses to join in, who recoils or who cannot participate is no longer included in the virile connection that unites a group of men through latent antagonism. The education of young boys is conditioned from the outset by the non-choice that orientated rivalry represents. This rivalry is generally reinforced by the idea that physical strength is needed to reduce the other to silence in a group of men (but there are also symbolic ways to reduce others to silence, which would be the form of domination preferred by intellectuals).

How does this belief in a normalising virility develop? It exists in our societies in many mono-gendered spaces that Daniel Welzer-Lang has termed "the house of men", in reference to the anthropological research of Maurice Godelier (2004). Among many peoples, the separation of the sexes is very strong, and there are specific places either for men or for women, which are prohibited to the other gender. There are also places in our society where boys are initiated among men into virility (e.g., school playgrounds, gyms, sports clubs, pubs, and stadiums), and socialised within the hierarchical picture of male–female relationships, where femininity (of which a part could also belong to men) becomes the negative central pole, the inner enemy to be fought against:

> The education of men is socialisation to gender violence, against women, but also and primarily against weak, fragile boys, who become scapegoats, a fate that threatens any man who is not overtly virile. But the homophobic socialisation of boys is also a form of violence against oneself, so that the body becomes what is expected of one of the lads. In this house-of-men, one learns how to exclude sensitivity, gentleness, and empathy, while also learning how to fight to be the strongest, the best, and the first. And woe to those who reject the codes of virility! They are downgraded from the group of men, and are regarded as women, or their symbolic equivalents, the homosexuals. (Welzer-Lang, 2009, p. 49, translated for this edition)

These sites of homophobic socialisation are often centred either around athletic performance, the capacity for action, or verbal agility, which are all areas likely to exclude, for one reason or another, those boys with disabilities who might be tempted to frequent them (or is it a form of prejudice to affirm that?). Rivalry sporadically plays a part, in the form of peaks of contained aggressiveness: a quick rush of physical aggression, resulting in a virile struggle, where two forces agree to be measured against one another; a sharp rise in verbal aggression, which one must be able to answer without fear, and especially without fearing to get drawn into the game of one-upmanship. This might eventually lead to mutual esteem between those partners capable of measuring up to one another. In fact, those who enter these places of rivalry are individuals who are not only able to react, but who also implicitly agree to measure themselves against others, sporadically. On this basis, a virile agreement is established, based on relationships of domination that are pacified, at least temporarily; privileged places for the expression of a *libido dominandi* that takes many forms throughout one's lifetime.

In such contexts, the disabled boy is summed up by his physical weakness, his "natural" disabilities being supposed to exclude him automatically from the "competition". It seems difficult to accept that he may enter, as others do, into adolescence, the age of male rivalry, of confrontation with the world, of the physical risk-taking particularly prevalent among boys (Le Breton, 2007). It seems clear to parents that their child will not be able to enter these zones of competition, where it is no longer possible for them to protect him from this symbolic or real violence.

> In general, the boy learns his social role at an early age, from his parents and the people around him, through the remarks made to him, people's attitude towards him, and any encouragement he receives. He quickly learns that it is good to be aggressive, "not to let himself be trifled with", "to have character", to impose his will, to be noisy, never to show pain or fatigue, to have a "virile" scatological vocabulary. He must be a "man" and not be tied to his mother's apron strings or behave like a "little girl", or he risks being disqualified as a male. (Le Breton, 2007, p. 65, translated for this edition)

The author adds a social aspect to the attributes of manhood: the femininity of a man might be accepted in bourgeois circles or among the wealthy, but not among the lower social classes, or in inner city areas, where "an insecure boy, in any situation of exclusion, tends to cling to models of virility that he will caricature" (Le Breton, 2007, p. 67, translated for this edition). His quest for limits and virile identity can take various forms: "dangerous games, drunkenness, speeding, whether on a bike or by car, suicide, delinquency, physical violence, contempt for women, etc. . . ." (Le Breton, 2007, p. 67, translated for this edition).

Driving at speed, or physical challenge, must, therefore, be part of the construction of masculine self-identity. But can one take risks to demonstrate one's virility, when one is dependent? Physical disability creates many more risks and, at the same time, the impossibility of taking risks as other adolescents do, due to the permanent presence of adults. One of the challenges for carers today is that of letting young people with disabilities refuse help, encounter difficulties, and be faced with their inability to accomplish what they desire, even when the outcome seemed obvious to adults even before the attempt. This confrontation with real life (even without genuine life-threatening risk) is present more or less patently among all adolescents. The ability to accept one's choices with complete self-awareness is not unthinkable, and neither is autonomy, if we regard it in the etymological sense (ability to create one's own standards of life), and not as the ability to cope alone in life by living "just like everyone else". But this path requires us to renounce the stereotypes of virility, which are generally a condition for inclusion in a group of young men, and in that way achieving an identity that is recognised by one's peers (unless, yet again, we are labouring under our own illusions, while disability might, in fact, be perceived by the peer group as one of those extreme experiences so sought after today by adolescent groups).

The next stage in the classic recognition of male identity is the socially recognised union with a woman, then access to fatherhood and parenthood (with the paternal authority that springs from this). Yet, even as we discover the modern-day father, who also adopts some more traditionally feminine values, it seems that men with disabilities must still remain dependent (even in their own representations) on the traditional figure of the Father.

However, this fundamentally dominant figure is not necessarily linked to an incarnation: the statue of the commander is not to be touched. Immaterial, it resists even death, and haunts with overwhelming power those who suffer its yoke. Why should authority still be associated with physical power? We will explore these issues through our previously mentioned discussions with Marcel Nuss.

Paternal virility and paternal authority

When asked about risk-taking and fatherhood, Marcel Nuss told us that, in his case, the two things were interdependent: at the age of twenty, he had chosen to remain hospitalised (for life, as he then thought) in an intensive care unit, in order no longer to be dependent on his parents. This was, for him, a way of entering the adult world. In fact, this decision allowed him to meet his first wife and have children with her.

Curiously, the plain fact of being married and becoming a father was not enough for his virility to be recognised, which meant that he ran the risk of internalising this refusal:

> Regarding the qualities required for one to be virile, life has taught me that it is the gaze fixed upon you at a given moment that will reveal your virility or extinguish it. You cannot declare yourself virile; you either become virile or you don't; it is a slow, contextual, and cultural transformation.

He adds, regarding the function of authority that fathers are thought to possess,

> How many times have I heard, particularly when my children were very young, that in my state of complete physical dependence, it was impossible for me to have any authority?

> This is a false premise. For if there is one thing that disability has taught me, it is that authority is a matter of presence and not of physical strength. It's not the scary people—those who represent a threat, or a potential danger—who possess authority, but rather those who "impress" others by their force of persuasion.

> Authority is a fundamental part of what we are, not what we do (along the lines of "I will hurt you if . . ."). Consequently, one does not need to compel by force, but rather to convince by experience; it is necessary to convince others that you are in the right, rather than compelling them by the principle that "might is right".

Finally, there can be no good authority without a minimum of trust, and, therefore, freedom. All existence is built on experience, whether good or, sometimes, bad. Confidence in others, trust in life, and self-confidence are essential to living and loving well. Furthermore, good authority must be able to teach its neighbours, whoever they may be, to be self-confident.

A person who knows how to inspire respect and give confidence has authority, even if that person is disabled. (personal interview)

The role of father figure can, therefore, be played by a disabled person, even more so when we think of the role of modern-day fathers, which involves listening and understanding, traditionally assigned to the maternal figure (Korff Sausse, 2009, p. 93). Why should disabled men need to be castrating fathers instilling fear, unyielding judges bearing the Law and the word, when so many contemporary fathers are no longer like that? Neither must there be any question of reducing the disabled father to a permissive and fragile father, which he certainly is not, but to perceive the difference between the image of the Father, with its normative constraints, and the reality of fatherhood as it exists today.

Sexuality and reproductive power in question

Although he has had two children with his first wife, Marcel Nuss has often faced doubts as to his paternity, with many people questioning the fact that he could really be sexually active ("How did he ever have children?" sniggered an applicant for a position as carer during a job interview with him (Nuss, 2008a). Others, despite the fact that they know him well, still wonder if he can *really* have sex. Sexual power is always linked to the image of physical domination by the male, the domination of an active man over a passive woman ... and it is far from common knowledge that a quadriplegic can have a fulfilling sex life when there is no rupture of the spinal cord.

The reasons for this denial of sexuality are probably also related to the fear of engendering and reproducing disability,[4] especially among the parents of disabled young men. These parents might themselves have experienced, at the birth of their children, a sense of procreative failure and guilt for having engendered disability. Fear is, therefore, associated with sexuality and procreation (as if they were necessarily related to one another), and the disabled man inherits much of these parental representations, which he encounters when he considers becoming a father himself.

For you can never become a father alone, without being part of a lineage. A man disabled from birth has to solve a problem of lineage from the outset, especially because of the cultural importance attached to resembling one's parents. The disabled son is an unrecognisable descendant, whom some parents even refuse to consider as their son, because they cannot see themselves in him. There was not reproduction in the strictest sense, but the engendering of an individual marked by difference. It is difficult to identify with this son, to survive through him, because he does not resemble his parents closely enough. This individual, who is less than a man, and only anecdotally sexual (with a penis serving merely as an indicator, like hair colour) will never attain a satisfactory phallic potency. He will not readily be able to take the place of a father whose physical abilities will always be greater than his own, even when he reaches adulthood. Worse still, sometimes the son is not even expected to live as long as his father. Under these conditions, the position of the Father is unassailable: he will always dominate you, and might even outlive you.

Negative sexual identity

People with disabilities are often placed in an intermediate status between children and adults, as if we expected them to recognise their inability to have a "serious" form of sexuality, marking their sexual identity. For a disabled person, the issue of homosexuality, bisexuality, or transsexuality seems minor, because sexuality itself is not equated with the real possibility of constructing self-identity, as identity is systematically brought down to the fact of being disabled, as if this were the only vector of individual identity (Korff Sausse, 1996; Nuss, 2008b). It is, therefore, far from certain whether we are concerned to the same extent by the homosexuality or bisexuality of a disabled person.

In the case under discussion, *negative* sexual identity is a more meaningful concept, since individuals are purely and simply denied the possession of a "real" sexual identity. The homosexual person may certainly sometimes be cast in a stereotypical and undervalued sexual identity, but although there is *negativity*, there is less often in our society the pure and simple *negation* of adult homosexual identity. In contrast, disabled people are sometimes asexual (considered as disabled, rather than male or female), and very often desexualised, as if their genital and reproductive power did not exist.

The risk of these representations, for the subject, is the early internalisation of negative sexual identity, where self-awareness of one's potential for seduction would come far too late (or never), as one would never have recognised in oneself the capacity to demonstrate virile potency. It seems that, whatever the situation, everything still remains to be done: it is necessary to rebuild, restore, and repair; or, even better, to explore other ways, other means. This can obviously be interpreted both in the physical and psychological sense. The idea is to create this construction of identity outside the normative networks largely internalised by the subjects.

This constantly renewed self-construction can be perceived positively, by reference to contemporary philosophy, where authors such as Michel Foucault (1976, 1984) or Judith Butler (1990, p. 23, 2008, p. 255) criticise the idea of "sexual identity" that could reveal self-identity. Fixing sexual identity can only take place at the expense of rigidification, which the subject is not required to undergo. Foucault would certainly have been interested in the idea of a subject for whom sexuality itself had been denied from the outset. It is precisely this form of negation that is at work in the case of the disabled person: not merely access to a "masculine" or "feminine" identity (which, incidentally, would make little sense to Foucault), but access to the recognition of sexuality in itself, under various conditions serving to indicate the case regarding each individual.

Hetero-sexual virility reifying identity

What is important for Foucault is not to claim an identity, which appears reifying, closed in on itself, but, rather, to claim a sexual creation at odds with the forms of identity produced by our scheme of sexuality. Sexuality, as it exists and develops, is more important than the "real" sexual identity of each individual, because that identity is illusory, unless some distance is maintained in relation to it:

if identity becomes the major problem of sexual existence, if people think that they have to "disclose" their "own identity", and that this identity must become the law, the principle, and the code of their existence; if the question they perpetually ask is: "Is this thing consistent with my identity?", then I think they will go back to a form of ethics very close to traditional heterosexual virility. (Foucault, 1984, p. 1558, translated for this edition)

Heterosexual virility seems to be a source of identity frozen in ethics, understood here as the way you lead your life. It is traditional for the man to embody "the law, the principle and the code of existence" in his own identity, and for the man to embody that which has no flaws, and that which lasts. This virility of reference is highly normative; it imposes both the rule and the law in society, and within the family. We understand that any flaw in this heterosexual virility can be daunting. However, by thus fossilising identity, do we not miss what makes human identity, which is the ability to be oneself through the quest for one's self?

Now the disabled person, even more than an ordinary person, is assigned a fixed identity. A disabled person is more clearly subjected to the norms that constitute each subject. Judith Butler adopts Michel Foucault's notion of subjection, in both senses of the term *subject* (autonomous subject, and subject submitted to power). Each subject denies this subjection; he refuses it, turns against it, but cannot escape it. For, to rip away these internalised norms would be to tear off one's own skin. They are part of identity (and, notably, sexual identity). Release, by moving out of a place to which one has been assigned, cannot be thought of without intense guilt, because there has been self-construction within these norms. The place one occupies is a place that has been assigned and accepted, without any feeling of deprivation. What one is deprived of is thought of as inaccessible, and it is not perceived as a loss or deprivation, but as something that it is shameful to want, or illusory to desire. We might well perceive that reality itself is also essentially the result of a social construction, yet it requires a great deal of work on oneself to realise that we are not organically or naturally fated to accept this or that condition. Feminism has shown this by denouncing the idea of any inability in women (to exercise parental authority or to manage the housekeeping money) based in nature on any organic condition. In addition, one may wonder if the incapacity of any person, disabled or not, might not also have a strongly normative aspect, through which it is not even possible for them to consider (their own sexual pleasure, or their own identifying worth, for example).

Reflecting on heterosexual identity and the forbidden nature of homosexuality, Butler notes that this ban masks that which it causes to be lost, so that the loss is not represented as such (by foreclosure). She compares this to the phenomenon of melancholy in the Freudian sense, where the object is lost and with it the consciousness of the loss, not without a strong internalisation of the object in the form of identification (Butler, 1997, pp. 132–137).

According to Butler, subjects do not desire in relation to what they are naturally destined to desire, but they internalise what they do not have the right to desire (male individuals when one is a boy, for example). Gender is based on what is forbidden. And this prohibition becomes part of the very identity of the subject, through that which may not be desired. Sexual identity is, therefore, built on the condemnation of some possibilities of love. One is a man in so far as one does not desire another man. Therefore, the fact of desiring another man calls into question the fact of being a man, as Butler says, "if one is a girl to the extent that one does not want a girl, then wanting a girl will bring being a girl into question" (Butler, 1997, p. 136).

We could say, by drawing inspiration from these analyses, that the disabled subject has been led to internalise that he does not really have the right to desire, or that he does not have the right to be fully a man. He is socially tolerated, in that a portion of his virility is condemned, because of a limitation seen as biological, or as "natural". In fact, it is the internalisation of the forbidden and the identification with the inaccessible figure of the stereotypical virile man that creates this impression of a form of nature against which it would be pointless to fight.

The renewed creation of sexual identity according to Michel Foucault

Faced with these limitations of sexual identity, Michel Foucault considered, in his later works, a continuous creation of identity, creation where one becomes man without rite of passage, without recognition of social status as a virile individual, without claiming a "core identity" to reveal and on which one may rely. The only nature available to us is a force, and this force has no form or scripted destiny.

Force is not to be found in stability, but in diversion and in play. Playing is not a sign of inconsistency: you can play very seriously. Play must be interpreted both in a playful and a mechanical sense: there is "play" in the machine, in the mechanics of norms. And playing this game acts as a dynamic and protean force. In this sense, if I am me, it is because I invent myself, and not just because I claim a form of heroism leading to self-discovery, the truth about oneself, which is, according to Foucault, connoted from a virile heterosexual perspective, because it bears a code of existence reifying identity.

Identity is, thus, seen by Foucault as being more related to the *uniqueness* of the individual (the character of being unique). However, if by identity we mean the characteristic of remaining the same over time, then "the relationships that we must maintain with ourselves are not relationships of identity; they are rather relationships of differentiation, creativity, and innovation" (Foucault, 1984, p. 1558, translated for this edition).

These aspects of Foucault's reflection seem particularly important for that which is automatically set outside the norm, since identity is not to be sought following a norm which structures the relationship with oneself, on the model of the statue of oneself. It matters little that one has not the stature required by the image of heterosexual virility: there might be, there must be, other forms of self-acceptance under the rules of play, of the play that one gives to the norms without plunging into uncertainty or guilt. Thus, there may develop forms of male seduction and forms of modern-day fatherhood that are not traditionally associated with virility. They can only be validated subjectively by noting their already very real social existence.

These other forms of the masculine can play on the creation of self, through the recognition of one's own power of seduction, through forms of existence that are not predictable in advance, since they originate in self-presence and presence for the other. They are the generally forgotten values of virility and masculine seduction. But what better guides may be found with regard to shared pleasure and self-discovery?

Conclusion

Virility, as an attribute of one's personal identity and in its power of seduction, is not based, as some common misrepresentations would have it, on a bodily condition. Rooting the concept in muscular and genital power is an illusion wherein one's view can become side-tracked in seeking to relate that dimension of virility with some primordial sexual potency, echoing an anatomic and physiological vision of how the male body should be. Now, such masculinity can for no man be considered to be a stable identity, no more so, indeed, than belonging in a clear-cut manner to the female or male gender. To a heterocentric vision of sexuality, there needs to be added the denunciation of a vision that would in some way seek to validate sexuality by reducing it to a form of naturalism, blurring the differences between sexual attributes and gender attributes, and confusing the power of seduction with physical integrity in the sense of being free from any form of invalidity.

We are not confronted here by claims to a form of identity that would appear to be reifying, closed in on itself, but, rather, a claim to sexual creativeness that makes a radical break with the identity-related forms generated in our general arrangement of sexuality by the irruption of a body considered to be different. This body, considered to be devoid of the power of seduction, incapable of acting genitally, and precluded from procreation, breaks in to bring into question all our perceptions of what a sexually attractive man should be, sexually proficient and able to become a father.

This calling into question of a form of identity seen to be invariable over time brings to the fore an identity that is granted to us only on a temporary basis and that can be withheld, but that we can also denounce. It then fits into a game scenario where there is both a playing out and play in the sense of freedom of movement in the machine, in the mechanics of social norms. This play is not the sign of inconsequentiality: one can be highly serious about a game, as Foucault insisted, on condition that its full force and proteiform vitality are safeguarded against any attempt to finally freeze identity and recognise oneself in it. By this token, the identity of being disabled before that of being a man then appears no more than one possibility with regard to one's identity, as being liable to change as one lives out one's life. Identity thus construed then becomes no more than a temporary process intended to boost the efficacy of one's quest for social relations and the pursuit of contacts conducive to sexual pleasure.

Notes

1. There are many valued male roles in which some form of indirect seduction occurs, but from which virility is abstracted: priests gratify by the quality of their presence. They are supposed to be understanding, caring, sedate, and devoid of sinful passions. The seduction exerted by a disabled man is somewhat similar, as there is no risk of seeing him throw himself physically at the other person. It is a way of letting the other person approach at the pace of their own desire, something rarely accepted by the majority of men. Note that in the erotic fantasies presented here, it is almost as though sexuality was as forbidden for the disabled man as it is for the Catholic priest, as if acting on such impulses involved a powerful transgression.

2. Marcel Nuss's power of seduction has been confirmed to me by many women ... including my own wife, who did not hesitate to describe him as more virile than me ... But, curiously, the narcissistic ways in which I tried to reassure myself were directly based on stereotypes of (muscular) virility and not on the presence of the other person. This personal example marks the imposition of gender and its normative character, to which we all fall victim, as we have constructed our identity through such normative references.

3. This perception is "feminine" to the extent that it is mainly present among women (but not exclusively female). A man may also possess this sensitivity to the presence of the other through the gaze.

4. Even solicitude and care might participate in the desexualisation of the disabled, who are considered, against all evidence, as latent children, sometimes even as asexual, even though many people with intellectual disabilities use sexual behaviour as a means of expression (behaviour that is often repressed by society, which fails to notice that such behaviour is one of the few ways the disabled have of clearly demonstrating their intentions). Many authors have emphasised the fears related to the sexuality of people with disabilities, and the subsequent denial of their sexual power as a source of pleasure, of their reproductive capacity, and of their adult genitalia.

References

Ancet, P., & Nuss, M. (Ed.) (2012). *Dialogue sur le handicap et l'altérité. Ressemblances dans la différence*. Paris: Dunod.

Butler, J. (Ed.) (1990). *Gender Trouble: Feminism and the Subversion of Identity.* New York: Routledge.

Butler, J. (Ed.) (1997). *The Psychic Life of Power: Theories in Subjection.* Stanford, CA: Stanford University Press.

Butler, J. (2008). Imitation and gender insubordination. In: J. Storey (Ed.), *Cultural Theory and Popular Culture: A Reader* (4th edn) (pp. 224–238). New York: Routledge.

Foucault, M. (1976). Dans La Volonté de savoir. In: *Histoire de la sexualité, I* (pp. 177–191). Paris: Gallimard.

Foucault, M. (1984). *Sexe, pouvoir et la politique de l'identité. Dits et écrits, Vol. II.* Paris: Gallimard, Quarto.

Godelier, M. (Ed.) (2004). *Métamorphoses de la parenté.* Paris: Fayard.

Korff Sausse, S. (Ed.) (1996). *Le miroir Brisé. L'enfant handicapé, sa maladie et le psychanalyste.* Paris: Calmann-Lévy, 2009.

Korff Sausse, S. (Ed.) (2009). *Eloges des pères.* Paris: Hachette Littératures.

Le Breton, D. (Ed.) (2007). *En souffrance. Adolescence et entrée dans la vie.* Paris: Métailié.

Nuss, M. (Ed.) (2008a). *La présence à l'autre: accompagner les personnes en situation de grande dépendance* (2nd edn). Paris: Dunod.

Nuss, M. (Ed.) (2008b). *Handicaps et sexualités—Le livre blanc.* Paris: Dunod.

Welzer-Lang, D. (2009). Homophobie, hétérophobie, multisexualité, égalité, signes de l'éclatement du corset du genre? In: *Des hommes et du masculin, études et travaux de l'Ecole doctorale TESC n°11.*

CHAPTER TWO

The traumatic effects of encountering disability: the bond and psychic transmission put to the test

Albert Ciccone

E ncountering their child's disability represents an especially traumatic experience for the parents. For the subject primarily concerned, the child, discovering their disability is also potentially traumatic.

In this chapter, I consider the traumatic effects of encountering the disability from the perspective of the bond and psychic transmission. I investigate the effects of failure in transmission as induced by the disability, as well as the specific features of bonds and transmissions that it generates, permits, or reveals over time.

The term disability here includes the somatic, cognitive, relational, and psychic fields. Clearly, each situation poses specific problems that have to be differentiated, but I attempt to distinguish and cover a certain number of sufficiently common issues.

First, I describe the effect of the break in filiation, the effect of the primal disappointment, with the host of violent feelings that accompany it (guilt, shame, and hatred), and also the effect of sudden and early psychic separation.

I then consider the various effects of transaction and transmission that this experience generates from the defensive adjustments it imposes. The effects of secondary symbiosis, with its different figures (incestuality, idealisation, destructiveness, and tyranny) are described. The deployments of transmission fantasies, with their functions of exculpation (innocentation), of reconstitution of the genealogy, and appropriation of the traumatic experience are also highlighted. I then concentrate on the affects of guilt and shame the trauma mobilises, and the psychic work these affects produce. I consider transmissions of the affects of guilt and shame, with the "affect bearing" function the child can fulfil. I stress the repetitions of the primal disappointment the disability imposes. Finally, I envisage the disability as an attractor, for the child as for those around it, of transmissions, identifications, and conflicts relating to oedipal, but also and above all, archaic and narcissistic, issues.

I describe the imago encroachment processes at work in these different bonds, and the way in which the child struggles with its parental imagos in those transactions and transmissions.

The effect on filiation, narcissism, and parenthood

Break in filiation

Disability defies genealogical bonds. It causes a fracture or a break in filiation. This traumatic shock above all affects the narcissistic aspects of the bond of filiation.

We are aware of the narcissistic issues any child bears. As Freud (1914c) so clearly put it, one of the essential functions of any child involves reviving and ensuring immortality for the parental narcissism of which he or she is both depository and bearer. "His Majesty the baby", in Freud's words, has to accomplish all the dreamt desires the parents were unable to achieve. Immortality of the ego, undermined by reality, thus finds a place of refuge in the child. The parents' love, so touching and so child-like, is nothing other, says Freud, than their narcissism reborn.

Disability disrupts this hope of narcissistic immortality. Thus, disability also causes a break in what Aulagnier (1975) described under the terms of a "narcissistic contract". The narcissistic contract, as a formation of an unconscious link, binds the child to the parents, to the previous generations, and, more particularly, to the entire social group. It prescribes the mission the newborn bears with it, meaning that of ensuring continuity of the generations in exchange for recognition by the new arrival's group.

The disability causes a sudden, radical, and unforeseen break in this narcissistic contract, or compromises its emergence. The child, too clearly differentiated from its ascendants, too much in a situation of otherness, finds itself in a condition of "degeneration", meaning in a traumatic separation from its generational or genealogical lineage. Of course, not all disabilities have an equivalent impact. There are ways more or less permitted by the (social) group of derogating from that narcissistic contract. There are deviations or singularities that are more or less tolerated, more or less capable of being subsumed in narcissistic contracts. It is, for example, much easier to be recognised and confirmed by social discourse as the parent of a child affected by a chromosome abnormality than be admitted as parent of a psychotic child—and the same applies to the child himself.

The trauma affects not only narcissism, but also the deepest layers of human identity. The disability poses the question of our very belonging to the human species; it attacks the feeling of humanity and leads to an experience felt of strangeness, of non-humanity. How can a seriously disabled child, affected in its intellectual and mental capabilities, in its ability to communicate and relate, be recognised as fully human, that is, endowed with psychic qualities, with a psychic life? This experience of strangeness, of non-humanity of the child, imperils the identification of the parents with their own humanity. The child affected by a disability (especially when of a serious nature) provokes, makes fragile and even disqualifies parental humanity.

Primal disappointment

This fracture, or traumatic break, in filiation generates (while also being the very result of) an effect of disappointment for which I have adopted the term primal disappointment (*déception originaire* in French, 1997).

Such a disappointment reflects the narcissistic wound experienced in a context of sudden disillusion. It causes a feeling of collapse, of internal disaster, that requires a reworking of things equivalent to a work of mourning, but different from such work in that, first, the object has not been lost, and second, that the traumatic event is persecutory by its

omnipresence: the disability is still there, ever visible, constantly recalling the original catastrophe.

The origin affected by disappointment concerns a child's coming
into the world, but also the desire to have a child, the origin of that
desire, and the origin of identity, that of the child as also that of the
parent, the origin of the feeling of humanity. The origin is marked by
the trauma, the wound, disqualification, and disappointment.

The primal disappointment, whose corollary will be despair, is
condemned to repeat itself inexorably. Indeed, the parents, through
their implicit expectations, through their illusory hopes that they
necessarily keep alive, are brought to place the child in a persecutory
situation of repetition of the disappointment. Moreover, each singular
event, each modification, each change (of school, of institution, of
carer), each new separation, each stage in the path of life, will always
summon the original traumatic experience ("You always have to start
off again from scratch" is the way parents often put it). The least problematic event recalls the traumatic origin, takes you back to the point
of the primal disappointment.

The repetition of disappointment, of the wound, will lead the child
to interiorise the image of a disappointed, hurt, and forlorn parent and
to identify with such an imago, or to develop defensive attitudes
against such a perception.

Sudden psychic separation and parental psychological prematurity

The encounter with the disability, in so far as it imposes a traumatic
experience of otherness, generates an effect of sudden and early
psychic separation.

We are familiar with the conceptions of Frances Tustin (1981), who
considers the autistic child to be "psychologically premature", a child
who lived the experience of psychic separation too early, before their
psychic apparatus could contain, tolerate, and metabolise such a trial.
It can be said that, in the case of a traumatic encounter with the child's
disability, it is the parents who find themselves in this condition of
"psychological prematurity". The parents go too early through the
experience of psychic separation with their child, who too soon
becomes another, a stranger. The disability asserts otherness in too
early, too violent, and too absolute a manner.

Parenthood, just like the child's subjectivity, develops through a
gradual work of mourning and disillusionment from an experience of

primary illusion. The child gradually separates out and individu-
alises, the parents too. The primary illusion is necessary to establish
the first bonds of attachment, the first intimate forms of communications, the first experiences of understanding of the child by the
parents.

The non-establishment or the sudden break in that illusion,
through the experience of psychic separation that the disability
imposes, will lead to the parents attempting to retrieve that primary
illusion, by reconstructing the postnatal symbiotic matrix. However,
that (secondary) illusion will then be defensive, as it will contain the
knowledge of otherness, of the sudden and early separation, and it
will be there to serve at all costs in maintaining the symbiosis, the non-
separation, so as to avoid the return of disintegrating effects due to the
traumatic experience of absolute otherness.

Thus, it already involves a defensive measure against the trauma
of encountering the disability.

Defences and rearrangements.
Effects on the bond and transmission

Secondary symbiosis and its forms

The effect of traumatic otherness and the testing of the narcissistic
aspects of the filial bond that the encounter with disability produces
will lead to the parents or the family arranging and maintaining a
state of secondary symbiosis with the child, to attempt to retrieve the
primary illusion suddenly wiped out by the primal disappointment,
and to struggle against the effects of catastrophic separation that the
disability imposes. This symbiosis can take different forms, or find
expression along the lines of certain of its aspects, all of which are
interconnected.

Narcissistic bond and incestuality

In the sealing of this secondary defensive symbiosis, the fantasy that
drives the parent or the family is a fantasy of reintroduction of the
child into the womb, into the family uterus, for it to be repaired, but
also for it to repair the family womb, for it to reconstitute the narcissistic completeness of the family body that became shattered.

The symbiotic nature of the parent–child bond, as generated by the disability, accounts for the hypertrophy of the narcissistic dimension of the bond of filiation (Guyotat, 1991). It also bears witness to incestuality in the sense in which Racamier (1992, 1993, 1995) talks about it the incestuality that is one of the figures of symbiosis (Ciccone, 2009a; Ciccone & Ferrant, 2009).

Thus, for example (and here is a clue to that narcissistic filiation), one can frequently observe situations of "abduction" of the child affected by a disability: the child might be abducted by the mother, enclosed in a position of child-of-the-mother, with exclusion and disqualification of the father and the paternal lineage (we shall look at an example later on); the child can also be taken by, or given to, its grandmother (often on the maternal side), who "sacrifices" herself to raise the child, to protect the mother from mental collapse, from melancholic destructiveness. While the child is sometimes "given" to the grandmother, it is sometimes the entire family that finds itself thus looked after, or even accommodated, by the grandparents.

While the disabled-child-of-the-mother bears witness to the narcissistic dimension of the bond of filiation, he or she also testifies to the oedipal problem that sometimes comes in to mask that narcissistic conflation. If the mother's status is borne by the fantasy I mentioned of the reintroduction of the child into the womb, that parthenogenetic status can also be defensive against a position of the child from the guilty infantile oedipal scene. The disability reactivates and feeds incestuous fantasies (the child given to the grandparents, for example, is thus designated as fantasmatically incestuous). He or she represents the expiatory punishment of the guilt-laden desire, the fault, the transgression.

The transgression also concerns the child's desire; in other words, the desire to take the parent's place. The disability answers in fantasy to the transgression. It represents the sanction against the desire to evince the parent, to kill them fantasmatically, and confirms the prohibition of parenthood or sexuality, the latter being reserved, in the (infantile) oedipal logic, to the previous generation ("I'm quite right to think that I'm not entitled to have children like my parents; only they have the right to do so . . ."; the parent who again becomes a child (of its parents) shows their debate with such a fantasy).

If incestuous fantasies are mobilised, if the child becomes a "child of sin", a "child of shame", we could also say that the disability authorises the incestuous fantasy or incestuous act as soon as it represents the measure of retaliation against guilty, transgressive desires. It enables the deployment of the incestuous fantasy or the incestuous act as, through the disability itself, the sin has already been expiated. Because the sin has been punished, expiated, the disability authorises the incestuous or incestual desire that the symbiotic bond comes in to wipe away (and that the sense of shame—as will be seen later—comes in to keep).

The narcissistic bond is maintained by the special relation to time that the disability imposes: time stands still; that child will be a child forever. One of the first questions that any parent asks when discovering the disability is: "What will become of him (her) when I'm no longer there?" The child is immediately placed in the situation of a child the parent will keep forever. Such a link, marked by pain, can also take on a form of sensual enjoyment, and the child can become an object of such enjoyment.

Let us recall how Racamier (1995, p. 41) thought of incestuality: the incestual is a "moral incest", it goes beyond the sexual and describes a link in which the other is a utilitarian narcissistic object, an "object–non-object", forbidden from its own desire, an idealised fetishist object that must idolise the subject, and an object of enjoyment.

Incestuality, figure of symbiosis, is frequently accompanied by forced identifications, imago encroachments (Ciccone, 1999, 2012), which will generate possible generational upheavals: the child will be strongly identified with an imago, with an ancestor bearing a stigma, an imago that will encroach on, and alienate, the child's identity. That forced search for identification in part responds to the break in the bond of filiation, to the break in the genealogical link, as generated by the disability. Such an encroachment sometimes concerns a heroic, grandiose imago, with the disability fostering idealisation, which is also a characteristic of incestuality.

Idealisation

During consultations, a young child affected by cerebral palsy was consistently interested in the figurine of an animal with a broken leg. His mother systematically pushed that figurine away to suggest other toys. She often talked of her own grandfather, a heroic figure who had lost an arm in the war and managed to overcome that handicap, had built his own house, etc. Whenever the child slumped over the table, the mother called on him roughly to "Sit up straight!"

It can be said that this mother projected on her son the image of the heroic, grandiose grandfather. What she was putting off by pushing away the figurine with the broken limb was the very image of the disability. But the child was unable to honour such a contract: "keeping up straight", like the mother's grandfather. What had to be upheld, kept up straight, was also the mother (both outwardly, preventing her from becoming depressed, avoiding disappointment, and the mother within her, maintaining the idealisation).

I stated earlier that the trauma can be considered as an experience that takes on the appearance of a punishment, a retaliation, and that these latter paradoxically authorise transgression. However, while they authorise that transgression, they also authorise idealisation. Idealisation is both an effect of the trauma and a defensive measure against the trauma. Many children affected by disabilities become idealised, mythical, messianic, saviours of the family that becomes invested by a narcissistically redemptive mission: that of saving a disabled child, then all disabled children. Similarly, many children, confronted by their powerlessness, develop fantasies of omnipotence.

One could liken that idealisation of the child, or even sometimes that exhibition, to those ancient practices of exposure. In ancient Greece, deformed new-born infants were exposed, that is, abandoned in some place far away from the community. They were exposed to the gods, handed over to nature and divine powers. Those who survived exposure were transformed from malevolent beings into heroes (which is what appears to have happened with Oedipus, according to certain interpretations of the myth). So it can be seen that while the disability relates to monstrosity, inhumanity, and the malevolent, it also approaches the divine.

The path towards idealisation is so often and so readily opened up before the child affected by a disability. As a result, the latter might show himself to be all-powerful and tyrannical.

Destructiveness

While the bond with the child affected by a disability is often of symbiotic nature, the figures of symbiosis being found there, one can frequently see in such bonds the work of destructive symbiosis. The child, for example, is all the more idealised in that it is disinvested; the parental discourse stating unfailing attachment and love is contradicted by attitudes or acts revealing denied hostility; in the place of that impossible separation there comes in rather a disproportionate remoteness, a brutal, urgent, and unexpected setting aside.

In the figure of destructive symbiosis, each mutually destroys the other. "With every day that goes by, a bit of me dies", said a mother of a seriously encephalopathic child.

Tyranny

Another figure of symbiosis or an effect of symbiosis (and/or incestuality) is tyranny (Ciccone, 2007b; Ciccone & Ferrant, 2009).

Clinical treatment of disabled children often shows a development of tyrannical bonds. The child is in the position of a tyrant, of omnipotence within a family whose guilt and despair prevent any position of organisational authority. Alternatively, then, the child might himself be tyrannised, sometimes by an older brother or sister, who takes advantage of parental ambivalence. As another option, hatred towards the child might be strongly counter-invested in positions of overprotection, of symbiosis that poorly mask the underlying ambivalence and tyrannical destructiveness.

Élisa is a two-year-old girl for whom a diagnosis of a chromosomal abnormality was revealed at the age of one year. Where initially she was a calm baby, "in a world of her own", as her mother put it, but who posed no particular problem, from when the diagnosis was made she became bad-tempered, prone to bouts of anger, hitting herself, and hitting her mother at the slightest contradiction.

The mother did not accept the diagnosis, became depressed, felt guilty, and herself was beset by a feeling of shame, a feeling that she could come to grips with only extremely furtively and painfully.

Here is a fairly typical sequence of interaction that can be observed.

> The mother talks about her pain and weeps. The child, previously busy with a game, approaches and tries to clamber up on to her knee. The mother then pushes her away. The child, with a toy in her hands, makes as if to break it. "Don't make me angry!" cries the mother. The child breaks the object. The mother scolds her. The child shouts. The mother

pulls the child towards her, vigorously, and continues to scold her while consoling her at the same time, folding her arms around her roughly. And the child bites her breast. The mother pushes her back again, complains of her daughter's tyranny, regrets the absence of the father, who is never there. And when he is there, Élisa only has eyes for her father: "When her father's there, I don't count any more", says the mother.

This banal sequence reveals some common elements in clinical experience of disability: the painful experience of loss and disappointment mother and child experience; the affects of guilt and shame mobilised by the trauma; the child's quest, her attempt to revive the object, and the maternal demand for narcissistic reparation (the mother asks to "count" as someone, she who has been disqualified in her function and in her parental identity); the difficulty in containing the child's violence and the maternal response that, under the effect of guilt and hostility, intertwines both reprimand and rough consolation. We could say that, by acting in such a way, the mother, while complaining of the child's violence, is at the same time telling the child herself how to behave in the same manner, mistreating her, and roughly taking her in by biting her (Ciccone, 2003).

The tyranny exercised by so many children can obviously be explained by the encounter with a collapsed and wounded environment, and by the necessity, among other things, of reanimating the object, which leads, in particular and paradoxically, to repeating the destruction, as in the logic of the antisocial trend Winnicott (1956) talks about.

The quest for the object is, of course, accompanied by enjoyment: exultation at the confusion of the powerless object faced by the imposed tyranny, and enjoyment through the feeling of revenge that such a defeat of the object procures the subject.

The failure of the object, of the environment in its containing and transforming function of violent pulsionality, clearly maintains the child's tyranny. This failure is, in part, brought about by effects of guilt (especially when combined with other factors) in so far as the reality of the anomaly, of the infirmity in the child, confirms a parental fantasy of having damaged the child. The parent cannot then exert ordinary authority as she feels guilty of being violent, "bad", if she is firm or if she sets limits, if she sets prohibitions. Thus it is that she will let the child deploy a violent and tyrannical form of self-assertion.

That "dysfunctional authority", as Carel (2002) put it, will produce effects of generational inversion. This can be seen in the way the parent announces authority, as through the expression: "Don't get cross!" used by the mother of Élisa, as mentioned above. Thus, the parent does not set a limit to contain the child's pulsionality, but, rather, asks the child to contain her own, not to arouse her anger, meaning to be an adult, a parent for her, the parent-child. This configuration favours, or bears witness to, the incestuality characteristic of tyrannical bonds.

While the tyrannical bond is marked by incestuality, it is also an attempt to treat incestuality, to resist it. The tyrannical child, for example, is often a child who is struggling against a parental, narcissistic, and oedipal seduction, while also realising, in the same movement, the incestuous desire of possessing the object for his own enjoyment. Tyranny produces incestuality, but also responds to incestuality, to enjoyment, to the narcissistic possession and use of the child by the parent. Indeed, the hold on the child's body, as can be observed, for example, in re-educational and functional demands, the investment of the child as a body to be repaired (even if such actions are, of course, necessary), can lead the child from babyhood to actively resist, to openly and tyrannically struggle for an appropriation of his or her own body, then later to lay claim to the disability in a provocative manner.

A deaf child, for example, whose mother wanted him to let his hair grow to hide his hearing aids (signs of the narcissistic wound, of shameful humiliation) demanded of his mother not only that he be allowed to have his hair cut, but also for her to buy him fluorescent red hearing aids . . .

Here, for the child, there is a reversal of the humiliation, of the shame and the narcissistic wound, in phallic exhibition (Ciccone & Ferrant, 2009).

Tyranny is a method for treatment of the despair, the powerlessness, and the humiliation with which the trauma is confronted.

Projective identification

Symbiosis is a stage of the bond constituted by the work of projective identification. The encounter with the disability exacerbates the need (on the parent's side) to resort to identificatory projective processes.

"She'll never be able to do without me," said the mother of a small, seriously encephalopathic girl. "I'm everything for her and she's everything to me. I am her and she is me. I'm her angel. 'Cos she can't defend herself, she can't talk or move. I do it for her. I think for her. I understand everything about her, I know her by heart. I know what she desires . . ."

Maintaining this symbiotic illusion, this conviction of clairvoyance, through the massive utilisation of projective identification processes is intended to avoid the mourning due to sudden and traumatic separation, to the traumatic effects of absolute otherness.

The transmission fantasy

While the encounter with disability represents a present traumatic experience, it also provides an opportunity for revelations on past traumas with which it will connect up, that it will bring back into one's memory, awaken, and revive. The present trauma produces a reinvestment of past traumatic experiences, whether real or imaginary, buried or forgotten, traumatic experiences belonging to the subject's or the family's history. Such traumas can, indeed, belong to the parent's childhood history: real events or traumas related to infantile (including oedipal) fantasies that reality has not sufficiently denied. They might also belong to prehistory: such and such a child with an infirmity will recall such and such an ancestor bearing a particular stigma.

This connection of the present and the past, especially when it calls up an ancestor, leads to the deployment of transmission fantasies (Ciccone, 1999, 2012). This involves built or reconstructed, conscious or unconscious scenarios in which the subject designates themselves as the inheritor of a psychic content handed down by another, whether contemporaneous (in an inter- or trans-subjective link) or ancestral (in an inter- or trans-generational genealogical link).

Such a fantasy has several functions. First of all, it has a function of exculpation (the subject has nothing to do with it, since the trouble comes from an ancestor). The transmission fantasy also has a function of representation or inscription of the subject in generation—the child subject with the disability, but also the parent subject from whom the child came. Indeed, the disability produces an effect of "degeneration", as I stated above, placing the child in a position of absolute otherness. Finally (and this function results from the two previous ones), the transmission fantasy has a function of subjectivation, of appropriation by the subject of a foreign traumatic history—in the same movement leading the subject to dispossess itself of it.

Thus, while the disability defies genealogical ties, while it causes a break in the bond of filiation, it also and simultaneously makes possible the suture of that break. Such and such a child is "late" in developing, as is remarked to his or her parents: yes, but "his uncle or great-grandfather . . . walked and talked very late," they answer. The infirmity is, thus, both recognised and denied. The child is recognised by those close to him as both a stranger and yet one of them. The transmission fantasy, thus, has a paradoxical effect, an effect of transitionalisation. It recovers the context of transmission and reorganises it, in a work of reconstruction aiming to preserve the genealogy, the generational.

Needless to say, transmission fantasies act independently of the existence of hereditary biological processes, even if biological heredity can act as a support or an ingredient in the construction of such fantasies, and can represent the bodily and event-related correlate of such fantasies whose issues concern the place of the subject in generation and genealogy, as also the treatment of contemporary traumatic experiences.

A large number of examples could be cited to illustrate and highlight the deployment of transmission fantasies. Here is one of them.

This involves a child, Arnaud, and his family. Arnaud was two years old when I met him for the first time. He suffered from a mental seizure in the first months of his life. This was well stabilised by the appropriate antiepileptic treatment and did not block his psychomotor and intellectual development. But the encounter with the "disability" was especially traumatic, above all for the mother, Ms T, and, before the wound and the maternal collapse, the child took on an omnipotent, sadistic, and tyrannical position towards the mother.

Very quickly, during psychoanalytic family therapy, the aetiological question came up, with a strong element of anxiety and guilt. Arnaud's maternal grandfather had a mentally ill aunt. She had been hospitalised for twenty years and died of cachexia, in a psychiatric hospital, fifty years before. This story was shameful and remained a matter of taboo in the family. When Arnaud had his problems, Ms T's mother remembered that her step-parents had told her of this story. She looked into the matter and thus found out the context surrounding that person's death. The step-parents told her that the aunt had fallen from her bicycle when she was eighteen years old and that everything had stemmed from that.

The family then wondered whether Arnaud had something to do with this story, whether that great-great-aunt had not herself been epileptic (hence the cycling accident), and so on. This was reinforced by the fact that Arnaud closely resembled his maternal grandfather. And, on a regular basis, as the sessions went by, there emerged behaviour patterns and traits of character interpreted by the family as behavioural responses or traits of character of the grandfather.

On the father's side, after a period of denial, we were to learn of the death some years previously of a seriously disabled cousin (also hidden away) placed in an institution unbeknown to all those close to him.

To summarise, transmission was, thus, a way of seeing things that was very much invested in by the family. The question of heredity was central, informed by the mental illness of the mother's great-aunt and the infirmity of the father's cousin.

Moreover, Arnaud's illness started (as recounted in family history) when his mother, suffering from angina, passed it on to him, after which he started having convulsions.

The (conventional) perception of things we see here at work thus concern heredity, madness, shame, and guilt (due to the contamination).

During a session, Ms T spoke about another major character: her father's maternal grandmother. She had brought up Ms T's father, who had been rejected by his parents. Ms T's great-grandmother had very dark skin, like Ms T's father and Arnaud. When Arnaud was born, "he was black" and Ms T asked, "Where did he come from to be black like that?" Moreover, Arnaud had a mark at the bottom of his back, a "characteristic of people from the south". This all goes back to the "invasion of the Huns", said Ms T. Now, the maternal grandmother of Ms T's father was from the south. Ms T said she had to work out a family tree. She had never taken such an interest in genealogy until Arnaud came along. Because with Arnaud, "plenty of genes came back".

Finally, I should mention the ties between Ms T and her father, described as being extremely eroticised: she was "cuddly" with him, sitting on his knees even when grown up, until she met her husband. Indeed, her father took it extremely badly that she should turn away from him to get married.

I shall just make a few comments concerning this example. First, to note how resorting to the transgenerational represents a process of exculpation: the subject is not concerned—it all comes from an ancestor. It all amounts then to the "genes", a past history of phantasm and subjects not to be evoked, a matter for embarrassment, associated with madness and shame. That embarrassment is tied up with a guilty primitive scene: the (original) fantasy is, in effect, a fantasy whereby a rape handed down the stigma. The "mark" that comes from the invasion by the Huns is handed down by an ancestor (the grandfather's grandmother). The mark leaves with it the stigma and the "genes" bring into the phantasm the primitive guilt of the founding act: the inaugural act of rape.

The (primitive, oedipal, and incestuous) scene of guilt is echoed back into phylogenesis, is transferred into a prehistoric time, into the genealogical.

Resorting to the transgenerational, thus, signals a need for exculpation, faced with the forms of guilt the disability (including maternal oedipal guilt) reawakens. But it also represents a defence against doubt as to filiation ("Where did he come from?" wondered the mother): the community of behaviours, the community of symptoms reconstructed between the child and one (or more) ancestor(s) place the child in the genealogical tie. The "stigma" is, then, paradoxically, a suture in the break in the bond of filiation.

The deployment of fantasies of transmission thus represents a way of repairing the break in the bond of filiation. Through these fantasies, the subject appropriates or attempts to appropriate the traumatic event, becomes subject of the strange history that imposes itself so brutally on him, and all this in the same movement that leads him to relinquish or evade it.

The construction of the transmission fantasy is supported by a process of imago encroachment. The encroachment of parental perceptions on the physical space of the child, the child's "identificatory seizure", the forced identification of the child with the ancestor, through channels of projective identification, answer to that need to build a fantasy of transmission that both restores the bond of filiation and treats the oedipal guilt that the traumatic encounter with the infirmity comes in to revive, a disability coming to the fore itself as the dramatisation of a measure of retaliation.

The work of guilt and shame: the fantasy of guilt and the effects of shame

Guilt and the fantasy of guilt: subjectivation of the trauma

While the fantasy of transmission has an effect of appropriation and subjectivation of the traumatic event, another fantasy also has that effect and that function: this involves what I have termed the fantasy of guilt.

The encounter with the disability generates feelings of guilt, as we have seen. With the previous example, I evoked oedipal infantile guilt. Several aspects of guilt are mobilised. Several forms of the feeling of guilt produced by the disability can be enumerated.

The encounter with disability first produces a form of guilt we could call "post traumatic", guilt to which one readily has access, often consciously: guilt at having given life to that child, of having imposed on it an existence imagined as being lifeless or devoid of hope, guilt, too, in not having been able to avoid the disability, the accident, and guilt at having desired the death of the child. But that guilt will connect with older and much more unconscious forms of guilt.

Old forms of guilt "already there", as we might say, are senses of guilt due to the ambivalence (fear of destroying the loved object) and the much more primary (cf. Roussillon, 1991) guilt due to the experience of only being able to create a poor, unsatisfactory world, and of being inherently bad. Such forms of guilt are dramatically confirmed by the encounter with disability, by bringing into the world a child that is "damaged", disappointing, "bad"; they will give its most dramatic impact to that experience, and might generate melancholic or masochistic processes.

Let us also note the guilt, or even the shame, relating to the sexual scene that any pregnancy reveals or exhibits, and that also see these things potentially confirmed by the trauma that begetting a child with a disability represents.

Thus, from these different forms of guilt, we may see develop in the parents what I call a fantasy of guilt. Even when the aetiology is known and recognised, the question of guilt nevertheless remains unresolved. Indeed, the parents will wonder what they did for such a tragic and unfair event to happen to them. They will then seize on these guilts, whether old, current, or renewed, to build a fantasy of guilt.

So many examples could be evoked, as with that of the mother who rejected her pregnancy, wanted to abort, feeling repulsion for the child she bore. All the same, she ended up keeping the child. That child was born and developed early autism. The mother was to say that her child rejected her because she herself wished for his death: "We talk of mothers who don't love their children, but we never talk about children who don't love their mothers", she says. Some doctors consulted suspected genetic problems in that child, but the examinations made revealed no anomaly. The mother failed to understand these examinations being prescribed and refused to pursue investigations. She held on to her psychogenetic theory, she held on to her guilt. First, that guilt enabled her to invest in the child (as she feared, indeed, that if a genetic aetiology were to be revealed, she would disinvest and again reject the child) and, second, it allowed her to mitigate the traumatic nature of the trauma.

It could, indeed, be said that while the subject is guilty of what he or she endures, being in some way responsible, if the event is justified, the trauma will then already be less traumatic, and will also be better mastered, controlled, as appropriated by the subject. The trauma is all the more unfair and scandalous in so far as it is inevitable and eludes the ego. It can be argued that the more the subject is innocent of what happens to him the more, in a way, the trauma is traumatic. The fantasy dramatising guilt will aim to ensure that the traumatic aspect of the trauma does not become too pronounced.

It is precisely such an accentuation that, paradoxically, medical and rational paths of exculpation achieve ("You aren't to blame, it's an accident"—but the subject, meanwhile, insists on being involved in the matter). One can say that exculpation in a way deprives the subject, taking away from the possibility of appropriation of what in his traumatic story belongs to him, as it accentuates the traumatic nature of the trauma.

Yet, if we respect and tolerate this movement of appropriation, if we allow the subject to conduct a work of elaborating (often crushing) guilt, if we let him share and explore through to its logical conclusion his feeling of guilt, we shall then be creating the conditions for him to be able, little by little (once the work of elaboration has been sufficient) to accept the idea of taking into account that which he is innocent of in his history, for him to be able gradually to distinguish the share, within reason, of what he is responsible for and for what he is not to be held to account.

The subject will then accede to a real position of innocence, that supposes a very different process from defensive exculpation, or imposed or prescribed exculpation, which do not lead to the feeling of innocence.

We can, therefore, refer to a real work of guilt in traumatic contexts.

The fantasy of guilt, the construction of a theory whereby the parent has something to do with it, takes part in this work, and, thus, has a dual function: first, it mitigates the traumatic nature of the trauma (the subject becoming active where he or she formerly submitted passively); second, he or she makes possible and accounts for a movement of appropriation (the subject becoming subject of a story that was foreign to him).

Guilt—current and post traumatic—that the fantasy puts on show concerns, as in the example above, investment of the child (the child is thus because the mother did not desire him, or because its conception followed an abortion or adultery, or because the mother abandoned him for a few hours or a few days after his birth—if the child was, for example, in a neonatology ward far from the maternity hospital ward—or, again, because the mother went back to work too early and, thus, left the child with an unbearable feeling of missing her, etc.). But these fantasies become compounded, as I have already stressed, by historic, long-standing guilts that concern the same things that, in the final analysis, psychoanalysis addresses, that is, death or sexuality (in the broad sense of the term).

The fantasy of guilt, just like the fantasy of transmission, thus achieves (at the same time as it is the effect thereof) that transaction involving appropriating a strange traumatic history, making it subjective by mitigating its traumatic impact. The fantasy of guilt, thus, gives the subject the illusion of control, of gaining mastery of the traumatic event.

The historic guilts that the fantasy of guilt will again come to grips with obviously concern, in part, the oedipal guilt attached to the desire of a child, always transgressive for the oedipal child having remained alive in the parent, and who remains convinced that he is not entitled to sexuality and parenthood, that these latter are reserved for the previous generation, and that their realisations would be equivalent to killing the parent to take his or her place. Moreover, any pregnancy is always the exhibition of the sexual scene that led to it, which can produce feelings of shame and guilt for which one will also grasp the fantasy.

Any experience of pregnancy, due to the ambivalence that characterises it, is accompanied by guilty and shameful thoughts that generate fears and anxiety (as to a malformation, a monstrosity, an anomaly in the baby). Reality gainsays these fears in the vast majority of cases, and they are then destined to be repressed. When, however, a problem arises in reality, everything happens as if reality came in to confirm the fantasy, producing a collision between fantasy and reality.

This traumatic realisation of the fantasy, this collision of fantasy–reality, generates fantasies of guilt, but can also lead to a sideration of thought, to an immobilisation, or a bringing into suspense, of the thinking processes. The sideration aims to silence guilty, shameful, and traumatic thoughts (despair, injury, injustice, death wishes, and abandonment). Yet, sideration is not repression, but a traumatic response to the trauma that reality imposes. Sideration evacuates unbearable emotional experiences, the mental pain, outside the field of perceptions.[1]

Again, getting to grips with traumatic experiences and the reorganisation of (primary and secondary) feelings of guilt in fantasy thus testify to an effort of subjectivation in an attempt to escape from sideration, to attempt to escape from the trauma, to try to control it.

An illustration of this mastery of things, in the very context of deployment of fantasies of guilt, is with the premonitory dream. Many parents of children with disabilities (as also many subjects having experienced traumatic experiences) report premonitory dreams where the disaster was announced. The premonitory dream, that is only "premonitory" after the event, is a figuration of the attempt to control the trauma by anticipating it. Convincing oneself that one can anticipate the trauma gives the illusion of possible control over the disaster. The subject can, thus, at the same time appropriate the event.

Finally, and to end discussion on the matter of guilt, it can be said that the experience of feeling guilt allows for access to a depressive position and its being surmounted, the only issue to the experience of absence. And this is what the work of appropriation and mitigation of the trauma (as achieved by the fantasy of guilt) leads to. Acceding to a depressive position and surmounting it presuppose being able to feel the absence, the loss, sufficiently. And guilt is one of its conditions or one of its means.

Shame and its work: conservation of the trauma

I have evoked shame and shameful thoughts a number of times. Shame is obviously mobilised by the encounter with disability, jointly with guilt. While guilt is felt before the superego, shame is experienced before the ideal of the ego, and in such an experience, shame measures the injury to the ideal of the ego that the trauma can cause. It strengthens the cruelty of the superego as generator of the feeling of guilt, and crushes the ego, stifles its creative appropriation capabilities. Shame accentuates the traumatic effect of sideration.[2]

Just as for guilt, different forms of shame and generations of shame are called up, given new life by the trauma. Current forms can be distinguished from older, historic forms, awoken or vivified by the recent event. Secondary forms and primary forms of shame can be differentiated. It can also be argued that at the origin, shame and guilt were not differentiated. Primary shame and primary guilt are intertwined.

Shame is often more difficult to explore than guilt. It has a number of sources in such contexts.

I already said that any pregnancy in a certain way exhibits the sex scene at its origin. Shame first relates to sexuality. For many couples, the arrival of a child with a disability has the effect of arresting their sex life in so far as the latter is associated with a primitive, monstrous, and inhuman scene. The disability defies, provokes the sentiment of humanity. It attacks, fragilises, and disqualifies parental humanity and creativity.

Shame is also born of the narcissistic wound the disability produces and the "primal disappointment", which affect the roots of narcissism, of identity and the feeling of humanity. Shame is especially related to the way others look at you, and mobilises—or is mobilised by—what is in itself similar to the other, or is not. The disability breaks the continuity of identity, produces a fault-line of being together within the human community.

Contrary to guilt, which derives from the experience of having lost an object of love, of having damaged it, shame derives from the experience of being lost or being damaged for the object. It is such a trial that the child's disability imposes on the parent, through that narcissistic wound, that disqualification of humanity, that disqualification of the ego, that failing in primary identification—and one can surmise that such a trial might impose itself on the child, too. Shame supposes the subject's identification with the depreciated, damaged object. It is from that place of the disqualified object having lost the subject as object of love, that shame is felt.[3]

Shame and humiliation are, among other things, at the source of the idealisations I have described. Many disabled children become in their parents' eyes mythical, messianic children with a grandiose destiny. Such idealisations and such grandeur are the effect of a reversal of shame.

I have mentioned the work of guilt, and we can also entertain the idea of the work of shame. Shame has functions and operates a psychic work in traumatic contexts.

Shame, first, has a function of burial of the trauma. Ferrant and I have described this special feature of shame: it cannot be repressed, unlike guilt, and is destined rather to be buried. We can say that shame leads into burial the traumatic experience that generates it and that it will thus treat. While guilt performs a potentially subjectivating interiorisation, shame has a less felicitous effect with the interiorisation it produces, preserving the trauma. Shame does not allow the trauma to be overcome; it makes do with burying it, incorporating it.

We could, thus, consider a function not just of burial, but of encapsulation of the trauma, rather like what Rosenfeld (1985) or Tustin (1986, 1990) describe on the matter of the function of "autism capsules" or "autistic enclaves" in non-psychotic personalities, who preserve the trauma as it is, who isolate it and keep it until a situation conducive to an elaboration, to a transformation, arises.

I shall highlight another aspect of the work of shame, setting out from a remark made by Rouchy as he was discussing the transmission of "crypts" and "phantoms", as discussed by N. Abraham and M. Torok (1987). One recalls that Abraham and Torok show how shame produces what they call a crypt: a shameful secret shared with an object in the position of an ideal, and that the subject loses, producing a crypt in the mental space. Discussing the transmission of crypts and phantoms, Rouchy (1995) raises the hypothesis whereby they may be thought of as infiltrating "into the hollow hiding place of forbidden games, of sensations, of unmentionable enjoyments . . . jealously guarded by feelings of shame" (p. 156, translated for this edition). Thus, shame would jealously guard unmentionable enjoyments.

Such enjoyments are especially bound up with anality. Shame is, indeed, strongly connected with anality, as also with the look—the looks of others and the look of one's own ideal on oneself. Shame concerns anality exposed to the gaze of others. We can say that the prototypical situation of shame is that of the child whom the world can see has defecated in his pants. Shame pushes one to flee from the stare and bury anality.[4] And such enjoyments as shame would arise to keep, in the traumatic experience of disability, will, among others, be related to incestuality buried in symbiotic links.

Indeed, in contexts of traumatic encounters with disability, we can observe enjoyment in the symbiotic link that parent and child develop, in the secondary symbiosis as I have just described, with the fantasy of reintroducing the child into the womb or into the family uterus, with incestual acts or the incestual fantasies that accompany that symbiosis, as we have seen.

Shame can, thus, be understood from the perspective of its function as guardian of secret enjoyments. It buries enjoyment. The affect of shame is not readily accessible as it is itself buried, masked, and shame can also be considered to be the guardian of burial, the guardian of the trauma, of what is kept secret, and secret enjoyment.

Let us note that shame will predominantly concern the incestual, while guilt will be more attached to incestuous fantasies (Ciccone, 2009a), if we retain the distinction Racamier (1992, 1993, 1995) establishes between the oedipal incestuous and the incestual, which is an act equivalent to incest but without fantasy, that overflows from the incestuous, and in which the other is denied in his subjectivity and is considered as a utilitarian object of narcissistic enjoyment.

We can, therefore, talk about a work of shame as of a work of guilt. And one can say that this work of shame, in such traumatic contexts, treats the traumatic experience by incorporating it, conserving it, and also treats, by keeping them buried, the incestuous or incestual desires mobilised by the trauma, as well as murderous, infanticidal desires— related to destructiveness, anal sadism, and to hatred.

If shame is an affect felt by the ego, shame can bear on the object, on the damaged, monstrous child, or, more exactly, on the disqualified ego of the subject who has created that monstrous child; but shame can also bear on thoughts, desires, things felt mobilised by and against that child, and, in particular, infanticidal desires, hatred.

While the work of shame treats hatred (buries it, encapsulates it, jealously keeps the secret enjoyment it can procure, etc.), we can also say that shame generates hatred, that child who shames becomes the object of hatred. This is something we often observe. Guilt and shame seal bonds where suffering and enjoyment, violence and attachment intermix. We have seen the tyrannical relation, as a form that symbiosis can take, as often being destructive.

I previously mentioned the matter of grandeur and anality. Moving on from one to the other can be represented, for example, from Meltzer's (1992) conception of the "claustrum", which describes that internal object whose prototype is the maternal body penetrated by projective identification, and inside which the ego gains refuge and navigates, passing from one "compartment" to another. The rectal compartment of the claustrum is the seat of tyrannical processes, of anal destructiveness, of violence and terror. The "head–breast" compartment is that of grandeur, of the swelling of narcissism. The reversal of shame and humiliation into a grandiose exhibition corresponds, in the fantasy and according to Meltzer's model, to the passage of the ego from the anal space of the claustrum to the head–breast space.

So, there is a link, an articulation, between narcissistic wound, humiliation, guilt, shame, grandeur, anality, hatred, and tyranny. One can say that the more idealisation is grandiose, the more the narcissistic wound and exposed anality will be humiliating, and the more hatred and tyrannical destructiveness is violent, the more guilt and shame will be mobilised.

If guilt produces a transaction in the form of potentially subjectivating interiorisation, and shame an interiorisation in the form of conservative incorporation, one can also envisage transmission of such affects, or even consider a relation of transmission between shame and guilt themselves, in traumatic contexts in general, and in such experiences of encountering disability in particular.

Guilt, shame, and transmission

The affects of guilt and shame will first be frequently transmitted. The subject unable to feel such violent affects will find an affect-bearer in another to carry and possibly treat those affects (Ciccone & Ferrant, 2009). That other might be the child himself.

The child and the infant do not initially suffer from guilt and shame. Shame and guilt are first felt by, and pointed at from, outside intervention. It is the look from outside that transmits the perception that the disability is a disability and that imposes an additional burden on the child, made up, among other things, of sentiments of guilt and feelings of shame. The child's guilt and shame will, in part, first be those of another, those of the parent.

It is hard to say to what extent the infant, and the young child can be affected by shame and guilt. The older child, the adolescent, may have accesses of, and possibly talk about, feelings of guilt and shame, in all events the conscious aspects of such sentiments—although this always remains difficult and, finally, fairly rare. Such affects are most often chased from consciousness, or changed into their opposite.

Moreover, the feeling of guilt can be transmitted in such a way as to cause shame in the recipient. Indeed, the idea can be argued that, in traumatic contexts, shame can be the effect of a transmission or a fantasy of cryptic transmission of guilt (Ciccone, 2007a,b, Ciccone & Ferrant, 2004, 2009).

While shame produces a crypt, guilt, too, can be encrypted, when it is not elaborated, when it crushes the ego, when it cannot be subjectivated and, thus, repressed (even if repression is a possible outcome of guilt, unlike shame). If we take up the model of the crypt adopted by Abraham and Torok, and the model of transmission of the crypt, we can state or assume that, in situations of transgenerational transmission of guilt, of the "fault", the feeling of shame or the experience of shame (a diffuse, enigmatic feeling that invades the person concerned) often emerges as the effect of a transmission of non-subjectivated, non-symbolised guilt. Shame would then be the effect of a cryptic transmission of guilt. Here, we are faced with one of the figures of traumatic transmission and transmission of the traumatic.

And one might well think that here is one of the potential effects of parental guilt (but also shame) on the children in the sibling group in general and on the child affected by the anomaly himself.

Parental guilt and shame when not treated, not elaborated, or even not experienced, unspeakable, will weigh twice as heavily on the disabled child as on the other members of the possible sibling group, condemned to look after them, assigned first to a function of affect-bearer, and also subjected to the toxic effects of cryptic transmissions.

Manic and melancholic defensive positions:
repetition–transmission of the primal disappointment

While access to a depressive position and its being overcome testify to an elaboration of the trauma, such a movement is obviously rare, laborious, and presupposes a long term, an adequate (both historical and topographical) distance from the traumatic impact to ensure and assume its elaboration. Close to the traumatic experience, when it is recent or when the subject fails to distance it by occupying a zone of the ego preserved and sufficiently remote from the traumatic zone (especially if the traumatic zone within the ego is too extensive, if the ego has been excessively broken in on), the subject will then occupy or organise various defensive positions to protect against catastrophic anxieties, anxieties of loss, and depressive anxieties.

One can see, in disabled children's families, a frequent oscillation between two extreme defensive positions the parental psyche is led to organise to get away from the traumatic impact of the encounter with disability: a manic position and a melancholic position.

The manic position is organised around illusions, denials; it is not so much the reality of the disability that is denied as the affects, the emotional excitements related to the encounter with the disability.

"My child was never a problem for me, I accepted him just as he was"; "When I learnt my child had Down's syndrome, I was delighted as everyone knows children with Down's are cuddlier than others", etc.

The manic position also contains idealisations, as referred to above.

"My child is an angel", said one mother about her seriously encephalopathic child, and when I took up her words and interpreted them as being metaphorical ("He's like an angel"), she bluntly took issue with me: "No, not like an angel, he *is* an angel."

Other parents reconstruct the image of a mythical child, like the mother who, hyper-attentive to the slightest intellectual progress of her child, became convinced that he was gifted and kept asking constantly for IQ tests.

The disabled child can become a marvellous, messianic child, who will save the family by giving it a narcissistically valorising mission, that of "saving a disabled child".

Idealisation is a schizoid process. It allows the persecutory, cleaved part as the object of depressive feelings or hostile feelings to be kept at bay, as well as violent feelings of envy towards happier motherhoods. And it is the real child who is, thus, kept at a distance. The more the child is invested in as an ideal, angelic, pure child, the more the parent is in contact with that ideal child and less he or she is in contact with the real child, who is then abandoned. But what is rejected is, above all, the mental anguish of which the child is the origin.

The manic position contains the illusion of possible magical repair, which can be expressed, for example, by an agitation seeking to do everything to fill in for what is lacking in what the child has to offer its parents in their daily life.

At the very opposite of this manic position we thus find the melancholic position, characterised by disinvestment (disinvestment in the child or disinvestment in any possible progress the child might be capable of achieving), and negative illusions (that are not forms of disillusion). The negative illusion is an illusion of absence of illusion (cf Roussillon, 1981): the illusion that all is lost, that nothing remains worthy of being attempted or hoped for. The melancholic position does not correspond to a state of mourning and does not allow for the work of mourning, but, rather, expresses a culture of mourning being fed by the love of mourning.

In the manic position, as in the melancholic position, despair and persecutory guilt are deeply at work in the parent, and these will place upon the child an additional burden whenever he has to deal with his parental imagos.

Indeed, the oscillation between manic and melancholic positions fails as far as repair of the traumatic experience is concerned. All it does is reproduce, while simultaneously being the effect of, a repetition of the primal disappointment; by that repetition the parent transmits the experience felt of the primal disappointment. He transmits destroyed, irreparable internal objects, condemning the child to interiorise destroyed imagos and inexorably to repeat the primal disappointment.

The disability as attractor of transmission

The clinical treatment I envisaged is that of the traumatic encounter with a child's disability. It mainly concerns the effects in the parents (and in how the family works) and in the child of such an experience. What I have described could quite well apply, in all or in part, to the possible sibling group of the disabled child, as well as to the professionals, to the teams of carers who commit to, and get involved in, accompanying such children and families.[5]

The disability obviously affects the subject most immediately concerned, the child with that deficiency. A certain number of the effects it produces in the child are dependent on the way the surrounding environment reacts when confronted with the disability. We have seen the effects of guilt, of shame, affects indicated, or even in part transmitted by, the object, by the environment, with the subject possibly being assigned to an affect-bearing function. We saw how the subject's shame can be considered as the effect of a cryptic transmission of the non-elaborated guilt of the object, of the parent. We saw the effect in the child, and in the bond, of the transmission of a shattered parental object. The child can interiorise a damaged, spoilt parental object, can identify with such an object. We can describe the imago encroachments in the internal world of the subjects themselves. The child may submit to or react against such transmissions. We saw the grandeur that can be deployed in the child, the tyranny he or she might develop. We saw how, especially in the oscillation of manic and melancholic positions, the child is condemned to reproduce the primal disappointment.

We can say that the disability is a real attractor for psychic transmission, in the subject as in those around them. It attracts for the subject, as for those around them, the transfer of psychic contents; it is the place of transfer for psychic problems, processes and conflicts, fantasies, imagos, and affects.

The disability attracts parental imagos, as we have seen, that will encroach on the child's subjectivity, and will potentially alienate his or her identity. It attracts oedipal scenes, incestuous fantasies, incestual, symbiotic desires; it awakens old conflicts, repressed, buried, and forgotten affects that will impose themselves on the child, which the child will inherit. The narcissistic wound that it represents, the undermining of the ego it brings with it, make sure the disability will preferentially attract the archaic, narcissistic aspects of psychic conflictuality. It will bring into play, on the very body of the subject, such conflicts. The disability will be a place of transfer of oedipal problems but also, and above all, of the most archaic, most narcissistic issues and conflicts of the subject as also of those close to them.

I put forward the idea whereby the disability (of a child, of a subject) can be seen as representing the imago incorporation of the parent damaged, destroyed, and hurt by the traumatic encounter with her child's disability (Ciccone, 1994, 2007b, 2010, 2012). When the child is confronted by a distraught parent, or a parent whose parenthood has been attacked, undermined, disqualified, his disability will potentially come to represent that hurt parent, that internal parent, or that damaged imago. It will be the trace thereof in the body, and it will be the trace of the process of interiorisation or incorporation of such an object.

The attraction the disability exerts on primitive and less primitive suffering and conflict thus works for those close, for the parents of a disabled child, and works, too, for the subject affected by the disability.

Notes

1. One of the forms of immobilisation of thought—-or one of its effects—is, for example, the centring of the entire family, and everything about the way the family works, around the disability and around saving the child affected by disability, the subjects being alienated from this desperate and illusory imperative of saving.

2. What follows concerning shame and work on shame resumes the theses developed in Ciccone and Ferrant (2004, 2009) and Ciccone (2007a, 2009b).

3. Such a situation is of the same order as that which characterises melancholic identification, which led us, A. Ferrant and myself (Ciccone & Ferrant, 2009) to postulate that shame is to guilt what melancholy is to depression.

4. To stress the link between shame and anal enjoyment, we may well recall Freud's observation when the Rat Man reveals to him, when pushed, the details of the haunting scene, that of anal torture with rats, a scene that disturbs the patient, inspiring disgust in him, a feeling of repugnance: "At all the more important moments while he was telling his story his face took on a very strange, composite expression. I could only interpret it as one of horror at pleasure of his own of which he himself was unaware" (Freud, 1909d, p. 167). Disgust, like shame, is here the guardian of unconscious anal enjoyments.

5. On the effects of disability, cf. also André-Fustier (1986) and Korff Sausse (1996). On the effects in the sibling group, cf. Scelles (2010). On effects of violence, guilt, and shame in teams of carers, cf. Ciccone (2008, 2009c); Ciccone & Ferrant (2009).

References

Abraham, N., & Torok, M. (Eds.) (1987). *L'écorce et le noyau*. Paris: Flammarion.

André-Fustier, F. (Ed.) (1986). *L'enfant "insuffisamment bon" en thérapie familiale psychanalytique*. Lyon: Presses Universitaires de Lyon.

Aulagnier, P. (Ed.) (1975). *La violence de l'interprétation*. Paris: Presses Universitaires de France.

Carel, A. (2002). Le processus d'autorité. Approche clinique et métapsychologique. *Revue groupal, 10*: 7–38.

Ciccone, A. (1994). Handicap et altérité. In: *Actes des Journées nationales de l'ANECAMSP: Entre prévention et évaluation, quelle place pour l'enfant?* (pp. 197–206). Paris: ANECAMSP.

Ciccone, A. (1997). Empiètement imagoïque et fantasme de transmission. In: A. Eiguer (Ed.), *Le Générationnel* (pp. 151–185). Paris: Dunod.

Ciccone, A. (Ed.) (1999). *La transmission psychique inconsciente: identification projective et fantasme de transmission*. Paris: Dunod.

Ciccone, A. (2003). Les enfants qui "poussent à bout": logiques du lien tyrannique. In: A. Ciccone (Ed.), *Psychanalyse du lien tyrannique* (pp. 11–46). Paris: Dunod.

Ciccone, A. (2007a). La transmission psychique à l'épreuve du handicap, In: A. Ciccone, S. Korff Sausse, S. Missonnier, & R. Scelles (Eds.), *Cliniques du sujet handicapé. Actualités des pratiques et des recherches* (pp. 75–92). Toulouse, Érès.

Ciccone, A. (2007b). La tyrannie chez l'enfant porteur de handicap. *Champ psychosomatique, 45*: 35–51.

Ciccone, A. (2008). Violence dans le soin au handicap. In: R. Scelles (Ed.), *Handicap: l'éthique dans les pratiques cliniques* (pp. 43–53). Toulouse: ERES.

Ciccone, A. (2009a). Potentialités incestuelles et mise en histoire générationnelle dans les contextes de handicap. *Le Divan familial, 22*: 67–80.

Ciccone, A. (2009b). Handicap du bébé et travail de la honte dans la famille. In: N. Presme, P. Delion, & S. Missonnier (Eds.), *Les professionnels de la périnatalité accueillent le handicap* (pp. 99–124). Toulouse: Eres.

Ciccone, A. (2009c). Faire violence sous prétexte de soigner. In: S. Korff Sausse (Ed.), *La vie psychique des personnes handicapées* (pp. 197–205). Toulouse: Eres.

Ciccone, A. (2010). Le handicap, l'altérité et le sexuel. In: A. Ciccone (Ed.), *Handicap, identité sexuée et vie sexuelle* (pp. 7–24). Toulouse: Eres.

Ciccone, A. (Ed.) (2012). *La transmission psychique inconsciente: Identification projective et fantasme de transmission* (2nd edn). Paris: Dunod.

Ciccone, A. (Ed.) (2014). *La violence dans le soin*. Paris: Dunod.

Ciccone, A., & Ferrant, A. (2004). Réalité traumatique et "travail de la honte". In: B. Chouvier & R. Roussillon (Eds.), *La réalité psychique: psychanalyse, réel et trauma* (pp. 177–201). Paris: Dunod.

Ciccone, A., & Ferrant, A. (Ed.) (2009). *Honte, culpabilité et traumatisme*. Paris: Dunod.

Freud, S. (1909d). *Notes Upon a Case of Obsessional Neurosis. S. E., 10*: 155–249. London: Hogarth.

Freud, S. (1914c). On narcissism: an introduction. *S. E., 14*: 159–215. London: Hogarth.

Guyotat, J. (Ed.) (1991). *Etudes cliniques d'anthropologie psychiatrique*. Paris: Masson.

Korff Sausse, S. (Ed.) (1996). *Le miroir Brisé. L'enfant handicapé, sa maladie et le psychanalyste*. Paris: Calmann-Lévy.

Meltzer, D. (Ed.) (1992). *The Claustrum*. Strathtay, Perthshire: Clunie Press.

Racamier, P. C. (Ed.) (1992). *Le génie des origines: psychanalyse et psychoses*. Paris: Payot.

Racamier, P. C. (Ed.) (1993). *Cortège conceptuel*. Paris: Ed. Apsygée.

Racamier, P. C. (Ed.) (1995). *L'inceste et l'incestuel*. Paris: Ed. du Collège de Psychanalyse Groupale et Familiale.

Rosenfeld, D. (1985). Identification and its vicissitudes in relation to the Nazi phenomenon. *International Journal of Psychoanalysis, 67*(1): 53–64.

Rouchy, J. C. (1995). Secret intergénérationnel: transfusion, gardien, résurgence. In: S. Tisseron (Ed.), *Le psychisme à l'épreuve des générations. Clinique du fantôme* (pp. 145–174). Paris: Dunod.

Roussillon, R. (1981). Paradoxe et continuité chez Winnicott: les défenses paradoxales. *Bulletin de psychologie, 350*: 503–509.

Roussillon, R. (Ed.) (1991). *Paradoxes et situations limites de la psychanalyse*. Paris: Presses Universitaires de France.

Scelles, R. (Ed.) (2010). *Liens fraternels et handicap. De l'enfance à l'âge adulte*. Toulouse: ERES.

Tustin, F. (Ed.) (1981). *Autistic States in Children*. London: Routledge and Kegan Paul.

Tustin, F. (Ed.) (1986). *Autistic Barriers in Neurotic Patients*. London: Karnac.

Tustin, F. (Ed.) (1990). *The Protective Shell in Children and Adults*. London: Karnac.

Winnicott, D. W. (1956). The antisocial tendency. In: *Collected Papers. Through Paediatrics to Psychoanalysis* (pp. 364–374). London: Basic Books, 1958.

CHAPTER THREE

Cultural interpretation of disability

Charles Gardou

This chapter is devoted to the cultural productions that determine how disability is viewed and that inform behaviour and practice. It derives directly from a trip made with researchers from twenty different countries (Gardou, 2011) to the Oceania continent (the Kanak region and the Marquesas Islands, where we lived for a number of years), to North America with the Inuits in the far north and Canada, South America (Brazil and the Amerindian territory, Surinam and Guyana), the Asian continent (China and the Lebanon), Africa (Senegal and Brazzaville in the Congo, Algeria and the Island of the Reunion), and the European continent (Italy, Norway, Germany, the United Kingdom, Portugal and France).

Our investigation sought to respond to three essential and closely interrelated questions. How is disability actually seen in daily life across the different continents? How can sense be made of the maze of conceptions surrounding disability? Finally, beyond cultural diversity, is there a central unity behind these different visions?

How is disability seen in daily life
across the different continents?

Since time immemorial, disability in its various forms has been a consistent and pervasive reality. This expression of fragility, universally present in time and space, is likely to affect the entire chain of life. No species is exempt. The plant world, too, knows its cases of divergence, as with the monotropa (also known as indianpipe or ghost flower). This strange flower growing in Asia, Europe, and North America has no green parts and is utterly incapable of producing chlorophyll and so is deprived of photosynthesis for sustenance. To survive, it lives in pine forests where, thanks to the filaments of a fungus attached to its roots, it links up to a conifer (without, however, invading its tissue, unlike a regular parasite). The host tree provides the plant with the nutrition it needs to survive and develop. The bird's nest orchid, with its russet flowers, found in Asia and Europe has the same deficiency, leading it to cleave to a deciduous tree (often a beech) to survive. Here, too, a fungus plays an essential intermediary role in passing on vital energy.

Such is the reality of the plant world, where failures and accidents actually contribute to creating the links needed to surmount them. The animal and human world shares many of the same features. Human imperfection, as ever the rule, makes myth of the ideal, the Superman. Between the infant's pram and the Zimmer frame of old age infirmity, those best preserved strive to hide the fact that their history, from alpha to omega whatever the geographical latitude, remains that of their basic puniness and the many constraints life throws up.

Now, wherever they are, people unfailingly seek (setting out from their inner self as fashioned by their culture) other explanations for their incontrovertible imperfection, on the rocky shores of which their Promethean dreams of control, absoluteness, and eternity come crashing down. This quest leads to a tumultuous series of collective perceptions with their lot of glories and accompanying miseries.

Despite their roots that plunge into the same Earth, perceptions of disability reflect the diversity of the soils that nourished them to offer a kaleidoscopic countenance of human life and the multiple nature of its universe. These perceptions have a history and geography, varying from one culture to another and even within the same society according to the period (Stiker, 2005). They impart an original shape to the social bond, tracing demarcation lines between people affected by a disability and others.

What, then, are the perceptions of disability, whether positive or negative, that different cultures generate, incorporate, and vehicle? How do they underpin social practices, specific forms of organisation, attitudes and behaviours towards disabled people? What origin and what meaning do we assign, according to our respective cultural backgrounds, to these different ways of life? The confrontation between the chapters of the great bible of cultures leads to deconstructing what, within any one single society, ends up by appearing to belong to the realm of the natural, the immutable. It gives an insight into what, subsumed within the framework of a particular culture, we are no longer able to distinguish; questions familiar concepts, as handed down by tradition and maintained by cultural conditioning, rooted in habit. It questions the meanings assigned to disability, the responses adopted to it and the specific institutions, arbitrarily fabricated by people, that finally are mere conventions (Douglas, 2004). What singularities do we discover from one stage to another on our trip around the world? Let's take a look at a few examples.

In Oceania, in the Kanak communities of New Caledonia, disability is perceived as a misfortune, just like other forms of adversity. Its interpretations are always relational. The disorder it represents is attributed to rifts, whether voluntary or involuntary, in the relational balance between the person, their family, the community (where the dead and spirits are considered to remain full members), and the cosmos. Identification of the disabled person's social origins is, thus, the business of seers and diviners. In such a context, the victim of misfortune can be either the elected spirit of the divinity or bear the stigma of infamy.

In a similar world view that takes in the terrestrial world, the beyond, and nature, the Maoris of the Marquesas Islands in French Polynesia sought among the powers of the invisible world the roots of the trials of existence. Evils, likely to affect adults or their children, were the sign of divine punishment for the violation of a civil or religious law. Only the mediation of prayers, offerings, and sacrifices that men give up to the gods could afford relief and heal. However, those who survived despite their disability could help others overcome their limits. Thanks to the art of compensation they were forced to develop, they could play a supportive role and act as guides for other mortals.

In North America, the Inuits of the Canadian Arctic interpret the nature, form, and origin of disability in accordance with cultural forms of logic that also take their source in a cosmology where the fate of the living is closely linked to that of the dead, whose names they are given at birth. In their world view, the negative effects of words, behaviours and wrongdoing collectively have an impact on a number of generations sharing the same name. In a harsh, or even hostile, environment, those people who, due to their disability, experience difficulties assuming their social role were formerly set aside, except where they showed outstanding abilities in surmounting the limits caused by their condition. Performativity still rules as an overriding concept to understand their experience and perceptions. Determination, courage, the ability to perform and go beyond one's condition remain bodily and spiritual dispositions valued by the Inuit culture.

In the Amerindian territory of inner Guiana, the Amazonian rainforest communities have managed to preserve their ancestral principles in their relations with the hazards of life and a sense of solidarity in the destiny of fellow creatures, be they human, animal, plant, or even mineral. As with sickness, bad luck or too much rainfall or sunshine, the disability is the sign in their eyes that the time is out of joint, harmony having been disrupted due to behaviour deviating from community rules, or (sometimes extremely ancient) hatreds or vengeances. While the shaman is likely to identify the precise root cause and possibly set matters right, the whole community is, nevertheless, concerned.

For the Saramaka, Djuka, Matawai, Paramaka, Kwinti, and Aluktu black Maroon peoples living alongside the forest rivers of Surinam, the Maroni River on the French Guiana border, and the Lawa, one of its tributaries, there is a whole range of active spirits potentially responsible for impairments to body and mind. Major divinities communicating with humans and some actively beneficial spirits offer their interpretations, their protection, their care, and the people are accustomed to resorting to propitiatory rituals, to prayers, and offerings to the ancestors.

Chinese society considers work as a movement immanent to the internal dynamism of life, and the "face" as the founding and organising mechanism for human relations. Nothing, then, can be worse than not being able to make oneself useful and lose face. As a result, those who, due to a disability (often seen to be the sign of a failing or a fault of the parents or ancestors) do not have a trade or skill, do not marry and, thus, have no offspring, find themselves deprived of social existence.

In the modern Lebanon, in a culture where war assumed the dimension of an existential framework, disability, a memory of tragic responsibility, takes on a near sacred aspect. It is a stark reminder of conflict and those spared remain somehow indebted to the injured. Its representations are loaded with feelings of indebtedness, duty, shame, and compassion, sustained by religion. It is through religion that you express repentance, salve your conscience, and find relief from guilt. Relations with people suffering from disabilities above all come under the sway of a notion of debt and duty combined. You bear in you the disability suffered by others, living this out as a form of handicap in itself.

In Senegal, God alone decides sovereignly, so people think, as to the lot of human beings, doling out happiness or unhappiness. Disability is, thus, an existential misfortune with a strong spiritual meaning attached to it. The depreciation and exclusion of those who find themselves victims are reinforced by a social and a symbolic order rolled into one. Those who approach it remain ambivalent—invested by ancestral fears, they seek to ward off the "danger" while simultaneously hoping, through offering alms, to obtain God's blessing. The disabled, thus, play the role of go-betweens for what is seen and remains unseen, the human and the divine. Despite belief in a unique and omniscient God, people also believe in spirits, both good and bad, who bestow bliss or bring down misfortune on human beings.

In the imaginary framework of the traditional Algerian family, disability is often equated with a curse on the parents that pursues the offspring, or the evil eye aroused by mysterious forces. That explains why the new-born baby is sheltered from the gaze of others for a period that varies from one region to another so as to afford protection against spell casters and other ill-intentioned individuals. This traditional matrix nowadays combines with more modern conceptions. So, the family will resort to the physician and the healer, the psychologist or psychiatrist, the taleb or the marabout. Similarly, there is a tension between fantastic perceptions of the disability and institutional practices that seek to remain rational.

In Italy, how disability is conceived of varies between north and south. Some perceptions of failings in the soma, the mind, and the psyche in the south are still under the sway of magical–religious thinking. But, more globally, the Italian cultural landscape bears the dual imprint of the popular pagan cultures of the south and that of Christianity, that went from a concept of disability as a sorrow-sin to one of sorrow-necessity, a sign of the divine will underscored by a link between suffering and redemption. The country also remains marked by the process of deinstitutionalisation, as commenced at the end of the 1970s, and by the contributions of some anthropologists (especially Ernesto de Martino) that led to defining disability as a set of interiorised social barriers, a loss of control of one's own story, told by others.

How to make sense of the maze of conceptions surrounding disability?

Our ways of construing and taking into account the disability proceed, as will be seen, from a cultural imagination as to ourselves, others, and our common human condition. Faced with the maze of meanings that are conferred on this human reality and the difficulties involved in identifying them in an operational fashion, let us try to characterise some different conceptions:

An "anonymous being" or an imbalance?

To adopt the expression used by Laplantine and Thomas (1986) in their remarkable work *Anthropologie de la maladie,* in an ontological conception, the disability is considered to be an isolatable reality: an evil in itself, an otherness, a foreign entity, pathogenic, lesional. This "anonymous being", having broken in "somewhere", can be identified. This is something that certain slang expressions on behavioural disorders reflect in a deprecatory fashion. In French, the common term for mad or crazy is *dingue,* a derivative of "dengue", itself coming from the Swahili expression *ki denga pepo,* that can be translated by "cramps" caused by an evil spirit. (The disease is actually caused by hematozoan parasites being inoculated into the blood by mosquito bites.) In English, the word "crazy" itself derives from the idea of something being full of cracks. There is, therefore, this pervasive notion of either a form of invasion or dislocation. The *International*

Classification of Impairments, Disabilities and Handicaps (World Health Organization, 1980) is largely based on this underlying concept, ascribing the handicap to the lesional aspect, that is, a locatable deficiency affecting an anatomic structure or an organ function, including of a mental or psychological nature.

This organicist, anatomical, and localising vision, inspired by the bio-medical model, reduces the disability to a lesion, commanding an exclusive relation with the body. In the name of scientific legitimacy and technical efficacy, the person's point of view is denied, to be succeeded by an entity in many respects imaginary, whereby our society defines the impairment. This is perceived as an individual problem requiring medical treatment. Failing a cure, normalisation, adaptation of the person, or changes in their behaviour are sought. Medical care constitutes the main preoccupation and, at a political level, the response involves amending or reforming health policies. A reductionist model of the body is adopted: anatomy, and anatomy alone. The fact that the body and its perception occupy a space between anatomy, the libidinal and the phantasmatic, as modelled by cultural and social factors, is disregarded.

In a functional or relational conception, the disability is no longer thought of in terms of "being". A dynamic approach comes in to replace the lesional perspective. Organic dysfunctions (of the eyes, the ears, or structures involved in movement) are not evacuated but, rather, an interest is taken in their functional impacts. The dysfunction is also seen as an impairment or imbalance; the consequence of a disharmonious, disturbed, upset relation between the person and their environment. The improvement process then takes the path of a relational rebalancing.

An external element or an internal process?

An exogenous conception reminds us of perceptions of the disability as accident, related to the action of an extrinsic element. Where does it come from? From nature or biology? From the social environment, the life-style or culture? From a pathogenic family? In the latter case, the mother is often the one suspected. She is the one in the wrong, it is her fault and maybe she wanted the child she brought into the world to be that way. The flawed assumptions attributing autism (whose aetiology has yet to be revealed) to a pathology in the mother–child bond come to mind. Perhaps a form of vengeance is the cause? A sorcerer, a genie, a spirit, a demon, God, or simply fate? Perceptions of the disability as a curse correspond to this conception.

Conversely, where an endogenous conception comes into play, the disability shifts to the side of the person affected. It comes from within, being an intrinsic process. Whence notions of dispositions or predispositions, of genetic heritage or heredity, of terrain and nature, constitution, temperament, or "internal environment", as in Claude Bernard's expression (1865), for whom stability of the internal environment predominated as clearly being the *sine que non* precondition for life being maintained. Interpretations of disability as a punishment are rooted in this conception: it is thought of as the consequence of what the individual or the social group have themselves caused, either unconsciously or deliberately, by negligence, excess, or transgression. If one looks to the Christian tradition, for the Hebrews of the Old Testament, the afflictions of the "impotent folk", the "blind, halt and withered" were handed down by God, who, thus, punished Man's lack of faith. Such is the story of Job and his many trials.

An excess or a loss

In an additive conception, the disability is represented as being an element that has penetrated the body or the spirit: an undesirable excess requiring an exeresis; a pathogenic excrescence to be removed. Something the person bears as a burden ("bearing a disability"). What counts most here are notions of excess. The very story of the word "handicap" is interesting in this respect. Once applied to the world of horse racing, it took on the meaning of an extra weight some horses have to carry to even the betting stakes. This additive conception also informs

> the historical and cultural basis of Christianity, for which the individual is born in a state of sin (original sin) and must seek to be relieved of this burden by the intercession of a third party (Christ, or the Lamb of God), of whom the biblical text states that he taketh away the sin of the world" (Laplantine & Thomas, 1986, p. 113, translated for this edn)

Under a subtractive conception, the disability is "something less" that has been taken away or has escaped from the person ("loss of reason", or, slang, "losing one's marbles"). It refers to the inability or the privation of being able to compensate the deficit, the deficiency to be made good, or the lack that has to be made up for. These are notions of prevailing absence, suppression, loss, hollowness, or emptiness and alienation. More popular expressions such as "off one's head" and "round the bend" echo such perceptions of disorientation and disarticulation. It was precisely this negative vision that the *International Classification of Functioning, Disability and Health* came in to redress by replacing the *International Classification of Impairments, Disabilities and Handicaps* in May 2011.[1] Based on a bio-psycho-social conception, it seeks to coherently synthesise biological, individual, educational, and social perspectives.

A calamity or a fecund experience?

In perceptions dominated by the conception of a malevolent influence, the disability is considered to be an absolute evil, an abnormality, a biological deviance and, at the same time, a social deviance. It becomes an object of devaluation, of humiliation and shame, becoming synonymous with stigmatisation, exclusion, and death. It is seen as a calamity, a radical non-sense; an absurdity, an abjection nothing could justify. The person affected is seen by others as being socially devalued, out of sync, and feels that, too, within himself/herself.

Conversely, as part of a more benign outlook, the disability may have a positive meaning bestowed on it. It fulfils an irreplaceable social balancing out. It makes for an especially fecund and meaningful experience, entailing knowledge, transcendence, and transfiguration of oneself, an opportunity to discover the invisible mainsprings of forces that emerge from vulnerability itself (Gardou, 2009).

Is there a certain unity beyond cultural diversity?

Beyond the multiplicity of cultural roots, discontinuities, and dissemblance, can forms of culture that are recalcitrant to uniformity nevertheless show a certain unity? Their system of perceptions of disability is, here as elsewhere, a cultural construction that is handed down, learnt, and interiorised from early childhood: a kind of common good.

Without for one moment denying the objective reality of physical, sensorial, mental, cognitive, or psychic deficiencies, whether congenital or acquired, likely to lead to a disability, the latter also stems from a cultural background, inherited, modelled, and woven from historic, social, relational, religious, economic, and political elements. It is a total social phenomenon (as Marcel Mauss would have put it) that can only be grasped in the real-life situation. How they are looked on depends, primarily, on the cultural context, as Michel Foucault so luminously showed in *Madness and Civilization* (Foucault, 1965). Its interpretation is never solely individual, but depends on a social order, that is, above all, a mental order. The latter, being determined by culture, relates to the quest for a meaning faced with the enigma that is Man. Indeed, if there is one search for meaning that affects every individual in any culture, then it is the possibility of disability, latent or fortuitous, that haunts us with a sense of dismay.

The system of perceptions takes root in the deepest strata of a culture. What is more cultural than that? Under the outward appearance of what is natural, it is difficult to disaggregate. The system encompasses forms of thinking into "normality" and "abnormality", theories, profane, institutional, or scholarly discourse, beliefs about disability, ideologies and values brought into play. Culture here plays a crucial role, much like a printer that draws and prints characters point by point. While the members of a particular society are differently influenced, they still tend mostly to fit into the mould, generating a new vein of unconscious constructions and other collective illusions.

Within a culture, the common belief thus creeps into individual thinking, irradiates it, and, to a certain extent, shapes it. Psychoanalysis, a discipline so complementary to anthropology, teaches us that bonds are close between the individual's unconscious and the social unconscious as defined by norms. Although human beings do not behave exactly like bees and ants, there nevertheless prevails a form of regimentation of personal and social life. This entails that each culture has its own way of defining markers to govern relations with people affected by disabilities. Marcel Sendrail (1980) wrote in his *Histoire Culturelle de la Maladie* that each culture makes claim to a style in terms of disability much as it does in matters of literary, decorative, or monumental style.

Only distorted echoes of the disability actually reach us, warping our vision, generating divisions and exclusion. Plato's famous allegory of the cave in Book VII of *The Republic* springs to mind. The men confined and shackled underground only know of things, of others, and themselves what they see in the shadows thrown by the fire on the part of the cavern wall facing them. Similarly, when confronted by disability, our minds are clouded by the sediment of mythology and the deeper alluvium deposited on the collective unconscious. These handed down beliefs prove to be much more pervasive than the objective observation of the eminently pusillanimous nature of human beings. Their strength and the difficulty in overcoming them derive first from their mythological and collective nature and, second, from the fact that their foundations are so rarely challenged.

It is, therefore, hardly surprising that it is so difficult to gain release from the cultural chains that bind a society together; tearing oneself away from the established format to question the particular vision of disability that a culture "imposes" on its members; ridding oneself of common perceptions; dissenting to accede to "transgressive", individual thinking. People's anxieties stem as much from the culturally constructed nature of disability as from its objective reality. Wherever they are in the world, they fail to make it "natural", to consider it as an eventuality in their existence and accept their fate in resigning to the failing or inadequacy. This "threatening" situation symbolises a wound, within themselves and outside them, they can no more succeed in eliminating as admitting. It "strikes" the person and their broadest environment, disrupting the reigning cultural order. It corrupts the ideal rooted in any culture that specifically delimits conformance and defines deviance (Durkheim & Mauss, 1903), elaborates categories, makes sure people comply with them, generates and maintains processes of interaction, opposition, and relegation to otherness or segregation.

In most cultures, people affected by disabilities are condemned to follow a separate path, to live out of the way (atopically), with no real place in the social structure, sometimes surviving as beggars. They are physically present but destined to live in a world outside, away from the general flow of life, corseted by myth and phantasm, or even physically strait-jacketed, in all events hampered from taking part in society.

While, according to the culture, some disabilities are more devaluing than others, none escapes from opprobrium. Wherever it may be, disability concentrates Man's eschatological fears such that those who experience it on a daily basis remain, to varying degrees, prey to an imaginary world nurtured by immemorial and deep-rooted fears. A constellation of images deforms their existential reality, compounding the "handicap". This results in them suffering from that form of alienation that Erving Goffman (1975) calls a negative, spoiled identity: a "handicapped identity" produced by the culture of belonging that impresses on their minds and bodies the representation it makes of them.

Such is the universal conundrum in thinking out what makes Man whole and accepting the human condition as it is, not as we would imagine it to be.

As can be seen, the multiplicity of cultures and religious beliefs, in which so many varying conceptions take root, nevertheless fails to erase the underlying unity of any human experience. The best shared thing in the world is maybe the anguished confusion human beings feel when confronted by their vulnerability, of which disability is just one of the many expressions, with various ways of evading, warding off, or evacuating it, but with ever the same paradoxical dream of being relieved of their common humanity.

Note

1.   The *International Classification of Functioning, Disability and Health* was endorsed at the 54th World Health Assembly of 22 May 2001 (WHA Resolution 54.21). Accepted as one of the social classifications for the United Nations, it takes in the *Rules for the Equalisation of Opportunities for Persons with Disabilities* adopted by the United Nations General Assembly at its 48th session on 20 December 1993.

References

Bernard, C. (Ed.) (1865). *Introduction à l'étude de la médecine expérimentale*. Paris: JB Baillière et Fils (Garnier Flammarion, 1966).

Douglas, M. (Ed.) (2004). *Comment pensent les institutions*. Paris: La Découverte.

Durkheim, E., & Mauss, M. (1903). De quelques formes primitives de classification. Contribution à l'étude des représentations collective. *Année sociologique*, 6: 1–72.

Foucault, M. (Ed.) (1965). *Madness and Civilization: A History of Insanity in the Age of Reason*. New York: Pantheon.

Gardou, C. (Ed.) (2009). *Pascal, Frida Kahlo et les autres . . . Ou quand la vulnérabilité devient force*. Toulouse: Eres.

Gardou, C. (Ed.) (2011). *Le handicap au risque des cultures. Variations anthropologiques*. Toulouse: Eres.

Goffman, E. (Ed.) (1975). *Stigmate. Les usages sociaux des handicaps*. Paris: Editions de Minuit.

Laplantine, F., & Thomas, L. V. (Eds.) (1986). *Anthropologie de la Maladie. Etude ethnologique des systèmes de représentations étiologiques et thérapeutiques dans la société occidentale contemporaine*. Paris: Payot.

Sendrail, M. (Ed.) (1980). *Histoire Culturelle de la Maladie*. Toulouse: Privat.

Stiker, H. J. (Ed.) (2005). *Corps infirmes et sociétés: essais d'anthropologie historique*. Paris: Dunod.

World Health Organization (Ed.) (1980). *International Classification of Impairments, Disabilities, and Handicaps: A Manual of Classification Relating to the Consequences of Disease* (Published in accordance with resolution WHA29. 35 of the Twenty-ninth World Health Assembly, May 1976). Geneva: World Health Organization.

CHAPTER FOUR

Prediction, disability, and genetics

Marcela Gargiulo

Introduction

G enetic science is both fascinating and disturbing. It can spark enthusiasm, but it can also feed fear. By delving into the possibly inherited genetic factors in the body, genetics sheds new light on what was previously regarded as an ungraspable and mysterious field of knowledge. Hence, genetic science makes a significant change in symbolic references.

A genome-based prediction possibility is more than mere scientific information. A test needs to be considered in the light of the patient's reality, lest its results spawn an "informative illusion" regarding the notions of body, time, and death.

DNA testing can reveal genetic mutations. Those mutations can be responsible for a considerable range of genetic disorders. We shall particularly confine our focus to late onset neurogenetic diseases leading to severe disabilities and dependencies. Some of these diseases are associated with cognitive impairment that can evolve into dementia.

When a parent is carrying a mutation or is already affected by a disease, genetic tests can supply information to healthy offspring as to their genetic status. Test results can provide answers to the following question: "Am I carrying the same genetic anomaly that is responsible for the disease or disability affecting certain members of my family?"

When dealing with cancer or cardiac pathologies, one may recommend medical supervision or possibly preventative measures once presymptomatic (or predictive) genetic testing has been done. The same does not apply with late onset neurodegenerative diseases where medicine is confronted by the paradox of, on the one hand, having to anticipate and predict the emergence of diseases and disabilities while, on the other, being unable to propose any remedial or preventative measures after an unfavourable result. Presymptomatic tests can reveal numerous neurodegenerative diseases, including cerebellar ataxia, autosomal dominant spastic paraparesis, Charcot–Marie–Tooth disease, facioscapulohumeral myopathy, oculopharyngeal myopathy, Creutzfeldt-Jakob disease, familial dystonia, Steinert myotony, CADASIL syndrome, Alzheimer's disease, and Parkinson's disease. Late genetic testing has also revealed some familial forms of amyotrophic lateral sclerosis as well as many other neurological diseases.

An unfavourable presymptomatic test result points to the risk of developing the disease and ensuing disability. Hence, learning a test result can stimulate an anticipated mourning process in which a patient begins to cope with the loss (as yet inoperative) of his or her "normal" reality. Such diseases can be passed down from one generation to the next, with a 50% risk that the child will become the recipient of the genetic anomaly where a parent carries the gene.

Anticipating the test result might well warp time perception. A time constriction can be felt between the healthy stage and the stage at which the disease manifests itself. Complete gene penetrance carries a shift from a potential to a real disability one has to accept. Hence, presymptomatic testing might have the effect of merging present and future through a telescoping effect.

The time factor affords a distance and space for elaboration and understanding. However, genetics and its insights challenge and disrupt this process, transforming lack of knowledge into clear information as to the future, how body and mind will evolve, the onset of disability, and possible subsequent loss. Here, it is worth recalling Masson's word of caution on scientific breakthroughs: "Genetic discoveries improve our knowledge regarding possible events. However, the information it provides belongs to the present time, it doesn't certify any future" (Masson, 1997, p. 179, translated for this edition). If we fail to heed this warning, genetic predictions can induce confusion between knowledge and truth. As a clinical psychologist and therapist with experience of genetic disease counselling, I have observed that no gene simply equates with fate or destiny. Learning a test result cannot be considered to mark a fresh start in a patient's life, but, rather, forms a part of their history and their unconscious mind (Gargiulo & Rosenblum, 2013).

How can one carry on with life once the results have been disclosed? Is it better to know or not to know? This proves to be a complex question when individuals at risk of a disorder's onset choose to undergo presymptomatic testing without any preventative measure. Such is the case, for example, with Huntington's disease, the first in medical history for which presymptomatic testing was proposed. This is a far cry from a neutral medical approach. Individuals "at risk" are induced to ponder their situation as well as on their free personal decision to know or not to know.

On a psychological level, presymptomatic testing highlights to what extent individuals may be unaware of something important, a vital issue, relating to themselves. But once the result is known, the emerging situation is characterised by the paradox that "while the disease and its subsequent disability prove to be real, its external manifestations remain for the time being imperceptible" (Gargiulo & Salvador, 2009). An unfavourable result means that while an individual is still healthy, they know they will develop the disease, and, thus, they start anticipating its emergence with the accompanying disabilities.

Presymptomatic testing for Huntington's disease: twenty years of experience since the first consultation in France (Pitié Salpêtrière Hospital)

Huntington's disease

Huntington's disease is paradigmatic in many respects. It is inherited in an autosomal dominant pattern. By delving into the family history, we often observe psychiatric, cognitive, and behavioural disorders, as well as uncontrolled movements.

Including all ethnic groups, the estimated prevalence in Europe is 0.5 to 1 in 10,000 (Kremer, 2002). This neurodegenerative disease especially targets the striatum in the mid-brain, the caudate nuclei, the putamen, and, subsequently, it will affect the cerebral cortex. It often affects people between the ages of thirty and forty-five. The condition gets gradually worse over time until uncontrolled movements and dementia appear, eventually leading to death after an average of twenty years. Meanwhile, we should bear in mind that each patient's medical story is unique and, thus, impossible to predict with any real degree of certainty. Carrying the disease presents a risk of one in two that each pregnancy will pass on the disease to the offspring. From one generation to another, we sometimes observe a phenomenon of genetic anticipation, with the offspring's gene mutation causing the symptoms to appear at an earlier stage in life than for their parents.

International recommendations

In France, presymptomatic testing is based on international guidelines providing a framework of recommended procedures for Huntington's disease diagnosis (International Huntington Association and World Federation of Neurology, 1994). Those guidelines are informed by five ethical principles. Testing should aim to benefit the individual being tested; that individual should be fully independent and have the required age of majority (testing is not possible before eighteen years of age); they must be in a position to make an informed decision; they must be availed both of full confidentiality in the matter and, finally, they also dispose of the right to choose not to know. The process of presymptomatic testing for a multi-disciplinary consultation includes a number of compulsory stages: (a) providing information about testing; (b) devoting thought to the matter; (c) decision-making; (d) blood test; (e) learning the results; (f) follow-up regardless of whether the result is favourable or unfavourable. This process gives the individuals the time to think things over between the initial test request and obtaining the results. Following on from the first consultation, at least three other interviews are proposed before decision-making and the blood test stage (Durr et al., 2005). Whether the result announced is favourable or unfavourable, the individuals have a further consultation with the same psychologist who helped them earlier in the reflection stage.

When considering the impact of such a process on a patient's future, the composition of the team (geneticist, neurologist, and clinical psychologist) and the time they can devote to the patient are of the utmost importance. This kind of medical consultation evolves gradually and requires the attention of a clinical psychologist who can help the patient adjust to such unsettling news and assist them in remaining committed to the process. The patient can still choose to remain in a situation of uncertainty. However, they need to be able to identify the consequences of such a result on their future life.

> So, a test refusal doesn't just imply a patient's refusal to know. It could also mean that they are just not yet ready to hear the results at that stage in their life. There is a possibility that the patient is not prepared to hear the results. (Gargiulo & Rosenblum, 2013, p. 173, translated for this edition)

Psychological interview and anticipation

Active listening through psychological interviews is important. The individuals concerned are reminded that we are not there to evaluate their choice but, rather, to help them listen to their own words, their own understanding of things. As the poet René Char put it: "The words which are going to come out know something about us which we don't know about them" (Char, 1977, p. 190, translated for this edition).

In such a process, the interview does not serve to analyse whether the test request is legitimate or not; it neither involves the expert's opinion, nor evaluates the patient's profile. Rather, the psychologist here considers the patient's reality based on their own statements and words. The patient is called on to take the initiative, whether they decide to take the test or not. This means the individuals concerned accept the consequences of their choice, while bearing in mind that the latter are well-nigh impossible to predict.

Such interviews emphasise the importance of mental anticipation. This forms part of a necessary process before the individual's decision to take (or not take) the test. When learning the results, whatever the outcome, patients are called on to plan for the future. Such anticipation is crucial in respect to the following three issues. First, by anticipating, individuals may gradually adjust to a new perception of time.

Second, they may learn to cope with waiting. Third, in some cases, by anticipating the impact testing might have on their future, patients may choose not to proceed with it.

How can testing impact patients?

Since 1992, 1,635 persons at risk for Huntington's disease have asked for presymptomatic testing at the genetics outpatient clinic at the Pitié Salpêtrière Hospital[1] (Paris) and initiated the testing procedure. After a variable delay and multi-step counselling, 1,078 (66%) decided to have the test performed and obtained their result, while 44% withdrew from testing for various reasons at different stages of the predictive counselling course, most of them after the first visit. The large number of those abandoning shows that requesting a genome test does not necessarily mean the patient really wishes to know. This clearly shows how important it is to listen carefully to the patient.

A number of studies have revealed that whether the testing result is favourable or not, learning the test results does not lead on to a significant number of dramatic outcomes, such as suicide or attempting suicide (Almqvist et al., 1999; Decruyenaere et al., 1995; Goizet et al., 2002; Timman et al., 2004; Wiggins et al., 1992). In Europe, 20% of persons at risk request testing for Huntington's disease (Almqvist et al., 2003; Mandich et al., 1998). A study on French groups reports that one person in two fails to follow this up after the first interview and that one person in ten finally refuses testing between the first interview and the moment scheduled for the blood test (Goizet et al., 2002).

Individuals who stick to the whole process and reach the result learning stage are generally thinking about having children or concerned to inform the children they already have of any risks (Gargiulo et al., 2009).

Individuals who, after careful consideration, decide not to go ahead with testing show to what extent an expression of intention and a request to know can be followed by a dismissal defence mechanism. If the desire to know prevails, this comes at the expense of an internal conflict. Most of those who request testing formulate their need to know and anticipate (Lesca et al., 2002). Where there is the likelihood of an unfavourable result, a test request expresses more than just a need to know. It signals the will to plan ahead and prepare oneself for future disease and disability.

When coming to a decision through the counselling process, many individuals at risk explain that through knowing whether they carry the gene or not, they can make arrangements: "I'm going to enjoy the time left before I become ill", "If I carry the disease, I'll leave my wife—I don't want her and my children to suffer from watching me lose my faculties", "I'm going to make financial arrangements so that my family doesn't go through hard times", "If I carry the disease, I won't have children". In some extreme cases, individuals mention their wish to commit suicide when the first signs of the disease appear.

The fact that a person is willing to anticipate both scenarios before taking the test is indicative of them seeking to overcome any passive attitude. While genetics dictates its laws, individuals will still seek to shape their lives. Anticipation provides a way of reclaiming one's future rather than being deprived of it. Thus, anticipation can be seen as an attempt by the individual to gain control over the scenario established by medical fact, which otherwise would reduce that individual to an object (Gortais & Gargiulo, 2000).

Decruyenaere and colleagues (1995) show that depression and anxiety levels decrease significantly five years after having learnt the result, no matter whether the test result proves favourable or not. Gargiulo and colleagues (2009) monitored 119 patients after the testing stage. Sixty-two individuals were carriers and fifty-seven did not carry the gene. At the end of a mean period of 3.7 years (range: 0.32 to 8.9) after the result was announced, depression was frequent in carriers (58%) and a significant percentage of non-carriers (24%) were depressed during follow-up. There was one suicide attempt and one hospitalisation in the psychiatric department for major depression after presymptomatic testing in carriers. It is important to note, however, that non-carriers also attempted suicide, one female non-carrier made two suicide attempts after the results and another woman non-carrier attempted suicide during a psychotic episode. After receiving the results of presymptomatic testing, 31% of carriers and 15% of non-carriers were under psychiatric care, a difference that was statistically significant ($p = 0.05$). Our clinical observations thus confirm some disturbing results regarding those patients not carrying the gene.

Paradoxical reactions and guilt

Indeed, both our clinical observations and extensive interviews revealed paradoxical reactions among individuals not carrying the gene. Those reactions appeared after learning favourable results. Those individuals had to manage and reorganise a change in their identity. Having considered themselves at risk, they ended up constructing their lives around the fear of carrying the gene: "I didn't marry, I didn't have children because I was convinced I would have the disease"; "My grandfather and my father died young, before the age of forty, so since I was thirteen, I thought I would be the next on the list". In certain cases, a favourable result would appear to feed "survivor guilt" with regard to carriers or those having already developed the disease. This guilt is a powerful force when it comes to their siblings.

The "survivor syndrome" has been described in the context of major disasters, as in the case of victims of war and former concentration camp inmates. Bettelheim evokes survivors' questions: "Why have I been spared? Consciousness would answer: . . . because another prisoner died in your place" (Bettelheim, 1979, p. 43, translated for this edition). When genetic hereditary diseases affect families, testing results become a family and group concern. Seeking to appropriate test results yields to a carrier–non-carrier polarity, based on a binary fate (Frischmann et al., 2008).

Siblings then experience a split in their connection with their fellow offspring. This connection is based on a myth of shared heredity. A gap ends up confronting their connection, leading them to differentiate radically. This constitutes a break-up in the sense that while being similar as brothers and sisters, they suddenly also become quite different. Brothers and sisters usually share a clear and unquestionable biological connection—a blood relationship. However, when a brother or sister carries a particular gene while their siblings do not, disillusionment sets in, the picture becomes demystified. They must then accept the fact that they might face a quite distinct fate from that of the other siblings. Thus, they perceive a tragic dissymmetry.

Caniou (1999) reports how a favourable test result can feed guilt and, thus, confront an individual. This guilt can be even felt towards their parents: "Why my mother and not me? That question has kept coming back to me since my earliest childhood. Very young, I was formed by that guilt. I felt my own life brought about my mother's decline. How can I bear this? How can I be worthy of my family, how can I pay for it?" Genetic disorders unfold an individual's understanding of their transgenerational history and of biological heredity.

Thus, when learning a favourable test result, a person can feel both a sense of guilt and indebtedness to their family.

We have observed that non-carriers need time to mentally recover after learning a "good result". Such reactions of failure to show joy or relief appear paradoxical. Yet, a favourable outcome to testing might well be perceived as a "wild interpretation" (Brun, 2001). The results might also generate a mental division. An illustration of this is reported by Caniou (1999) where a tested patient, having learnt of the favourable result, declared, "On the outside, nothing has changed in my life. However, the statement 'you are not carrying the gene', which I fully understood, shook me up, triggered my consciousness of finitude, and made me feel exposed."

Prenatal diagnosis

A European study reveals that requesting a prenatal diagnosis does not necessarily follow on from unfavourable presymptomatic testing results (Evers-Kiebooms et al., 2002b). In dominant diseases, prenatal diagnosis is a special matter. Parents who pass on the gene will themselves be affected. There is a 50% risk of passing on the gene to offspring who may then carry the altered gene. In some cases, couples eventually request a medical abortion.

Lesca and colleagues (2002) observed that women are twice as demanding for presymptomatic testing. Expectant mothers seem to be more concerned about being affected and passing on the disease than men are. The discovery of the gene responsible for Huntington's disease gradually led to an increase in the number of presymptomatic test requests. However, the number of prenatal diagnosis requests following on from unfavourable results remained low.

A European study was conducted on a population of 180 carriers of the Huntington's disease gene and 271 non-carriers, in Aberdeen, Athens, Cardiff, Leiden, Leuven, Paris, and Rome (Evers-Kiebooms et al., 2002a). Considering the reproductive age group with an average age of 31.5, the study revealed that for 85% of carriers, as well as 72% of non-carriers, there was no pregnancy. Only 60% of carriers who had children after testing requested a prenatal diagnosis. Such a low rate of requests among carriers suggests that the desire to have a child might be over-determined by concerns other than genetic risk. Moreover, an unfavourable result might actually trigger the individual's narcissism and desire to procreate. Consequently, an individual's desire to have a child might prevail over the perceived risk of passing the gene on to one's offspring.

Being in a state of anxiety

Being at a high risk of carrying the gene generates ambivalence. It yields a sense of opposites: carrier/non-carrier. These opposites leave the patient in an unprecedented situation. Caught up in this dualism, individuals might be overwhelmed by a sense of doubt—am I a carrier or not? Such doubt is redolent of obsessive ambivalence. It may overwhelm, disable, or inhibit individuals' thinking and acting.

When experiencing doubt, a patient needs to know their real genetic position. Doubt is often unbearable when dealing with the anguish of waiting and self-observation. Any change in behaviour, any abnormal movement, could be interpreted as a sign of disease: "Is anything getting out of my control? Am I forgetting any word, any work to accomplish, or any meeting? When this distressing question comes back to my mind: is it the beginning of the disease?" (Caniou, 1999, translated for this edition). Anything can trigger anxiety. However, we should not confuse a carrier's anxiety with a psychotic anxiety. It is not the kind of anxiety Pasche (1996) described as death anxiety among healthy patients with no external threatening sign. It is not a hypochondriac anxiety either: "the withdrawal from unconscious representations of an organ, a function, or their immobilisation can generate a void to be filled by disturbing physical sensations in the body" (Brusset, 2002, p. 64, translated for this edition). When repeatedly exposed to several family members' disability, individuals question their genetic risk. We might here be assisting in the emergence of a new clinical approach, with these unprecedented situations leading to new complaints and forms of anxiety.

The notion of anxiety proves to be a good tool to understand experience through a testing process. Minimal anxiety proves to be a protective signal, preparing individuals to learn the test result. Freud insisted on the positive side to anxiety, as being an anticipation and preparation for danger (Freud, 1916–1917, 1933a).

> Fright, fear and anxiety are improperly used as synonymous expressions; they are in fact capable of clear distinction in their relation to danger. Anxiety describes a particular state of expecting the danger or

preparing for it . . . fear inquires a definite object of which to be afraid. Fright, however, is the name we give to the state a person gets into when he has run into danger without being prepared for it . . . there is something about anxiety that protects its subject against fright. (Freud, 1920g)

In a presymptomatic testing situation, those three notions seem to be well represented. Anxiety is experienced while waiting for a possibly threatening result.

Fear of the results is experienced under knowledge that resolution of the uncertainty will come through an announcement of the result in binary form: carrier/non-carrier. Fear is based on excessive anxiety, with a primary danger "overwhelming the defensive ability of the body-ego" (Freud, 1923b).

If not prepared by the anxiety signal, an inflow of external energy would force the stimulus barrier and, thus, generate a trauma. "The Ego is concerned with its security. It uses anxiety sensations as a warning against any danger that may threaten its integrity" (Freud, 1940a). Accordingly, as a signal, anxiety is a self-protective and a self-organising mechanism for the ego. Such anxiety may be considered normal and necessary in the waiting context of genetic testing. By contrast, automatic anxiety would be a sign of distress and trauma, leading the ego to actual neurosis.

Prior to testing, successive consultations are used in order to helping trigger anxiety as a signal so as to reduce the pathogenic and traumatic effects announcement of the test results might induce. However, for two reasons, it would be illusory to believe that a result will have no traumatic effect. This is, first, because learning the results raises questions of identity, of filiation, and, particularly, of prediction as to the future. Second, anticipation does not spare individuals from suffering mental collapse, from coming adrift. When unprepared, individuals might feel fright, becoming overwhelmed by their instincts: it becomes impossible for them to frame such an unfathomable, unthinkable event.

Laplanche (1980) emphasises the paradoxical nature of the situation: "Fright continues, when we thought the individual would be prepared through the number of experiences he went through" (p. 58, translated for this edition). Anticipating does not completely prepare against fright, since the attack can be internal and can overwhelm the ego.

Hence, anxiety has a dual status: its intentional aspect (as an alarm signal) is closer to fear. Its irrational aspect (which is automatic and attacks the subject from the inside) is closer to fright.

Deferred action

Revealing a genetic diagnosis can be considered as a way of triggering a latent event. In our clinical practice, we observed that the traumatic announcement brings back to consciousness a more or less dormant past event. Freud often used the notion of "deferred action" to explain his conception of mental temporality and causality. This notion can be defined as a retroactive consideration of earlier experiences, impressions, and memory traces in the light of new experiences. This definition reveals the relevance of such a concept in the testing context. In this case, time is reversed. It extends from present to past, with a belated understanding, generating new meanings through deferred action.

Announcing a test result is a form of detonation. This does not eliminate its traumatic effect; however, it can still be brought into the subject's historical perspective, relativised. An individual's past will significantly influence the way they experience such an announcement in the present. Through putting things into their historical perspective, the individual may be induced to remember and build connections between past events. Whether those events belong to reality or to fantasy, they will be endowed with new meanings.

The traumatic potential is greater against an unprepared background.

Reflecting on how we handle the announcement consultation is extremely important. Accordingly, we need to devote much thought to the announcement concept, not as a unique act, but as a process unfolding through a temporality. An announcement is a process of putting things into words. However, the follow-up will not be only focused on listening to an individual's experience, but also on listening to its meaning: what does it signify? How do patients relate to themselves in reconstructing events? What is the patient's position and where are others to be situated? Such an elaboration is important, lest abreaction alone be of no benefit.

While announcing a result, a doctor should bear in mind that "saying goes beyond what is said". Such revelations will "inevitably deal with values and ethics" (Gori & Del Volgo, 2002, p. 135). While revealing test results, a doctor must appreciate the consequences of such an act, as well as the impact it could have on the individual.

Prediction and anticipation

Missonnier (2006) distinguishes between anticipation and prediction: "anticipation is moderate and different from the omen's omnipotence. An oracle's power to *prae dicere*—tell in advance—is justified by its complicity with the divine at the cost of its human soil expatriation" (p. 213, translated for this edition). The author highlights the danger of excess in anticipation. He considers such excess as manic behaviour that might lead to acting in a disorganised manner. He also points to the refusal and lack of anticipation we can observe among depressed individuals.

Porée (1998) compares presymptomatic testing with melancholy. The melancholic establishes temporality in the past. The future is already lost for sure, and life itself is experienced as a kind of death. In this same perspective, does not testing fix temporality? Does a presymptomatic test not imprison an individual in a forecast of disease and disability? Does the possibility of anticipation lead to better control, or does it bring in an omnipotent form of anticipation? Does a presymptomatic test suggest that the disease and disability are already programmed? Can it anticipate death and a life unfolding as if it were already a kind of death?

An unfavourable result might alter an individual's perception of time. Triandafillidis (1990) described it among depressed people by stating that

> a depressed individual cannot foresee: when immobilising time, putting it on hold, when living in an expectation mode—expectation of nothing—isn't it because they cannot conceive the future as possibly different from the past, which means a future free of fear of disappearing, free of the shock of devastation? (p. 151, translated for this edition)

Prediction involves the risk of taking away the unknown part of the future one might create. Carriers of the Huntington's disease's gene have to deal with the sight of affected relatives who are heavily disabled and its attendant anxiety: fear of declining, fear of disability, and fear of an early social death become more real.

Prediction belongs to the realm of medical knowledge. Meanwhile, anticipation belongs to the individual's conscious or unconscious quest. Thus, in many situations, anticipation can be understood as an attempt to control presentation of the self, whose continuity could be threatened by the traumatic break of a prognosis. The psychic activity of anticipation might have a stimulus barrier function to afford protection against the violent invasiveness of the announcement. Indeed, test results can generate a mental split that might disorganise psychic activity and integrity.

Sutter and Berta (1991) define anticipation as a

> number of phenomena. They may be physiological, psychological, intellectual, sensory or emotional. Those phenomena unquestionably belong to the future. Yet, they are already manifest, alive and active in the present. They can be rational or not, conscious or not. (p. 9, translated for this edition)

Thus, through anticipation, patients may go from prediction, generating a break in time and existence (prediction deprives individuals from feeling any future, since they sense they are predetermined by genetic information), to assuming their fate. Accordingly, anticipation could be considered as an avenue towards individuation and subjectivisation.

In summary, when prediction is a necessary medical act dissolving uncertainty, anticipation is the individual's quest to grasp knowledge that is announced to them. Such knowledge may be read as a kind of prophecy. When facing this kind of knowledge, anticipation becomes vital because individuals cannot yet feel or express the visible and perceptible signs of the disease to come. The potentiality for disease acts as a reminder of the limited time left and can entail representations of future losses.

Effects on temporality

Human temporality is different from object temporality. Human temporality is distinguished by the ability to experience a new start through deferred action and by the ability to anticipate the ending. In *Prometheus Bound*, Aeschylus points to an essential element in understanding how knowledge of the future can generate paralysis and anxiety. When giving fire to human beings, Prometheus also made them forget the time of their death. Gadamer (1998) emphasised Prometheus's essential gift:

> such is his essential gift. As other animals in their den, human beings would have spent their lives idle and sad, waiting for death. Once deprived of the knowledge of the date and time of their death, they woke up with hope and started building their world, changing it into a livable world. (p. 75, translated for this edition)

By withdrawing this knowledge, Prometheus instilled hope and the desire to live in this world. The fire taken from the gods to be given to men was a symbolic vindication of humanity.

How can predictions made on the basis of genetic testing results be used to anticipate when, as Missonnier (2006) puts it in the following statement,

> an anticipation's strength lies in its openness to the unpredictable! A moderate adaptive anticipation cannot be a (chimeric) precise prediction of the future. It is rather a symbolising process of diverse and complex possible scenarios to come. (p. 209, translated for this edition)

When confronted by a medical prognosis as to a future disease and/or disability, individuals clearly need this less drastic and more open anticipation of future events in order to overcome the harshness of the hard-cut genetic diagnosis's announcement. Failing this, the announcement might well be experienced as a form of sentence.

Conclusion

Nowadays, the clinical approach to disability does not simply deal with disabled individuals and their families. It also has to address the needs of a new population of those who, having undergone presymptomatic testing, are aware of a future disability. This notion is vitally important since, in the coming years, progress in predictive medicine is sure to lead on to major debate on public health and bioethics. As clinical psychologists, psychoanalysts, and psychiatrists, we all need to take an active part in thinking out new practices in the field of predictive medicine and be aware of its consequences for individuals, couples, and families, including present and future offspring.

Geneticists and clinical psychologists work together during such consultations. Each contributes according to their speciality, affording time to the patients for subjectivisation following on from pre-symptomatic testing, time during which one can look back to the past in order to open the way towards possibility of narration. Such elaboration might prevent the crystallisation of psychic symptoms, precluding the event from remaining within the obscurity of the unthinkable.

Note

1.   The consultation team includes two geneticists (Dr Alexandra Dürr, Dr Josué Feingold), two psychologists (Ariane Herson, Marcela Gargiulo) and two genetic counsellors (Elodie Schaerer, Celine Bordet).

References

Almqvist, E. W., Bloch, M., Brinkman, R., Craufurd, D., & Hayden, M. R. (1999). A worldwide assessment of the frequency of suicide, suicide attempts, or psychiatric hospitalization after predictive testing for Huntington disease. *American Journal of Human Genetics*, *64*(5): 1293–1304.

Almqvist, E. W., Brinkman, R. R., Wiggins, S., & Hayden, M. R. (2003). Psychological consequences and predictors of adverse events in the first 5 years after predictive testing for Huntington's disease. *Clinical Genetics*, *64*(4): 300–309.

Bettelheim, B. (1979). *Survivre*, "Comportement individuel et comportement de masse dans les situations extrêmes". Paris, Hachette, Pluriel.

Brun, D. (Ed.) (2001). *L'enfant donné pour mort*. Paris: Eshel.

Brusset, B. (2002). L'hypocondrie : thématique ou organisation spécifique? *Revue Française de Psychosomatique*, *22*: 45–64.

Caniou, M. (1999). "Vous n'êtes pas porteur du gène"? Médecine prédictive. Quelle place pour l'Homme? *LAENNEC* (Special edition), *47*(3–4).

Char, R. (Ed.) (1977). *Eloge d'une soupçonnée*. Paris: Gallimard, 1991.

Decruyenaere, M., Evers-Kiebooms, G., Boogaerts, A., Cassiman, J. J., Cloostermans, T., Demyttenaere, K., Dom, R., Fryns, J. P., & Van den Berghe, H. (1995). Predictive testing for Huntington's disease: risk perception, reasons for testing and psychological profile of test applicants. *Genetic Counselling*, 6(1): 1–13.

Durr, A., Gargiulo, M., & Feingold, J. (2005). Les tests présymptomatiques en neurogénétique. *Medical Science (Paris)*, 21(11): 934–939.

Evers-Kiebooms, G., Nys, K., Harper, P., Zoeteweij, M., Durr, A., Jacopini, G., Yapijakis, C., & Simpson, S. (2002a). Predictive DNA-testing for Huntington's disease and reproductive decision making: a European collaborative study. *European Journal of Human Genetics*, 10(3): 167–176.

Evers-Kiebooms, G., Zoeteweij, M. W., & Harper, P. (Eds.) (2002b). *Preatal Testing for Late Onset Neurogenetic Diseases*. London: Bios Scientific.

Freud, S. (1916–1917). *Introductory Lectures on Psycho-Analysis (Lecture XXV)*. *S. E.*, *15–16*. London: Hogarth.

Freud, S. (1920g). *Beyond the Pleasure Principle*. *S. E.*, *18*: 7–64. London: Hogarth Press.

Freud, S. (1923b). *The Ego and the Id*. *S. E.*, *19*: 3–66. London: Hogarth.

Freud, S. (1933a). *New Introductory Lectures on Psycho-analysis* (Lecture 32). *S. E.*, *22*. London: Hogarth.

Freud, S. (1940a). *An Outline of Psycho-analysis*. *S. E.*, *23*: 141–207. London: Hogarth.

Frischmann, M., Gargiulo, M., & Gortais, J. (2008). La fratrie confrontée aux inégalités de la génétique. In: C. Bert (Ed.), *La Fratrie à l'épreuve du handicap* (pp. 149–161). Paris: Eres.

Gadamer, H. G. (Ed.) (1998). *Philosophie de la santé*, M. Dautrey (Trans.). Paris: Grasset et Mollat.

Gargiulo, M., & Rosenblum, O. (2013). L'éloge de l'incertitude en consultation génétique. In: *Du soin à la personne,clinique de l'incertitude* (pp. 171–176). Paris: Dunod.

Gargiulo, M., & Salvador, M. (Eds.) (2009). *Vivre avec une maladie génétique*. Paris: A. Michel.

Gargiulo, M., Lejeune, S., Tanguy, M. L., Lahlou-Laforet, K., Faudet, A., Cohen, D., Feingold, J., & Durr, A. (2009). Long-term outcome of presymptomatic testing in Huntington disease. *European Journal of Human Genetics*, 17(2): 165–171.

Goizet, C., Lesca, G., & Durr, A. (2002). Presymptomatic testing in Huntington's disease and autosomal dominant cerebellar ataxias. *Neurology*, 59(9): 1330–1336.

Gori, R., & Del Volgo, M. J. (2002). L'éthique: un renouveau de la clinique dans les pratiques de la santé. In: D. Brun (Ed.), *La guérison aujourd'hui: réalités et fantasmes, 5 e colloque de pédiatrie et psychoanalyse* (pp. 127–150). Paris: Editions Etudes Freudiennes.

Gortais, J., & Gargiulo, M. (2000). Génétique, prédiction et anticipation. *Contraste. Revue de l'ANECAMPS, 12*: 67–78.

International Huntington Association (IHA) and the World Federation of Neurology (WFN) Research Group on Huntington's Chorea (1994). Guidelines for the molecular genetics predictive test in Huntington's disease. *Neurology, 44*(8): 1533–1536.

Kremer, B. (2002). Clinical neurology of Huntington's disease. In: G. Bates, P. Harper, & L. Jones (Eds.), *Huntington's Disease* (2nd edn) (pp. 28–61). Oxford: Oxford University Press.

Laplanche, J. (Ed.) (1980). *Problématiques 1: L'angoisse*. Paris: PUF.

Lesca, G., Goizet, C., & Durr, A. (2002). Predictive testing in the context of pregnancy: experience in Huntington's disease and autosomal dominant cerebellar ataxia. *Journal of Medical Genetics, 39*(7): 522–525.

Mandich, P., Jacopini, G., Di Maria, E., Sabbadini, G., Abbruzzese, G., Chimirri, F., Bellone, E., Novelletto, A., Ajmar, F., & Frontali, M. (1998). Predictive testing for Huntington's disease: ten years' experience in two Italian centres. *Italian Journal of Neurological Science, 19*(2): 68–74.

Masson, A. (1997). L'autorité du médecin entre le savoir génétique et le malade. In: A. Joos de ter Beerst (Ed.), *Génétique et temporalité* (pp. 163–208). Paris: L'Harmattan.

Missonnier, S. (2006). Périnatalité prénatale, incertitude et anticipation. *Adolescence, 1*(55): 207–224.

Pasche, F. (1996). Peur de la mort, angoisse de mort, défense du moi. *Revue Française de Psychanalyse, 60*(1): 49–53.

Porée, J. (1998). Prédire la mort. L'exemple de la maladie de Huntington. *Esprit, 243*: 17–26.

Sutter, J., & Berta, M. (Eds.) (1991). *L'anticipation et ses applications cliniques*. Paris: PUF.

Timman, R., Roos, R., Maat-Kievit, A., & Tibben, A. (2004). Adverse effects of predictive testing for Huntington disease underestimated: long-term effects 7–10 years after the test. *Health Psychology, 23*(2): 189–197.

Triandafillidis, A. (1990). Temps du savoir et temps de l'incertitude. *Psychanalyse à l'Université, 15*(60): 139–153.

Wiggins, S., Whyte, P., Huggins, M., Adam, S., Theilmann, J., Bloch, M., Sheps, S. B., Schechter, M. T., & Hayden, M. R. (1992). The psychological consequences of predictive testing for Huntington's disease. Canadian Collaborative Study of Predictive Testing. *New England Journal of Medicine*, 327(20): 1401–1405.

CHAPTER FIVE

The psychoanalytical approach to disability

Simone Korff Sausse

U ntil recently, disabled people had seemed to have eluded psychoanalytical investigation and treatment, with very few psychoanalysts taking an interest in them. Why was this? The first reason is the general tendency to misunderstand the psychic life of subjects affected by a disability. Also, as objects of study, analyses, and commentary, the idea that they may have self-knowledge is rarely entertained. Little interest is taken in their subjectivity. Faced with the suffering induced by the disability, we prefer to think that the person is not aware of their condition and imagine that they do not have the intellectual capabilities to think out their own situation. As a result of this, it is thought that they cannot benefit from psychotherapy. This resistance derives from the dual nature of the disability that, on the one hand, is irremediable and, on the other, is inscribed in organicity, both insurmountable obstacles for conventional psychoanalysis, as they counter the ideal of the therapeutic vocation. As a result, few psychoanalytical research works have been devoted to these fields of investigation. The impact of a traumatised and traumatic reality, whose mesmerising effect causes a sideration or rejection, produces a blockage of the thinking processes. Clinical work on disability is neglected by psychoanalysts, hurt as they are in their narcissism by these patients who arouse an "uncanny strangeness" and produce the effect of a broken mirror (Korff Sausse, 1996) within which we fear to recognise ourselves.

Clinical background

The thoughts exposed in the present section derive from my practice as a psychoanalyst in institutions receiving disabled children with their families where they receive multi-disciplinary care and psycho-dynamic guidance. Consideration is then extended to adolescent patients and adults, with the new problems that arise in relation to the disability, and present work with aging, both in relation to the disabled people themselves and their entourage, throwing up new problems.

My research on the disabled child led me to identify a certain number of clinical and theoretical aspects that I extended to what I call clinical work of the extreme. In the extreme, I gather together clinical fields (traumatisms, disability, somatic illness, palliative care, Alzheimer's disease, perinatal care, the extremely premature, aging, deported people, torture, war traumas, brain-damaged patients, social insecurity, the homeless, serious crime, etc.) whose common theme is the notion of the extreme, meaning what takes us up to the limits:

- of what is thinkable,
- of what can be symbolised or subjectivised,
- of what is shareable,
- or, above all, to the limits of what is human, for that is indeed the question that underlies these clinical studies and treatments, that inevitably questions our basic humanity and the legitimacy of our existence. Is that disabled person, who fails to correspond to the norm of humankind's future and who, further to that, reneges on his anthropological duty to perpetuate the species, really entitled to live?

What can psychoanalysis contribute to these clinical situations? The psychoanalyst will give room for subjectivity and refuse to reduce the person to his disability. He or she will devote attention not just to what the subject cannot do (will never walk, will not go to school, never have children, etc.), but will make the most of what he *can* do, or *might* be able to do in the future. Our ethical position refers back to Canguilhem's inaugural and pivotal theses (1991[1943]) whereby "abnormal" or "pathological" forms of life do not enter into a relation of binary opposition with normality, but, rather, that there exist two regimens of the way life works. "There is no fact which is normal or pathological in itself. An anomaly or mutation is not in itself pathological. These two express other possible norms of life" (1991, p. 91). This idea allows the anomaly to be approached as a form of the living that is not inferior, but different, and the ensuing discourse eschews the theme of what is lacking to favour notions of potentialities.

But to address the specific features confronting the clinicians who care for disabled people, the usual concepts of psychoanalysis are not adequate; there is a need to change paradigms and refer to the model of a contemporary psychoanalysis that we could qualify as being post-Freudian and that gives pride of place to new concepts such as projective identification, intersubjectivity, empathy, reflexivity, and the alpha function (Korff Sausse, 2010b)—a psychoanalysis that places greater emphasis on the body and less on language. A psychoanalysis that postulates that there is a non-verbal psychic dimension, meaning that care can be devoted to people lacking, or having limited access to, language.

In practical terms, in this clinical approach, it is not enough to be attentive to what the patient has to say (as so often caricatured by the analyst in his or her office who "waits for the demand"). You need to get ahead of the patient, as did Ferenczi before us, who invented "active techniques" to precipitate matters with patients who had suffered from early traumatisms and recommended adjustments to the psychoanalytical framework. But, above all, the therapist has to have commitment, empathy, and conviction (Scelles & Korff Sausse, 2011).

The conviction is to think that abnormality has something to teach us. Failing this conviction, there could be no clinic for disability. Wilfred Bion was a pioneer in this field, speaking as he did of faith, he who took just as keen an interest in the psychic life of the great geniuses as in extremely retarded people. Bion (1984[1962]) shows the analogy of the thinking processes at work in both these apparently opposed cases. The thought mechanisms in their origin and their working out are elucidated equally (or, even better, in a combined manner) by both these two extremes: on the one hand, high level intellectual and artistic works, and, on the other, the psyche in its stumbling progress and incompletion.

Traumatism

Psychoanalysis allows for an understanding of the traumatism that occurs when there is a disabled person in a family (Korff Sausse, 2001). When a child "not like the others" comes into the world, or when a child becomes disabled due to a disease or an accident, the family's entire universe is shaken to the core (Korff Sausse, 1996). Having heard the diagnosis, the parents are devastated and lose their bearings, much like those traumatised by war or the survivors of an earthquake. Confronted by an unexpected event ("it only happens to others") or one that, conversely, was overly awaited (the phantasm of the abnormal child is always present during pregnancy), they suffer from a state of shock that shows all the characteristics of the trauma as described by Freud and Ferenczi, with its suddenness, the feeling of unpreparedness when confronted by something that breaks in on you, frustrating the subject's capacity for symbolisation, something indescribable, causing dismay, sideration, and fragmentation of the ego.

The announcement of the diagnosis is a shock that divides family life into a "before", that seems to have disappeared for ever, and an "after", that has to be built and developed. "From that moment, we tipped over into another world, the world of handicap", as one mother put it. The arrival of a disabled child causes a change in the family atmosphere, often even changing the material conditions of existence (with the mother stopping work, moving house to live closer to a centre, etc.). A child's disability leads to chain reactions, with the upheaval of the relational network within the family and an impact on the psychic balance of each member of the family group. The resulting shock waves span the generations. It is not just the disabled person who is affected in their somato-psychic integrity but, rather, the whole family that is hurt in its identity. The parents, of course, for whom the disability constitutes a deep narcissistic wound, but also the grandparents, who feel concerned through the question of heredity and filiation. (Where did it come from? Who was at the origin of this stigma?) It is their position as ancestors, and, as a result, their role and responsibility that is involved and that will influence their behaviour. Yet, more than the grandparents, the brothers and sisters of the disabled child will be deeply affected (Scelles, 1997). They feel abandoned, sidelined by this brother or sister who becomes a pole of attraction for all the parents' energy and concerns. They cannot speak out freely, as any manifestation of aggressiveness will make them feel guilty. And they wonder as to their future: will they have to be responsible for the brother/sister after their parents' death? Will they be able to have normal children or is there a real or imaginary risk of passing the condition on to *their* children?

Psychotherapy of the disabled child

My psychotherapeutic approach follows the basic principles of the psychoanalytical method, but psychotherapy for disabled children raises a number of specific difficulties that relate to the characteristics of such rather special patients.

- they have little or no powers of verbal expression;
- they are highly dependent on the people around them, due both to their age and their disability;
- they have often suffered from early emotional traumas, whose full story they are not aware of;
- the parents are very much present in the treatment for various reasons;
- the disability introduces the parameter of organicity and the irremediable nature of the condition;
- the disability arouses a worrying strangeness, thwarting identifications;
- it leads, as a result, to special countertransferential effects.

The same characteristics will be found with adult disabled patients. In such cases, the analyst will encounter even more complex countertransferential problems due to the fact that these patients, who are of the same generation or even the same age as he or she is, give rise to closer and sometimes more disturbing identifications. Due to intellectual disabilities, there are special transfer processes that need

to be identified and understood that might otherwise remain unno-
ticed and cause awkward countertransferential movements. How, too,
should the eroticised aspects of the transferential relation be
addressed? This is an extremely difficult question that probably
explains the unwillingness of many analysts to receive disabled
adults.

There is a basic asymmetry in the primal human relation between
the mother and her child that can be discerned in the therapeutic relation. According to Piera Aulagnier (1981), the inaugural encounter of
the *infans* with the mother is marked by a fundamental and founding
dissymmetry that is reproduced in the therapeutic relation. With the
concept of "enigmatic signifiers", Jean Laplanche (1987) shows in a
similar manner that, through transference and countertransference,
the psychoanalytical situation reproduces the original seduction.
What the analyst has to offer (offering words, offering thoughts, offering a framework within which the links A, H, and C, as Bion described
them, can be deployed) outstrips the child's capacity to be able to use
them. The presence of a disability accentuates this dissymmetry, since
what we have is a child who probably will never acquire the mental,
verbal, and intellectual faculties of the analyst due to the deficiency in
thought mechanisms and failings in verbal expression.

Another characteristic (another difficulty) also results from the
psychoanalytical process with the disabled patient on the question of
reciprocity. Construction of the psychic apparatus, according to the
Bionian model of the α function, implies that the subject encounters
another containing subject who will receive his projections and return
them transformed, digested, and psychicised. This model risks being
endangered by the disability, first because the adult will find it hard
to assume their alpha function with a child who is thought unable to
respond to it, and, second, because the child might encounter difficulties integrating the restored elements. More time will be needed
and the cognitive specifics related to the disability will have to be
taken into account. Thus, the psychotherapy of a person afflicted by a
disability required to deal with both universal elements (the child
goes through the same stages in psychic development, resorting to the
same conventional mechanisms of splitting, repression, identifications, etc.) and specific elements.

Mireille is five years old, suffers from Down's syndrome and in
sessions and games expresses her preoccupation with being alike: like

the other children, like her mother, like her therapist. Among the game themes emerges the desire to have babies. What attitude will her therapist adopt? Will she take it as a phantasm? What significance will she attribute to the reality of the syndrome? The therapist risks being impeded by the idea that, unlike other small girls, Mireille might never become a woman and a mother like her therapist.

But, after all, why should a child with Down's syndrome not wish to have babies? What is more, the question of procreation for women with Down's syndrome is not definitively settled as being impossible. On such questions, attitudes and possibilities are undergoing considerable change. Disabled people's rights to sexuality are gaining increasing recognition, and, with that, the right to parenthood. Nevertheless, the expression of sexual desire and the wish to have babies arouses emotional effects and ambivalent phantasms in the family and the professional entourage.

Another characteristic of psychotherapy for the disabled child is the much larger space occupied by the parents, as the existence of a disability fosters projective identification and produces fusional mother–child relations. It is the child's abnormality that causes these indissoluble bonds, woven by both a shameful hatred and unbounded love. It should be borne in mind that the parents we shall be dealing with have suffered from a traumatism. They, therefore, deserve attention, vigilance, and changes in the framing and the method, as needed for any approach involving traumatised patients, as has been corroborated constantly since the ground-breaking work of Ferenczi. That is why it remains unthinkable to exclude them from the child's therapy or reject their requests in the name of analytical purity. That also explains why it is difficult to direct them to another therapist than the one caring for the child.

Works devoted to the symbiotic relation with the disabled child customarily focus always on the mother, either "forgetting" to mention the suffering of the father, or because they argue that fathers are less affected by the shock of the disability and by the narcissistic wound it provokes. In my experience with families, this vision is a false one, especially when the disability affects a son. Failure to acknowledge the narcissistic wound suffered by fathers also fits in with the frequently negligible attention given them by institutions, forming an often essentially feminine universe devoted to childhood, where the disabled child is seen to be an eternal asexual child. The problem is, therefore, not so much that the fathers have less to say about their disabled child, or that they are less affected, but that the medical teams have greater resistance to understanding their suffering (Korff Sausse, 1996).

In a leukaemia ward, a child asked the psychologist, "Aren't you contaminated, having to come here?" A truly relevant question! With the astonishing lucidity shown by children, this small girl, afflicted by a life-threatening illness, challenges the therapist to say what she was doing there, what she was after. She provides the key to understanding the fear and the reticence that the clinical field of the disease or disability inspire in the therapists. This, perhaps, explains why few analysts are ready to launch out into such an adventure. The superstitions, stemming from the magical thinking that Freud intimated was still active, are never far away, including the completely irrational phantasm of contagion. Thus, psychotherapy for a disabled patient puts psychoanalytical tools to the test and probes deeper into the analyst's countertransferential capabilities (Heimann, 1960; Searles, 1979).

Specific aspects of countertransference in the clinical treatment of disability

Clinical treatment of disability mobilises especially intense countertransferential reactions relating to the parameters that characterise the disability: organicity, its irremediable nature, intellectual disability, retardation, absence or abnormality of language, the body deformed by uncontrolled movements, and anomaly or deficiency in the organisation of thought processes (Korff Sausse, 2006c, 2007). This is clinical treatment that arouses excessive reactions, as with horror or banalisation, rejection or fascination, fusion or indifference, and that can readily pitch one from direct avoidance to boundless affectivity. The disability inevitably activates desires for reparation and generates a relation of mastery and dominance that provides an open door for tyranny (Meltzer, 2008[1968]). Dependence fosters perverse sadistic and/or masochistic tendencies on both sides. The vulnerability of the disabled person arouses sadistic tendencies in the other and the disabled person will find gratification in masochistic submission.

How can the aspects of countertransference that mobilise over-whelming power, hatred, archaic fusion, violent rejection, the restorative illusion, and the idea of murder be managed? This comes down to questioning the unconscious psychic issues that drive health professionals. What, then, can be said about the motivations of the therapist when it comes to taking care of an incurable patient? Taking on abnormality, strangeness, or even the monstrous? What function does this relation with a person so hurt, vulnerable, irremediably affected in their physical and mental integrity have for the therapist? We suggest that the therapist takes care also of his own infantile and wounded parts. We need our patients as the patients need us.

To explain these countertransferential phenomena, one needs to refer to the notion of projective identification. This fundamental concept was introduced by Melanie Klein (1946), then developed by Bion (1984[1962]), who gave to it another meaning, showing its positive function and emphasising the introjective pole more than the projective pole. From being a pathological mechanism with Klein, it becomes with Bion the first procedure for exchanges between human beings. Based on this concept, another model of the therapeutic relation can be defined, corresponding to the disabled patient's needs and capabilities.

Psychic contents, words but also non-verbal communications, expressed through a transferential relation, are received by an analyst ready to accept the projections and subject them to her transformational psychic activity. The information the analyst receives from her own psychic activity, echoing that of the patient, can then adopt forms that are not necessarily representations but, rather, perceptive–hallucinatory or psychosomatic forms. A therapist reported that having left an analysis session with an athetotic patient, she suffered from severe body aches. Other somatic signs—fatigue, nausea, and headaches—are frequent.

Mourning and depression.

The notion of mourning is frequently mentioned in relation to illness, disability, or any other form of anomaly. The parents are wounded in their own narcissism through their child. We then say that the mismatch between the imaginary child and the real child is so great that a real work of mourning seems necessary for the disabled child to gain his place. But what can be observed clinically with the parents is that this mourning process proves impossible.

The notion of mourning for the imaginary child appears as a too commonly entertained obvious fact, or even a cruel error. For the parents confronted by this trial, is not the idea of mourning really equivalent to accepting the unacceptable? A signal feature of the disability is that it remains an individual event. It does not fit in with history, but in filiation. It would appear to be like mourning without the rituals. Failing such rituals, the parents retreat into a silent solitude, with the feeling of living out an experience that separates them definitively from others. That is why early management, as practised in France, is essential. This also explains why parents find such consolation in associations of parents.

Another reason why mourning remains impossible is that time, rather than soothing the pain, actually accentuates the difficulties for various reasons relating specifically to the disability. The consequences of the disability are exacerbated as the child matures. For the parents, as time goes by, new problems constantly arise or difficulties that seemed to have been settled are again revived. But the main reason that makes mourning impossible is that the disabled child is well and truly alive. The task facing the parents is, therefore, pernicious in that they have to go through mourning for an object and at the same time invest in that very object.

For Freud, His Majesty the Baby is a projection of the parents' narcissism that assuages all suffering, satisfies all desires, and ensures the ego's immortality. That sick or damaged baby cannot hold to such promises, since, first, the parents have to worry about his fate beyond their own deaths and, second, there is every likelihood of him not, in turn, having descendents. The contract is broken. If the child cannot ensure that function of narcissistic restoration, it ends up being a persecutor. Indeed, it is not enough to say that the parents have death wishes towards their child, but, rather, that they have cravings for murder. Through turning into their contrary, these destructive urges are transformed into their very opposite attitudes, compassion and overprotection, corresponding to a defence mechanism that psychoanalysts call counter-investment. Counter-investment is a process postulated by Freud that involves actively preventing representations or unacceptable desires from emerging in the conscious. They are replaced by other representations, reaction formations that come in to replace forbidden thoughts and have the function of masking them.

These counter-investments are not to be found only with the parents. They form the basis for all social attitudes with regard to disability. They are also present in the teams and institutions that care for the disabled. Such ideas on death are especially difficult to bring out into the open because the real risk of death relating to the disability brings them dangerously close to their effective accomplishment. The reality of the disability introduces confusion between phantasm and reality. In the light of my clinical experience, I would put forward the hypothesis that what is pathogenic relates not so much to the murderous instincts in themselves as to the fact that they are dissimulated. Valerie Sinason (2009a,b) insists on the need to take up the issue of "the fear of being killed" with patients with an intellectual disability.

In a remarkable paper, Winnicott (2007[1956]) showed that such a patient imposes a "heavy emotional burden" on the therapist, arousing in the latter an intense form of hatred. "However much he loves his patients he cannot avoid hating them, and the better he knows this the less will hate and fear be the motive determining what he does to his patients" (p. 49). Instead of seeking to minimise or evade these negative aspects of the countertransference, quite the opposite is involved in bringing them out into the open.

That child, who obliges others to renounce so much and calls so pressingly for a work of mourning that proves impossible, risks becoming the object of an incorporation, whose characteristics are described by Maria Torok (1976[1968]). What then emerges is what is known as a fusional or symbiotic relation. This is an impossible mourning for a narcissistically indispensable object, in this instance, the image of a healthy child; shameful grief is felt for an object related to a secret shame, here the death wish. These symbiotic organisations are largely inaccessible to therapeutic intervention. There is a need to cater for the indissolubility of bonds and, thus, seek to arrange for a therapeutic space that can contain both of them.

That is why psychotherapeutic care must compulsorily associate the mother with the treatment. This is also valid for adult patients, as the parent–child bond lives on where there is a disability, through adolescence, then up to adulthood. There is the risk of a frozen, infantilising, and alienating relation being established if the parents are not helped and encouraged in the work of separation with the child who, having attained adulthood, nevertheless remains an eternal child, as it represents the injured and vulnerable child in them. There is the need for a third party to intervene, otherwise the family unit is likely to close in on itself, in deathly seclusion, facing what is felt to be a hostile world.

Another consequence of the impossible mourning is that the imaginary child keeps its place as an unattainable ideal or a malevolent double. The question then arises as to what the child himself can do with this double he constantly perceives in the gaze of others.

Just like his parents, the disabled child is confronted with a work of mourning: mourning for his normality, his integrity, and his independence. And, unceasingly, he must renounce. The revelation of being different, as repeated day after day through all the situations of daily life, inevitably brings on moments of depression. This is the oedipal period, where the child takes his place in the dual difference that goes to make up his identity—sexual difference and generational difference—where this depression becomes organised and manifests itself. Disabled children then go through periods of instability and excitement that alternate with periods of refusal or discouragement that are the different expressions of a real depression. But the disabled child's depression remains unknown to those close to him and neglected by health professionals, first because it often fails to appear in a direct way and also since it is unbearable for the adults, in whom it will revive their own depression. The parents are blinded by their sense of guilt that is expressed by the desire to see the child make progress, while the re-educators are similarly affected by their therapeutic ideal.

Suzanne is a ten-year-old girl suffering from a rare chromosomal disorder causing mental deficiency. Her parents take her in for consultation due to her bed-wetting problem. That day, she spends a large part of her session playing with a doll that constantly urinates (as Suzanne herself does, much to her mother's despair). The doll "drinks", then "pees", everything's "wet" and has to be dried out with a large number of paper handkerchiefs. What is she trying to say through this repetitive game where she wets everything? I think, and tell her so, that she is expressing to me through this game and to her mother through her bed-wetting, her fear of her disability and her rage at not being a normal little girl like her sister, whom she admires and at the same time persecutes. My interpretation has an immediate effect: now, instead of peeing, the doll "weeps", and the paper hand-kerchiefs are used to wipe away the tears from "baby's" eyes. The anger and depression relating to her singular situation can be expressed and very quickly the bed-wetting symptom disappears.

Infantile theories of disability

There is a general trend in the childish mind to construct theories to provide oneself with explanations of all the mysteries it encounters on the lines of the infantile sexual theories described by Freud (1905d). Disabled children perform all sorts of interpretations as to their dis-abilities. We know that an objective knowledge of sexuality will not prevent children from having irrational, personal, and changing sex-ual theories as to the way babies are brought into the world. Similarly, the theories that disabled children construct to explain their disabilities are so many fantastic explanatory constructions that fail to comply with the rational or medical information they have available to them. They are the reflection of their unconscious phantasms and vary according to the stages in their mental and emotional development.

Mireille, a five-year-old girl suffering from Down's syndrome, comes out with the following statement about her brother: "Antoine has a willie and I've got Down's syndrome." She shows how, for the child, at that stage in her maturation, her condition is experienced as the equivalent of gender difference. I have had the opportunity to observe such a parallel between the mark of the anomaly and the mark of sex difference in other children, with the confusion it entails between that difference of a genetic nature and sexual identity.

Within the framework of the conventional hypothesis of psycho-analysis, the sex difference is the prototype for all differences and the child perceives his or her abnormal condition on the model of sexual difference. But the difference relating to the disability cannot feature entirely in an opposition between masculine and feminine. Further-more, the child then risks univocally designating an abnormal form in relation to a normal form. As far as sexual difference is concerned, the child is similar to one of his parents, the one of the same sex, and different to the parent of the opposite sex. But when it comes to the difference relating to the disability, the child is dissimilar from both his parents. With whom does he or she share a similarity? From what mother or father does he or she come? From what couple is she or he the fruit? And to whom or to what can he or she give life? The disability mobilises singular aspects of the phantasm of the primitive scene, evoking an idea of deformation or of an anomaly in the process of procreation prior to birth. Therefore, disability studies can be compared to gender studies because they produce modifications in the way of thinking about any difference in a binary or a multiple approach (Korff Sausse, 2011b).

Four-year-old Nathalie suffers from Down's syndrome and shows severe learning difficulties. Her language remains impoverished, being reduced to poorly articulated sounds. However, she loves to name toys or pictures: boy–girl, mister–lady, and hen–cock are referred to repeatedly, but in evident confusion over sexual identification. Her first drawings are monochrome: she only uses a single colour per session. One day everything is blue and the next week there is only green, but she does not want to, or cannot, mix or juxtapose two colours. She finds it difficult to differentiate people, genders, colours, and phonemes. I try to find out how, within her family, they talk with Nathalie about her disability. The parents, traumatised by the situation, cannot manage to talk to Nathalie about her condition. The expression shocks and hurts them. Like many such parents, they are afraid of causing Nathalie to suffer.

Nathalie meets other trisomic children at the care centre and socialises with children from the neighbourhood at the nursery school. The parents think that Nathalie fails to see the difference. Unlike them, I think she can very clearly see that difference. But how to address a difference that cannot be stated in words? From there on, nothing can be said out loud with this small girl who is relatively alert and has evident symbolic capacities: all language is blocked in this situation.

Having talked about this with the parents, I take up the issue of her Down's syndrome condition with Nathalie, putting a name to it. Then, spectacularly, in the following weeks, Nathalie starts to pronounce words. With the next session, she produces drawings with two colours. As from when the adults around her have named the disability, put into words what makes her different from others, Nathalie can associate words and colours, identify them, differentiate them, and articulate them. A whole field of communicative meanings opens out where words, drawings, and thoughts can be rolled out.

Finding the words to talk about the issue

I advance the hypothesis that any human being, however helpless they might be, has something to say about their subjective position. Therefore, you have to leave room for that person's real-life experience and take an interest in what they themselves have to say about their disability. The fundamental reference for such a position is that of Sandor Ferenczi (Korff Sausse, 2006a), who revealed the child in the adult and sought therapeutic channels to address early traumatisms (Korff Sausse, 2006b). Like Ferenczi, I think it is necessary to listen to this child and seek to understand what he or she has to say.

But how to listen and talk to a child who does not talk? How can we imagine they have something to say to us when they have no mastery of language? Indeed, there remains the stubborn idea that a disabled person will, in any case, be unable to understand the message. In such cases, adults quickly give up on any verbal exchange.

We may also prefer not to listen to a disabled person so as not to hear what they have to say to us, as their way of talking disturbs us. These are questions that any child asks but that become a matter of greater anxiety when a disabled child is concerned. The question as to the origin and cause arouses a phantasm and a disturbing primitive, or even monstrous, scene.

Naming the disability and using the words to describe it brings up a host of problems. There is the risk of reducing the person to his disability, as the word can have a stigmatising effect. The words for the disability have that terrible power of freezing the child's identity within a reductive image. The words that describe the anomaly or disease are dangerous as they arouse superstitious beliefs. In *Totem and Taboo* (1912–1913), Freud refers to superstitious prohibitions and beliefs relating to words and names. Here, we are in the field of magical thinking and omnipotence: pronouncing the word is the same as making the thing concrete; not saying it would be a way to cancel it out magically.

For parents, telling their child "You are trisomic" implies the statement "I made you trisomic", and risks in return leading the child to put the question, or, rather, express the reproach, "Why did you make me trisomic?"

"You aren't the child your parents wanted." Here, maybe, is the crux of the matter. All questions and all explanations come back to the life wish or the death wish towards that child and explain why parents, and adults in general, have difficulties stating matters clearly. They are paralysed by this immense sense of guilt of having, at one time or another, more or less consciously, thought that it would have been better for the child not to have come into the world or that it should have disappeared.

For the disabled child asks questions, or, rather, *is* a question: he or she bears the basic questions faced by mankind. But children's questioning is rarely heard by adults. The child's understanding of his disability, much in the same way as that relating to sexuality, remains scandalous, forbidden knowledge. More so, perhaps, in that such knowledge reveals a feeling of shame relating to parental sexuality combined with the sense of guilt of being oneself the cause of that exposure. The disabled child bears with him a dual form of knowledge, or a twice forbidden knowledge. If adults refuse to talk about it, or talk about it with so much equivocation, then such thoughts must surely be forbidden.

The consequences of this unspoken theme are serious. If the disabled child does not hear the words to name what he is or has, that silence is likely to lead to a secondary intellectual inhibition that is tied up with that avoidance of any questioning. An inability to think of the disability leads to an inhibition of the thought processes themselves. Better not to think at all than think of what is forbidden. But setting aside such thoughts, it is the entire "apparatus for 'thinking' or dealing with thoughts", as Bion (1984[1962]) put it, that is cut out.

"They must be right"

Seventeen-year-old Magalie comes into her session each week announcing: "I've got nothing to say." She has plenty to say though, but is convinced that it has no value. At the first interview, she acts like a robot, expressing herself mechanically, completely absent while her parents told her story. Following a cerebral tumour operated on when she was five, she has an intellectual impairment and retarded ideation. During their account, Magalie remains as if frozen. What share do the neurological factors play in this slowness and what is due to inhibition? What is going on in her mind? Does she know herself? What can she say about her disability?

"She lost everything", say her parents. I wonder what remains for her, of all she has lost. Of that small girl she was before she was five? In fact, Magalie is perfectly able to explain to me what happened to her. She speaks of the tumour, "like a stone in the brain that I had to get rid of". For, while Magalie talks very slowly, her sentences are, nevertheless, perfectly constructed and her vocabulary is even extremely precise. During conversations with her I feel as if I were acting in a play by Marguerite Duras directed by Bob Wilson . . .

But Magalie has lost track of the past. She is like a stranger to her own story. Magalie's world is dull, immobile, a dead-end. She lives in a flat, futureless present, without ramifications towards the past. Like many disabled adolescents, Magalie seems to be deprived of her own childhood. Of course, in order to explain this "strangeness" of the past, we could mention factors relating to mental disability and cognitive disorders. But it seems to me that we need to seek another explanation for this opacity of mental operations. Anthropologists, such as Mircea Eliade (1963), tell us that any myth is a myth as to origins. Similarly, any questioning by the child is a questioning as to origins. And that is why the questions put by a disabled child, adolescent, or adult are so dangerous, for they relate directly to the question that makes everyone ill at ease: that is, the origin of the disability.

During our sessions, Magalie first remained silent. I encouraged her to tell me things about her life, but as soon as there was an element of conflict, Magalie immediately came out with the same phrase: "They must be right." "They" meaning parents, educators, and adults in general. This plural encompassed in an undifferentiated manner all others, all those who are not, like her, afflicted by a mental disability. Magalie constantly submits to this generalised, omnipotent reason. Caught up in a reductive image as projected on her by those around her, convinced that on any matter she does not know and cannot know, Magalie has no other issue possible than to comply with what is expected of her. She depreciates or cancels out her own opinions and desires.

One day, Magalie talks of her sister and her sister's girlfriends. She trivialises matters. They get on well together, no quarrels, no rivalry, etc. One thing emerges, however.

"My parents tell me I was jealous."

"Oh, really?"

"But there was no reason to be, it was just some ideas I got in my head."

"What ideas?"

"That they gave more to my sister than to me, but I know that wasn't true. My parents say they always did the same for my sister and for me."

"Yes, but what about you, did you feel differently?"

"In any case, I knew that I was different to my sister because I'm handicapped; for my parents, it wasn't the same."

Here, finally, Magalie could bring up her repressed feelings: jealousy, the feeling of being different, the certainty of not being the girl who was wanted, the guilt of causing her parents to worry, the questioning as to the origin of the disability. While talking of all this, her face lights up and her voice becomes livelier.

However, the next week, the parents announced that due to financial or organisational issues, they will have to put an end to the sessions with Magalie . . . "After all, nothing much happens during the sessions . . . she hasn't got that much to say . . .".

Unconscious representations

Disqualification of the sessions, discredit being heaped on the therapist, and, above all, undervaluing the disabled patient's word. I am struck, over and over again, by the difficulty people have in admitting that the psychic productions of the disabled person have value. How many times have I heard "he says nothing", or "what he says makes no sense" (Korff Sausse, 2011a)?

The situation becomes reversed as from when another person, the analyst, offers herself countertransferentially, meaning that she offers to receive the patient's messages. That is why there is often a spectacular effect with such patients at the start of psychotherapy through the simple fact (not as simple as all that in reality . . .) that the sessions grant existence and value to the patient's psychic productions since they can be expressed transferentially and received countertransferentially, opening out spaces where symbols can emerge, allowing for a subjective appropriation of those devalued or even discredited psychic contents. For the disabled person has an extremely negative self-image.

He or she is constantly confronted by unconscious representations of both a collective and individual nature that the disability activates and that determine the social practices of the social players, often unbeknown to them. Over the years, I have managed to identify the main representations aroused by disability that are probably the source of the rejection it continues to provoke. They emerge along three main lines (Korff Sausse, 2010a):

- culpable filiation: the abnormality is experienced as the punishment for an incestuous transgression that it brings out into the light of day;
- a hazardous transmission: the abnormality comes to show us, in a painful and worrying way, that we do not have control over the process of transmission, much as we would like to, and as the scientific illusion would have us believe. We do not know what we hand down; neither do we know what has been handed down to us;
- forbidden procreation. From then on, filiation and transmission must be halted: procreation must be stopped.

Here, then, are the representations that are activated by situations of disability and that weigh so heavily on what the disabled person has to live through. These are what are behind the lack of knowledge of the psychic life and stigmatising attitudes. During psychotherapies, it is essential to address these issues, as Sinason (2009a,b) has taught us.

"Nothing to say"

Pascal is a young man suffering from Down's syndrome who has been coming in for psychotherapy for three years. Sometimes, he ends a session with the words "Nothing to say", which seems a way of ending the interview for that day. He then adopts a fairly depressed tone of voice that contrasts sharply with the somewhat maniacal joviality that usually marks the sessions. Is that not a denial? I take a guess: "It seems to me that there's something here that you find difficult to say . . ." After a moment's hesitation, he comes out with two words: "sexuality . . . trisomy." If economy of means put to serve the power of the message is one of the characteristics shared by the great writers, one can only admire here Pascal's ability to deliver such a highly significant message in so few words.

> The extraordinary thing is the tour de force by which primitive modes of thought are used by the patient for the statement of themes of great complexity. And I find it significant that his ability to do this improves concurrently with more welcome advances. I say more welcome because I have not yet satisfied myself that it is right to ignore the content of an association because dealing with it would keep the analyst talking at infinitely greater length than the patient. (Bion, 1967[1957], p. 72)

Here, Bion shows, with clinical cases, that the patient says little about the matter and that the analyst is led, like an auxiliary ego, to say a great deal. But, in fact, that little is a lot if the analyst is attentive to it, and that little is only made possible by the special receptiveness of the therapist who, in a way, "lends" his psychic apparatus and alpha function to the patient.

Just two words to raise the existential question of any human being as to sexuality, but that for a being born with a chromosome anomaly will always awake disturbing phantasms and a sense of guilt. So, how do things stand for Pascal when it comes to the possibility of an affective, sexual, and possibly reproductive relationship? "Nothing to say" . . . What, indeed, to say about his situation that shocks everyone?

The same formula is recurrent: sometimes "nothing to say", then "nothing say". It would appear that Pascal is saying, on the one hand, "I have nothing to say", but, on the other, "mustn't say". On the one hand, the inability of a man affected by mental impairment to say things and who deprecates or negates his own opinions, taken up by a reductive image that is projected on him. On the other, the prohibition of speech, and, even more radically, of thought, as far as his wishes, oppositions, and conflicts are concerned.

The difficulty of speech and the slow emergence of ideas create the conditions for a sponge-like psychic apparatus that absorbs projections from others. Pascal finds himself invaded by thoughts that are not his own, words coming from others that he reproduces but that he has difficulty making his own. Psychotherapy is the place where his thoughts can take form because they can be shared. Sharing is the condition to constitute a psychic apparatus to "think thoughts without thinking", as Bion would have it.

This is the concept of empathy that allows the experience to be thought of as shareable. To be in empathy means sharing partially and by sectors, although actually lived out, the inner experience of others through feeling it and also managing to represent it to oneself, whatever it may be. Empathy, thus, enables us to understand what is foreign to us in the other. To recognise, in this disabled child, this adult affected by a mental impairment, that we would tend to consider as monstrous, a fellow human being.

The mirror and reflexivity

The disability questions the enigma of the origin in the dual sense of the word with respect to the meaning of beginnings, but also the meaning of causality. The parents set forth on a quest to find an explanation for that abnormality where the perceived causes entwine beliefs, superstitions, and magic layered on to medical knowledge that, in any case, fails to convince.

"Why?" "Why us?" are the questions that keep coming back. "Where does it come from?" There is questioning from the parents and the child on the matter of the primitive scene that caused the abnormality.

Like Oedipus, each child, even (or, perhaps, above all) one affected by a disability wonders: who am I? Where do children come from? The brain-damaged adolescent Magalie would appear to be remote from any frantic oedipal quest for identity and truth. And yet, she, too, seeks to retrace the origin of what makes her different from others. She, too, needs to be able to pose the fundamental question any thinking human being will ask. "*Why?*" With the disabled child, this spirit of enquiry intertwines with questioning as to the disability. The question as to how babies are made blends in with the question as to the why and wherefore of disabled babies being born. But his or her questioning, just like infantile sexual investigation, rubs up against resistance from adults who prefer to keep the image of the innocent child and the illusion of the happy idiot. As a result, the quest for meaning is often minimised, or even denied by the entourage.

Any child seeks a mirror that can reflect back his or her own image. Winnicott (1999[1967]) sees this mirror in the face of the mother, and above all her gaze, that has a reflexive function. "During the emotional development of an individual, the precursor for the mirror is the face of the mother". He reads in that look the injury he has inflicted on her and seeks desperately, as Narcissus, a mirror to see himself in. Winnicott pursues the matter:

> What does the baby see when he or she looks at the mother's face? I am suggesting that, ordinarily, what the baby sees is himself or herself. In other words the mother is looking at the baby and what she looks like is related to what she sees there. (p. 24)

Thus, what the baby sees in this inaugural mirror of his mother's eyes is not merely himself but his mother's feelings towards him, that is, what he provokes in the emotional life of his mother. But, then, what does the disabled child see? A look that is stricken, depressed, fleeting, rejecting? The child reads into the look of its mother the wound he has inflicted on her. What can be done with respect to this stigmatising look that inaugurates his first encounter with the world and that he will never fail to confront, everywhere and at all times, throughout his life?

For Winnicott, the mirror does not just reflect an image, which is a perception, but implies an apperception, meaning all the affects she feels for that child. There is a sentence where he states that the baby sees in the gaze of his mother everything he does to her, everything he arouses in her emotionally. Winnicott says that when perception takes the place of apperception, the mother's face is not then a mirror: the baby no longer sees himself but sees the face of his mother. Nothing is reflected, nothing is returned to him; there is no meaningful exchange with the world. The child perceives something, but fails to take cognisance of himself from what he sees.

A failure in reflexivity, whether for cognitive and/or identity-related reasons, hinders this duplication and causes a "bonding" to the other. External objects are over-invested, if internal objects are not solidly established, as the latter are too fragile, or are rendered fragile by the demeaning and disqualifying attitudes of those around. Infantilising one's entourage and internal dependency go together; they feed and strengthen each other. In patients affected by mental impairment, a difficulty in organisation of reflexivity can also be seen, meaning the organisation of the "internal mirror" of the ego.

Failing this, the person with an intellectual disability oscillates between depressive withdrawal to being subject to the avid quest for never satisfactory narcissistic contributions. The therapist will be the locus for reception of these contradictory transferential projections, requiring a special countertransferential work and the need to resort to different levels of psychic operation. He or she is called on both to be extremely active as an auxiliary self to ensure the impaired functions of the patient's self, but also to adopt a position of extremely attentive passive receptiveness so as to be able to capture the archaic, incomplete, fragmentary, and non-degraded messages the patient sends out.

Conclusion

Disability (and, above all, perhaps deficiency) is little explored in psychoanalysis, although it has been a recurrent theme in mythology, literature, and arts (Korff Sausse, 2010c). How can it become an object for psychoanalytical thought? It is time now to produce a psychoanalytical conceptualisation of disability and invent the appropriate therapeutic tools. Bion charted the path to model this new paradigm. "I wish to emphasize that all that has been said about the problems of knowledge applies with particular force to psycho-analysis and that psycho-analysis applies with particular force to those problems" (Bion, 1984[1962], p. 48). With Bion, we can thus propose this fairly radical reversal, postulating that science or philosophical thinking are "defective" if they do not cater for disturbances of the thinking processes, meaning that such disturbances are necessary to think about thinking.

References

Aulagnier, P. (Ed.) (1981). *La violence de l'interprétation: du pictogramme à l'énoncé*. Paris: Presses universitaires de France.

Bion, W. R. (Ed.) (1967)[1957]. *Differentiation of the Psychotic from the Non-psychotic Personalities: Second Thoughts*. London: Karnac.

Bion, W. R. (Ed.) (1984)[1962]. *Learning from Experience*. London: Karnac.

Canguilhem, G. (Ed.) (1991)[1943]. *Le normal et le pathologique* (3rd edn). Paris: Presses Universitaires de France.

Eliade, M. (Ed.) (1963). *Aspects du mythe*. Paris: Gallimard.

Freud, S. (1905d). *Three Essays on the Theory of Sexuality. S. E.*, 7: 125–245. London: Hogarth.

Freud, S. (1912–1913). *Totem and Taboo. S. E.*, 13: 1–161. London: Hogarth.

Heimann, P. (1960). Counter-transference. II. *British Journal of Medical Psychology, 33*: 9–15.

Klein, M. (1946). Some notes on schizoid mechanisms. *International Journal of Psychoanalysis, 27*: 99–110.

Korff Sausse, S. (Ed.) (1996). *Le miroir Brisé. L'enfant handicapé, sa maladie et le psychanalyste* [reprinted, 2009]. Paris: Calmann-Lévy.

Korff Sausse, S. (Ed.) (2001). *Le trauma: de la sidération à la création. Figures et traitements du traumatisme.* Paris: Dunod.

Korff Sausse, S. (Ed.) (2006a). *De l'enfant terrible au nourrisson savant (Préface à Sandor Ferenczi, L'enfant dans l'adulte).* Paris: Payot et Rivages.

Korff Sausse, S. (Ed.) (2006b). *Ferenczi pionnier méconnu. [Préface Ferenczi S, Le traumatisme, 1932].* Paris: Payot.

Korff Sausse, S. (2006c). Contre-transfert, cliniques de l'extrême et esthétique. *Revue française de Psychanalyse, 70*(2): 507–520.

Korff Sausse, S. (2007). Handicap et contre-transfert. In: S. Korff Sausse, S. Missonnier, R. Scelles, A. Ciccone, C. Bon, A. Herson, L. M. Streito, S. Pagani, E. Tesio, M. Mercier, J. Berrewaerts, C. Delhaxhe, R. Salbreux & G. Saulus (Eds.), *Cliniques du sujet handicapé: actualité des pratiques et des recherches* (pp. 39–58). Toulouse: ERES.

Korff Sausse, S. (2010a). Filiation fautive, transmission dangereuse, procréation interdite. L'identité sexuée de la personne handicapée: une pièce en trois actes. In: R. Scelles, A. Ciccone, S. Korff Sausse, S. Missonnier, & R. Salbreux (Eds.), *Handicap, identité sexuée et vie sexuelle* (pp. 43–60). Toulouse: Eres.

Korff Sausse, S. (2010b). Sans désir, sans mémoire, sans connaissance. Une approche psychanalytique du handicap et du vieillissement. In: A. Blanc, A. Anchisi, B. Despland, C. Eynard, M. Francoeur, C. Gucher, S. Korff Sausse, A. J. Mazuy, M. Myslinski, A. Ruffiot, G. Seraphin, & A. Weber (Eds.), *Les Aidants familiaux* (pp. 123–142). Grenoble: PUG.

Korff Sausse, S. (Ed.) (2010c). *Figures du handicap: mythes, arts, littérature.* Paris: Payot & Rivages, 2000.

Korff Sausse, S. (2011a). Un étrange déni. La méconnaissance de la vie psychique de la personne handicapée. In: P. Ancet & N. J. Mazen (Eds.), *Ethique et handicap* (pp. 141–167): Bordeaux: Les Etudes Hospitalières.

Korff Sausse, S. (2011b). Des gender studies aux disability studies: repenser les catégories. *Champ psy, 2*(58), 37–52.

Laplanche, J. (Ed.) (1987). *Nouveaux fondements pour la psychanalyse*. Paris: Presses Universitaires de France.

Meltzer, D. (2008)[1968]. Tyranny. In: *Sexual States of Mind* (pp. 143–150). London: Karnac.

Scelles, R. (Ed.) (2010). *Liens fraternels et handicap. De l'enfance à l'âge adulte*. Toulouse: Erès.

Scelles, R., & Korff Sausse, S. (2011). Empathie, handicap et altérité. *Le Journal des psychologues, 3*(286), 30–34.

Searles, H. F. (Ed.) (1979). *Countertransference and Related Subjects: Selected Papers*. New York: International Universities Press.

Sinason, V. (2009a). Psychothérapie psychanalytique de patients atteints de déficience intellectuelle. In: S. Korff Sausse, A. Ciccone, S. Missonnier, R. Salbreux, & R. Scelles (Eds.), *La vie psychique des personnes handicapées. Ce qu'elles ont à nous dire, ce que nous avons à entendre* (pp. 206–210). Toulouse: Eres.

Sinason, V. (2009b). Le handicap secondaire et ses rapports avec le traumatisme. In: S. Korff Sausse, A. Ciccone, S. Missonnier, R. Salbreux, & R. Scelles (Eds.), *La vie psychique des personnes handicapées. Ce qu'elles ont à nous dire, ce que nous avons à entendre* (pp. 211–225). Toulouse: Eres.

Torok, M. (1987)[1968]. Maladie du deuil et fantasme du cadavre exquis. In: M. Torok & N. Abraham (Eds.), *L'écorce et le noyau* (pp. 229–251). Paris: Flammarion.

Winnicott, D. W. (1999)[1967]. Mirror-role of mother and family in child development. In: D. W. Winnicott (Ed.), *Playing & Reality* (pp. 111–118). London: Routledge.

Winnicott, D. W. (2007)[1956]. Hate in the countertransference. In: *Collected Papers: Through Paediatrics to Psycho-Analysis* (pp. 194–203). London: Karnac.

CHAPTER SIX

The normality of the abnormal: disability, norms, and normality

Roger Salbreux

T he abnormal has always inspired fear; "sameness" reassures. Clearly, everyone needs to assert their identity, their uniqueness, and, thus, by opposition recognise the difference of otherness, but at the same time, we all experience the need to feel included in a system of belonging, a linguistic community, a group of peers, a family, a filiation.

We suffer when we see another with the same style, the same clothes, the same look as us. At the same time, racial, religious, cultural, and social class differences worry us and make us ill at ease, even if we are convinced that there is really no reason to consider those other people as belonging to a different form of humanity, to another species.

Herein lies the whole question of the same and the different that underscore the notion of otherness and that has so largely influenced the (sometimes contrasted) place occupied by disabled people in our societies according to the prevailing religious, epochal, and cultural functions (Stiker, 2006). Now, the contemporary movement in favour of integration and inclusion tends to erase the border between the normal and the pathological as studied so pertinently by Canguilhem (1991).[1] This necessarily poses questions around the issues of rights, identity, and reality.

The identity and group related contradictions mentioned above are banal although not always readily surmountable. However, they take on a much more violent aspect when the nature of the difference is rooted in pathology, and here there are a number of reasons. First of all, the pathology reminds us of our own vulnerability before the inevitability of disease and its consequences (disability); it also confronts us with our own finiteness before death (Kristeva, 2003); all eventualities that we prefer *a priori* to set aside from our fate, just as Freud noted "the timelessness of the unconscious".

Thus, we tend spontaneously to shy away from these pregnant realities when they cross our path: is this a fear-related avoidance or, rather, a denial of the differences inherent in pathology? We also, no doubt, flee from them for the sake of facility, so true it is that it remains more difficult to identify with another person when you have to reach out across the gap that separates us that is all at once bigger, more physical, and more tangible, and that could well arouse in us our aggressiveness.

The handicap is something to be detested

The word "handicap" is polysemous. First introduced in France in 1957 in a law on sheltered work, it went on, in 1967, in the report by Bloch-Lainé (1968), to take a distinctly ethical meaning, that of equalisation of opportunities, in accordance with its etymology and its origins in horse-racing. This came well before its entry into scientific vocabulary in a publication on intellectual impairment (Stein & Susser, 1974), as representing the "social disadvantage" of deficiency or incapacity. Its use was then generalised by Wood (1975) and adopted by Wood (1980).

From then on, this vocable became all the more successful in so far as at that time there existed only ambiguous terms, like that of "maladjustment", to designate, especially, the educational difficulties of the mentally retarded (Salbreux, 1996, 2005). The long career it has had since then has not prevented the word handicap from retaining, in the commonest and most widespread sense, the meaning of something lacking, a reduction, and from being connoted by values of exclusion (Gateaux-Ménnecier, 1990). It is under this latter connotation that it will meet up with infirmity and even madness, in all that opposes people afflicted by it to the current stereotype of beauty, efficacy, and success. This is all the more striking in the case of severe disability (Salbreux, 2000a).

Now, in its major forms, as with serious malformations or alienation with severe behavioural disturbances, the anomaly has always been shunned (this being true in all societies). There is no lack of hypotheses to explain this ostracism: fear of contagion no doubt, a poor example certainly, useless mouths to feed, clearly.[2] Ponder, for example, the simple fact that, at least in my country, the founding myth of psychiatry goes back no further than the French Revolution (Garrabé, 1994; Gortais, 1980). Philippe Pinel and his nurse, Jean-Baptiste Pussin, "freeing the insane of their chains", tell us (to phrase things in a more contemporary fashion) that we must recognise for them an "equality of rights".

More than this, the anomaly at birth has practically never been tolerated and is still proscribed nowadays. Indeed, from being exposed to the elements on the mountainside,[3] to abandonment in the forest[4] or abortion on so-called medical grounds, the only basic difference is that of technique. In the disappointment felt by the parents in having a child who is not the one they had hoped for, there is a seriously adverse effect on narcissism and on the process of filiation, taking the form of a disaster, affecting the child, the mother, the father, brothers and sisters, and grandparents.

To weigh the amplitude of this true malaise in filiation, all one needs to do is listen, in what the parents have to say, to the cataclysmic metaphors they use "the world crashed in on us; the ground shifted from under our feet; nothing is like it was before and nothing will ever be like it was before; the Earth stopped turning". The gap between what Soulé (1982) once called the child in one's mind, "the imaginary child", and the real child no longer enables these families to see themselves in that child born abnormal and "recognise" it (Salbreux, 2006b).

If the birth defect calls into question the lineage to such an extent, that is because the monstrosity suggests an abnormal conception, related, as has been usually contemplated over the centuries, to a sexual transgression. Thus will it awaken an ancestral sense of guilt (Korff Sausse, 1996, 2001). Such an observation is in no way surprising when you consider, for example, the fact that, in the Bible, people affected bodily or intellectually are subject to violent rejection: "Only he shall not go in unto the veil, nor come nigh unto the altar, because he hath a blemish; that he profane not my sanctuaries, for I the Lord do sanctify them" (Leviticus 21–23).

The disability strikes the whole family

The traumatism (truly the disaster) for the family that is the arrival of a child affected by a disability (or at risk of becoming so—which obviously has considerable significance in antenatal diagnostic practice) hits the parents with considerable violence from the moment the condition is announced. Furthermore, this upheaval is something enduring, for the announcement is not just momentary, but constitutes a real process that can sometimes last all life long. Thus it is that the issue of guilt and anxiety that accompanies it recurs at each stage in the child's development. As a result, this suffering concerns all the members of the family group (Salbreux, 2006b; Scelles, 1998).

This bringing into question of the narcissistic bases of the entire family arises both with respect to their project to have descendents (desire to have a child, the dreamt of child, etc.), and also in terms of the very bases of their origins in relation to their own parents (on the matter, for example, of "family defects" the said parents handed down to them or are assumed to have done so). However, it also challenges their own competence as parents. Indeed, the latter only rarely dispose of a family model to become the parents of a disabled child.

This "tsunami" hits the brothers and sisters and the grandparents alike through problems of responsibility relating to that "abnormal" filiation, the role of assistance or parental substitute they will have to assume, or that of guardian of a family secret, but also due to the imbalance caused by the concentration of energy and time on a single child, the disabled one, the said child's "eternal pampering" (Buck, 1950; Racamier, 1995), and, as a result, the isolation of the family in relation to those close to it, its friends and relations.

Examples of such harmful consequences are legion:

- a mother reproaches her very young normal son for having taken everything away from his disabled twin brother, metaphorically evoking the case of the twin-to-twin transfusion syndrome so well known to obstetricians;

- a young woman cannot manage to present her premature baby to her own mother, feeling herself guilty of having, unlike the grandmother, been unable to take her pregnancy to its term;
- a grandfather, perhaps a bit of a heavy drinker, wonders as to his responsibility for the malformations he observes in his grandson;
- an eleven-year-old boy cannot invite his classroom friends to the house as he does not wish them to know he has a handicapped sister, but he reveals this some days later at school when the teacher announces that they were to talk about disabled children on that day;
- a ten-year-old girl wonders as to her future when she has to look after her sister suffering from Down's syndrome; she also ponders whether she will be able to get married, concerned as she is not to give birth to another child like her sister . . .;
- the siblings who are called on "not to cause trouble as we've already got enough to worry about at home!" or who feel obliged to sacrifice their youth or their projects on the altar of family atonement.

The passage Winnicott (1957) devotes to the ambivalence of thoughts during pregnancy provides additional proof of the fact that this problem of filiation is central in the consequences of disability arising at birth.

He recalls that if the mother wants to see her baby, touch it, hear it, it is, among other things, to check it does not have a "defect". Indeed, she fears it will not be as perfect as she dreamt it would be. It is because she has doubts as to its perfection and that of the father, that she fears giving birth to a disabled child. Meanwhile, the father doubts his capacity to father a perfect child. Winnicott concludes that it is urgent for the father and mother to see their child to be reassured.

I add: "And if bad news was involved, if reality confirmed the phantasm."

Disabled people and their families are normal "people"

Considerable clinical experience in following up families with children afflicted by disabilities of all natures, both in CAMSP[5] and in specialised institutions, as also in community and voluntary organisations, has enabled me to understand that such parents consider themselves to be quite "ordinary" parents. Even after the period (prior to the French law of 30 June 1975[6]) during which families strongly felt a sense of guilt that was, alas, very real[7] and where they got together in associations, these mothers and fathers of disabled children claimed loud and clear their role as parents and their right to have an opinion on the care and education offered their child, just as for their other children.

They have consistently pointed out the negativity of the look of others (Saladin et al., 1990) and the propensity of professionals to describe their children rather by their failings than by their competences. They instance the prevailing prejudices and taboos when it comes to disability, which are received by the public only in the sense of depreciation, a particularity to which the professionals fall victim, indeed, much like society as a whole. One striking example of this was afforded me during a training session on the announcement of the disability by a mother who had raised a young girl with cognitive deficiencies well beyond her expected twenty years of age, before losing her.

Why, she said, when the child comes into the world in such a banal fashion, are his parents not told:

"'You know, before ten years of age, he'll pinch some money from your handbag or wallet, after ten he'll smoke in secret, first tobacco, then a joint; a bit later, he'll no doubt try ecstasy or heroin, he'll only come back home late at night, or even not at all and will end up slamming the door and leaving for good!'

"But we, as parents of disabled children, are told without further ado:

'He'll walk late or not at all, he won't be able to speak, he won't go to school . . . Get on with having another child!' There must be a reason for this difference," she concluded.

There are probably a number of reasons, starting with that special condition that singularly complicates the announcement of the pathology and whose management can hardly be learnt at the medical faculty. That is the panic fear of the professional, deprived of any experience in the matter (who does not know that you first need to listen to be in a position to help) and who fills in the void with predictions[8] that will prove to be all the more harmful in so far as at that precise moment they have no reliable knowledge as to the chain of events they feel such a need to talk about.

Indeed, a certain number of these parents explain how, having once overcome the initial state of shock, they adapted to the multiple constraints relating to the care and education to be afforded to that particular child. They went through hard times, sought solutions, fought an uphill battle, then finally found an effective form of organisation thanks to a sort of patchwork of different occupations, open to constant reorganisation, that gradually they managed to make more coherent and more effective in relation to the life of the whole family.

They testify (or, at least, some of them do) to having managed to keep family life going, having other children (though not always[9]), having known moments of undeniable joy, that most unconcerned observers cannot succeed in "understanding". They readily concede that these "successes", which suffer from so many exceptions, are the fruit of a draconian form of "organisation", allowing them to face up to so many unexpected situations and win some free time in a jungle of multifarious constraints. Also, how can one not recognise that, in such families, the children, even ones with a disability, are quite naturally happy.

These parents sometimes themselves suggest, and, in all events, show to the attentive observer, that narcissistic suffering, which is always present, has enriched them, made them more mature, that they have learnt to defend themselves against unpleasant remarks ("when you have children like that, you keep them at home"), embarrassed or inquisitorial looks, pitying condescendence, etc. In short, they have fought back, learnt from life, faced up, and often find themselves in the position of normal families who have done their "duty" as much as, or even better than, another and that, while not accepting the disability, do not necessarily regret what it "brought them". Here, of course, I exclude religious, fatalistic, or jubilatory connotations that can add a special tonality to these various discourses.

The disability is banal, the anomaly fits in normally with life

The traumatism of a disability arising within a family affects all the members of that family group (Scelles, 1998, 2007), their relations among themselves[10] and with those outside the family, with respect to their history, transgenerational mandates they have received, and the family myths that are theirs. Let us here again stress the isolation of such families. This traumatism, thus, "warps" their normal construction and their evolution but does not for all that make such families pathological or abnormal, at least not frequently. Moreover, the arrival of a disabled child can just as likely awaken the pre-existing dysfunction within the couple. It has long been noted that, in such circumstances, more fragile unions break up while happy couples combine forces.

The referral back by the disability to our own vulnerability and finiteness, as mentioned earlier, definitively forms part of the human condition, as Kristeva recalled in her letter to the President of the Republic (2003). It is maybe through this mechanism that disability accompanied by major dependence, as with the profound mental disability situation, deficiency psychosis, or epilepsies with severe psychopathology, teaches us most on the desire to live and about ourselves (Salbreux, 2000b; Titran, 1983). This contagious determination to lead life, this human quality of communication, even if it is sometimes reduced to a simple exchange of glances, this joy, sometimes, in again finding the object of love, the companion, this all leads us to pose implicitly the crucial question: do these people form part of our common humanity or do they belong to a different species? The answer is obvious, even if we nowadays hear some talk about elimination, taking us back to still recent and even darker periods in our history. It is this evident fact that drives the fight led by parents and professionals for these people's dignity (Salbreux, 2006a).

This interrogation overlaps with the central question of filiation: is this child really part of our lineage?

Indeed, the "monster" necessarily represents an enigma in filiation (Grim, 2001; Korff Sausse, 1996, 2001). Castration and death are not far away.

As stated by Richard (2001, p. 234): "The handicap or its threat, confronts (us) with the unacceptable of difference and solitude, meaning castration" (translated for this edition).

Recognition of that child as belonging to the family, affiliation in other words, is made difficult, with divisive mechanisms between the child, "flesh of our flesh", and the disability, with the same people exclaiming almost all together, "We haven't got a child like that in the family."

This initial separation must be reduced for the child with a disability to be "adopted" (Roy, 1999; Salbreux, 2006b), which merely constitutes, in reality, a variant in the normal process of attachment.

Indeed, everyone knows that such motherly love is neither innate, nor automatic, but, in reality, it is the child who will charm the mother, who will only become attached to her secondarily, as in a process of adoption. So it is indeed the child, as is commonly argued, who "makes" the mother.

More generally still, whether in the scope of the announcement or in that of observing the effects of the traumatism on the entire family group, the need emerges to be heard and for sharing. The narcissistic injury is a major effect, with a violent sense of injustice as expressed forcefully by the parents. This naturally calls for a response that must be of the order of fraternity or solidarity more than charity and compassion (although these latter are not forbidden, they might well not be enough and are, above all, considered offensive by disabled people themselves).

If, coming back to Canguilhem (1991) and observing that the able-bodied person knows that accident or disease can draw them into a situation, but that their "normality" is thinkable only in relation to their own ability to avoid that debilitating accident or disease, we can then go on to attempt a transposition. Indeed, Canguilhem (1991) wrote that "The human risk of one day becoming ill forms part of the one's state of health's perspective" (p. 217). We could, perhaps, in turn, hazard the view that "confronted by disability, the able-bodied person can no longer consider that other, different person as being of another nature than one's own".

To look at things from another perspective, let us take an example: if we try to compare ethnic diversity on the one hand and normality *vs.* disability on the other—meaning the diversity of personalities— the difference immediately appears quite considerable between the two sets of oppositions chosen. Furthermore, the social representations at work, especially as far as monstrosity and sexuality are concerned, in the contrast between the two situations retained, are extremely remote from each other.

Pursuing matters further with Canguilhem (1991), we are led to concur that much more than a radical opposition, what we have, rather, are variations in degree within the norm or different normative references. Clearly, the same applies for the disabled situation.

Now, in my view, there is an essential ethical need, that of considering the disabled child, adolescent, and adult as examples, among others, of variations on the normal, or even illustrations, instances, of extreme situations, with which our very humanity confronts us. Whether that imperative results from those few considerations set forth above or constitutes the source thereof, this leads us inexorably to thinking out the status of those differences. Even if the gap observed here is of a particularly unbearable nature, related as it is to pathology, one may surmise as to whether the variable expression, the diverse facets, of that same human vulnerability do not lead back, in themselves, to a remark that is both paradoxically disturbing and trivially banal: the "normal" nature of the anomaly or the malformation. In other words, should we not share the view expressed by Stiker (2006) that it is urgent to ensure that the cultural models we construct take into consideration these differences as a law of reality?

Conclusion

To summarise matters, whether personal representations are concerned (as with the phantasm of the monster) or social representations (as in the near systematic deduction of an irremediably spoilt future, which is the equivalent to a social death, whether it involves vulnerability and finitude or sharing, solidarity, and justice), all notions that revolve around disease, infirmity, deficiency, and disability (the social side of the previous notions) are profoundly related to the human condition and, thus, in a way, humanly "normal", in all events within the order of things.

Disability, thus, forms part of the *ordinary* in life (Gardou, 2005; Kristeva et al., 2006) and the families into which the disability erupts must be taken just like any other families. One can, thus, "live" oneself with a disability or share the abnormality of a person one holds dear but who is different. That society should shun that person or the families concerned is completely unjustifiable.

The specific needs of children and people with disabilities have to be taken into account and catered for with the appropriate resources, fitting in as often as possible with the "ordinary framework" of existence, or, failing this, in institutions and services that remain "open" towards normality, with freedom of movement in both directions from one to the other. However, so much progress remains to be accomplished, in the very interest of all citizens, whether able in mind and body or not, to overcome fear, look on others more kindly, and build that human community that will not deny difference, but from which nobody is excluded and that one may, henceforth, call an inclusive society.

Notes

1. Above all, this is true as far as the dialectical relations between illness and "good" health.
2. In this respect, it is relevant to recall the increased mortality through famine in hospitals during the Second World War. In France, this affected 40,000 mental patients (Caire, 2006).
3. As was Oedipus, the child with with swollen feet.
4. As was practised not so long ago in Africa.
5. A Centre for early medico-social action: one of the out-patient services of the French medico-social sector that is responsible for prevention, screening, treatment, education, and family accompaniment of babies who are disabled or at risk of so becoming, in their natural living environment and with the latter's support.
6. Policy Act No. 75–534 of 30 June 1975 in favour of disabled people, the first major law in France to transform the place occupied by disabled people in society. The second stage is constituted by the current law No. 2005–102 of 11 February 2005, for equality of rights and opportunities, participation and citizenship of handicapped people.
7. See, on this matter, the enthusiasm over this period for the book by Maud Mannoni (1972), and for that of Bruno Bettelheim (1967).
8. Prediction is not prevention: see what oracles can trigger off!
9. It sometimes happens that the disabled child is the first and the only.
10. For example, in her chapter in "*Cliniques du sujet handicapé. Actualité des pratiques et des recherché*" (2007), Toulouse, Érès, republished 2013, pp. 13–38, Scelles reports that disabled children can "blame themselves for having deprived their brothers and sisters of parents".

References

Bettelheim, B. (Ed.) (1967). *The Empty Fortress*. London: Macmillan.

Bloch-Lainé, F. (Ed.) (1968). *Etude du problème de l'inadaptation des personnes handicapées. Rapport présenté au premier Ministre (décembre 1967)*. Paris: Documentation Française.

Buck, P. (Ed.) (1950). *L'enfant qui ne devait jamais grandir*, L. Tranec-Dubled (Trans.). Paris: Editions Stock.

Caire, M. (2006). A propos de l'hécatombe par carence dans les hôpitaux psychiatriques français sous l'Occupation. *Histoire des sciences médicales, 40*(3): 313–319.

Canguilhem, G. (Ed.) (1991). *The Normal and the Pathological*, C. R. Fawcett & R. S. Cohen (Trans.). New York: Zone Books.

Gardou, C. (Ed.) (2005). *Fragments sur le handicap et la vulnérabilité. Pour une révolution de la pensée et de l'action*. Paris: Eres.

Garrabé, J. (1994). De Pinel à Freud? Le traitement moral: son évolution de Pinel à nos jours. In: J. Garrabé (Ed.), *Philippe Pinel* (pp. 71–93). Paris: Synthélabo, coll. Les empêcheurs de penser en rond.

Gateaux-Mennecier, J. (Ed.) (1990). *La débilité légère: une construction idéologique*. Paris: CNRS.

Gortais, J. (1980). Le rôle du mythe de Pinel dans l'organisation et le fonctionnement de la psychiatrie du 19e siècle. *Psychiatrie française, 11*(1): 77–82.

Grim, O. R. (Ed.) (2001). *Quelques figures cachées de la monstruosité*. Paris: Centre technique national d'études et de recherches sur les handicaps et les inadaptations (CTNERHI).

Korff Sausse, S. (Ed.) (1996). *Le miroir Brisé. L'enfant handicapé, sa maladie et le psychanalyste*. Paris: Calmann-Lévy.

Korff Sausse, S. (Ed.) (2001). *D'Oedipe à Frankenstein: figures du handicap*. Paris: Desclée de Brouwer.

Kristeva, J. (Ed.) (2003). *Lettre au président de la République sur les citoyens en situation de handicap: à l'usage de ceux qui le sont et de ceux qui ne le sont pas*. Paris: Fayard.

Kristeva, J., Gardou, C., & Chapelain, B. (Ed.) (2006). *Handicap, le temps des engagements: premiers états généraux*. Paris: Presses Universitaires de France.

Mannoni, M. (Ed.) (1972). *The Backward Child and His Mother*. New York: Pantheon Books.

Racamier, P. C. (Ed.) (1995). *L'inceste et l'incestuel*. Paris: Ed. du Collège de Psychanalyse Groupale et Familiale.

Richard, J. T. (Ed.) (2001). *Clinique de la castration symbolique.* Paris: Editions L'Harmattan.

Roy, J. (1999). Psychodynamiques parentales et handicaps: les effets sur l'enfant. *Contraste. Revue de l'ANECAMPS, 11:* 33–46.

Saladin, M., Casanova, A., & Vidali, U. (Eds.) (1990). *Le regard des autres.* Paris: Editions Fleurus.

Salbreux, R. (1996). Le modèle de PHN WOOD. Histoire, pertinence et devenir d'un concept issu de la déficience intellectuelle. Paper presented to the La terminologie en déficience intellectuelle. Journée d'étude de l'Association Internationale de Recherche scientifique en faveur des personnes Handicapées Mentales (AIRHM), Paris X-Nanterre.

Salbreux, R. (2000a). Évolution historique de la notion de polyhandicap. La personne polyhandicapée et son devenir. *Empan, 37:* 9–18.

Salbreux, R. (2000b). Les états déficitaires de l'enfant et de l'adulte. *Revue Santé mentale, 52:* 20–25.

Salbreux, R. (2005). Le modèle de P. H. N. Wood: histoire, pertinence et devenir d'un concept issu de la psychiatrie. Actes des 3èmes Journées de l'AFP. *Psychiatrie française, 36*(SP): 100–110.

Salbreux, R. (2006a). Vie, grande dépendance et dignité. 8ème Forum des États généraux du Handicap: le temps des engagements, Paris UNESCO, 20 mai 2005. In: J. Kristeva & C. Gardou (Eds.), *Handicap: le temps des engagements* (pp. 247–281). Paris: Presses Universitaires de France.

Salbreux, R. (2006b). Naître et reconnaître: les mots ont-ils un poids? In: P. Ben Soussan (Ed.), *À l'aube de la vie, L'annonce du handicap autour de la naissance en douze questions* (pp. 89–114). Toulouse: Erès.

Scelles, R. (Ed.) (1998). *Fratrie et handicap.* Paris: Editions L'Harmattan.

Scelles, R. (2007). Famille et handicap: prendre en compte les spécificités du trauma de chacun In: A. Ciccone, S. Korff Sausse, S. Missonnier, & R. Scelles (Eds.), *Cliniques du sujet handicapé. Actualité des pratiques et des recherches* (pp. 13–38). Toulouse: Erès.

Soulé, M. (1982). L'enfant dans la tête. L'enfant imaginaire. Sa valeur structurante dans les échanges mère–enfant. In: T. B. Brazelton, B. Cramer, L. Kreisler, R. Schäppi, & M. Soulé (Eds.), *La dynamique du nourrisson* (pp. 134–175). Paris: ESF.

Stein, Z. A., & Susser, M. (1974). The epidemiology of mental retardation. In: S. Arieti (Ed.), *Child and Adolescent Psychiatry, Sociocultural and Community Psychiatry. American Handbook of Psychiatry* (2nd edn) (Vol. 2) (pp. 464–491). New York: Basic Books.

Stiker, H. J. (Ed.) (2006). *Corps infirmes et sociétés: essais d'anthropologie historique* (2nd edn). Paris: Dunod.

Titran, M. (1983). Naître pour vivre. *Les cahiers du nouveau-né*, 6: 53–69.

Winnicott, D. W. (Ed.) (1957). *The Child and the Family. First Relationships.* London: Tavistock.

Wood, P. H. N. (1975). Classification of impairments and handicaps. Geneva: World Health Organization/ICD, 91. *Rev Conf*, 75(15).

Wood, P. H. N. (1980). Comment mesurer les conséquences de la maladie: la classification internationale des infirmités, incapacités et handicaps. *Chronique O.M.S.*, 34: 400–405.

CHAPTER SEVEN

The enigma of disability: talking about it with children, listening to them, letting them talk to each other

Régine Scelles

W hile many works address the impact of the way parents' view their disabled children, few seek to analyse what happens between children themselves in their constant and step-by-step discovery of their deficiencies and the ensuing consequences on the real, phantasmatic, and imaginary levels. To subjectivate the reality of the pathology and its consequences and share the images and the thoughts it gives rise to, the child sees it reflected in other people's eyes, first almost exclusively in those of adults who are supposed to know, then, more and more, in the eyes, the ways of doing and saying, of their peers. This chapter focuses precisely on such co-construction of meaning and representations between children.

It is, first, adults who let children know the questions they may ask others and ask themselves and those that are not to be formulated before other people. Each child, then, imagines the reasons for such prohibitions and restrictions when it comes to talking and knowing of such matters.

Having stressed the extent to which shame and guilt have a major impact in this process, we evoke approaches to foster the development of thought and knowledge in the child.

To resolve, at least temporarily, the enigma the disability poses, it must not be thought of as coming under a taboo, as part of the secret that, once out in the open, could threaten oneself or others.

Disability: an enigma that brings gender and generational differences into question throughout life

While the disability remains a traumatism, it is also an enigma that can, and, indeed, should, stimulate thought. This involves finding and generating images and words that enable children to construct and further develop their perceptions of the disability. For this process to be pursued, children, both individually and with their peers, must feel allowed to know, hear, and talk about things, and for them to be listened to.

The word "enigma" is defined as follows in the *Shorter Oxford English Dictionary*: "A riddle. An obscure or elusive speech; a parable . . ."

This sense of the obscure, the ambiguous, the desire to get to the bottom of the mystery, leads on to a search for the hidden meaning. Ambiguity results in not knowing which path to follow; some are lined with pitfalls, while others lead to dead ends.

Thus, the child contemplates the meaning attached to the specific nature of his or her impairments or competences in other people's eyes, observes and feels their effects in different ways at all stages in the life cycle of the family and each of its members.

Kaës (1988) recalls a number of fundamental oppositions that underlie what it is to be human: those of "pleasure/displeasure"; that of the link/non-link and the me/not-me (ego/non-ego), that generate a feeling of loss of unity; those of the ego/total object (ego), non-me/total object (alter-ego), related and separated, that presuppose the thought of separation. The subject then recognises the differences between genders and generations; those of differentiation between the world of the family and the society that introduces it, under the meaning "us/not-us".

Awareness of the existence of differences, between generations as between the sexes, organises the relation the subject harbours towards absence and desire; the various forms of social belonging provide the grounding for shared identity and lay the foundations for psychological alliances.

Among these "differences", whose meaning and effects are built up gradually, the child will seek to grasp the meaning of the difference that deficiencies introduce between "non-disabled" and "disabled" people.

Children understand rapidly that if the disabled person has a female or male anatomy, that does not imply that they will be treated, thought of, or even dreamt of as belonging to the imaginary and phantasmatic dimensions of "boys", "girls", "men" or "women". The disability can then feature as a kind of third sex that would still entitle one to be referred to as a "girl" or a "boy", but much less readily as a "man" or "woman". This might open out to sexuality, but less readily lead to the idea of forming a couple or experiencing parenthood.

The disabled subject is always someone's "son" or "daughter". Yet, so often we hear circumlocutions whereby the family includes "three children and a disabled child". That disabled child might, then, be forgiven for considering himself, or being thought of, as somehow straddling two generations, as being neither parent nor yet a child endowed with the potential of, in turn, becoming a parent.

Disabled people are of the world of the living, but a child will so often hear mentioned the fact that an ultrasound examination could well have led to the pregnancy not being taken to its term. This is bound to arouse in the child, whether disabled or not, speculation as to the conditions necessary to acquire legitimacy as a living being.

It often arises that a disabled person of, say, thirty years of age will be addressed in the familiar manner usually adopted when speaking to children (with use of the second person singular in French, for example) and dubbed with children's pet names like "Billy Boy". Their first name will be more readily resorted to than their family name.

The child confronted by the enigma of disability becomes sensitive to all these signs, quickly grasping those quite specific distinctions.

According to the child's age, such differences will take on different meanings. For example, a four-year-old stating "My brother's a boy, but I'm disabled" might signify a sense of doubt relating to gender differences, with all that may entail in relation to the idea of castration. Such questioning evolves considerably over time and never really ceases, with each stage that the child goes through leading on to a new series of questions and answers (of a sort) being found either alone or in the company of others.

The enigma of differences between children

The presence of brothers and sisters in the family poses the question as to origin, to the difference between the sexes, and the necessary encounter between two people from the opposite sex from one generation to give birth to a new human being of the next.

The body of the brother is both an external reality (capable of being seen, touched, maltreated, handled, and felt) and, at the same time, belongs to the subject's inner reality. The brother is another from whom you have to distinguish yourself and another with whom you need to identify to act and think "like him", yet without becoming him, differentiating oneself from him.

While brothers and sisters are given by parents, in what follows each child takes his own special position in relation to each of his peers and within the group of siblings, thus forming elective and changing ties. Via these interactions, the children gradually become creators of their own bonds as siblings and then feel both the benefits and the risks that belonging to a group entail, such belonging having an impact on their individual and group-felt narcissism.

Within this group (that provides such fertile ground to learn social life), the child measures up to the other person, creates pacts with them, is rejected, rebuffs in turn, is accepted, accepts, seeks freedom from adult interference while also, at other times, feeling protected by an adult presence, can threaten and be threatened without breaking the bond, abandon and is abandoned, too, in a subtle and ever changing game.

This contact between children encompasses an essential dimension of reciprocity: "If I touch him, he feels me and touches me; if I can try out my power and throw him down, kill him, then through holding back from doing so I can experience the difference between thinking it and doing it and feel the power of 'letting live'." This reciprocity is conducive to co-learning between children. Unfortunately, the way the child suffering from a disability is rendered vulnerable (as attested to by the protection afforded by adults) leads to the reciprocity normally played out in such sibling groups not working in the ordinary way.

Within this group, sheltered from the gaze and judgement of "grown-ups", from those who "know", children jointly create for themselves a magical world, invent their own rules, resolve enigmas that will only make sense within that particular group, and will contribute to instilling in its members a reassuring sense of belonging.

The movements of identification that organise and provide the basis for bonds between children when one of them is affected by a disability are problematic and can, on the phantasmatic plane, in the child's imagination, work as a real process of contamination ("If I identify with my sister, won't I become, or be thought of, as disabled like her?"). Now, such hampered movements of identification can lead either to a cleaving to the other ("I am the other person so as not to have to take into account our differences"), or a radical separation ("I have nothing in common with her").

Thinking about the functions of bonds between peers, in the process of subjectivation of the disability, obliges one to think out the bodily contact perceived and experienced by children during their games, where aggression and tenderness combine, with the pleasure of dominating the body of the other and the pleasure of submitting to them and being dominated. This takes place in a changing dynamic that allows the child to occupy different places and roles with each of his brothers and sisters as also at successive stages in his respective development. Indeed, the sensoriality and sensuality that find expression in such bodily struggles contribute material to give substance to oneself and the other, self and one's likeness, self and one's complement.

The bonds between children are elective and constantly changing: "having to be nice to Jules because he's disabled" comes down to the same thing as excluding him from bonds between pairs. Indeed, Jules, like others, must be able to forge alliances, seal pacts, refuse them, be chosen, be rejected, pay to form part of the group and then suffer the price for having breached the rules. Giving credit to Jules as being someone able to arouse sympathy or rejection for what he is, rather than for reasons of his disability, is important. If Jules cannot manage to gain his place as a peer within that group, then the full meaning of his individuality will turn out to be affected. Indeed, a part of the enigma for the child is in knowing where they come from; what meaning is attached to them; how they take their place in the organisational differences of humanity.

What has been stated above shows all that a child loses when he does not manage to feel himself, be thought of and recognised as belonging to a group of peers; unfortunately, this is the case for many disabled children.

Emerging differences between children: the subjectivation process

Certain stages in the life of the group of siblings are crucially significant in determining the way in which each of the children, whether alone or with the others, subjectivates the disability. To illustrate this, two of these stages will be considered: the moment when a younger child becomes more capable than an elder disabled sibling and adolescence. There are other moments, but these two are paradigmatic in the co-construction between children of the sense of difference.

Gaining seniority over an elder sibling

When a younger child achieves greater maturity than the elder disabled brother or sister, this arouses ambivalent reactions in the parents and in both children concerned. The younger sibling observes the parents' pleasure or sees it confirmed that he or she is free from disability and, at the same time learns that this reality obliges the parents to recognise the scale of their other child's deficiencies. In this manner, a younger child can, much to his or her dismay, take on the role, through their patent normality, as a revelatory factor of the elder sibling's disability. Moreover, he or she might have the feeling that they are usurping their position or, as one young girl put it, "being the elder one at the expense of my sister". The elder sibling, thus dispossessed of their "natural" position might, even if they take advantage of the protection afforded, feel wounded and, thus, denied recognition as "growing up". It is in this relational context that deficiencies take on their full meaning for both children.

Adolescence

Gutton (1993) reveals the importance of identification with the brother or sister in the process of adolescence. Thus, at adolescence, brothers and sisters are often the first to notice that the light kiss, the caress given their friend of either sex by their disabled peer is manifestly eroticised. Brothers and sisters might intervene to help the disabled adolescent work what psychoanalysts call "the second process of separation" (Blos, 1967). As it is advantageous for them for their sibling to become more independent, having his or her own leisure activities and friends, they might intercede in their favour to oblige their parents and, sometimes, professionals to give the disabled child greater freedom. Thus, they underline the fact that adults sometimes overestimate deficiencies and, therefore, hinder the process of attaining adulthood. Thus, it is at adolescence that siblings contribute to re-evaluating the consequences of deficiencies.

The disabled adolescent girl cannot indulge in the fantasy of no longer being disabled, of having children and finding a husband without her close relations and professionals making it their duty, at best by telling her, at worst by seeking to prove to her, that all that is and will remain forever impossible. Thus, the child often turns out to be deprived of a share in the dream that feeds the imagination of adolescents and adults alike. Brothers and sisters are better able than parents or professionals to accept the idea of dreaming with the disabled adolescent so that the pleasure enjoyed in such projection opens up the way to thinking of a future in which, gradually, real life events may take shape. Accompanied in their reveries, the subject feels vindicated in the perceived difference that exists between the real and the imaginary worlds and experiments with the perspectives this opens up for his or her personal life to unfold.

Thus, on adolescence, the group of peers has a central role in how the adolescent and then the adult manages to fulfil his desires, his pleasures, and choices with his deficiencies that, as a result, are subjectivated in a more personal way that is less dependent on what the previous generation thinks or yearns for.

Siblingship bonds to social bonds

Having taken his place within the family nest, the child must find his place in other groups (the kindergarten, school, leisure activities, work, etc.). All stages in the cycle of life involve crossing from one place, group, or condition to another, a passage that is signified and orchestrated by the prevailing culture, customs, and laws and, thus, by a societal context.

While the non-disabled brother can play the role of "go-between" towards social life for the disabled sibling by acting as a link towards "non-family" and "non-disabled" objects, this cannot be reciprocated; indeed, while the disabled person has friends at the social and medical institution, he is only extremely rarely invested in as a friend in turn by that person's brothers and sisters. This is something of which the disabled person is well aware.

Seven-year-old Marc is kept down in the last year of nursery school. He walks, but is unsteady and often falls during recreation. He can write, but with great difficulty and has serious elocution problems.

As from the age of three, he went to the local school with his twin brother but in different classes. While his brother went on to primary school, Marc stayed on at the nursery.

I met him at a time when his teacher was complaining that Marc was becoming more and more disruptive in class, especially by talking very loudly, dribbling a lot, and falling over more often, which aroused reactions among the other children that were sometimes difficult to channel. This attitude contrasts with the fact that, until then, everyone was delighted by what was considered by both teachers and parents to be a perfectly successful integration at school.

At the end of the previous year, it was decided to keep Marc on at the nursery school because Marc was "slower" and had only come to school half time for the first two years. Reasons of intellectual deficiencies were not mentioned then, but now his teacher starts to bring up the issue of cognitive deficiency.

Marc explained that last year the other pupils played with him because his brother forced them to, but now, with this support lost, he found himself alone during recreation. He added that lessons went too fast for him, that the teacher became too demanding, and that he could not put up with having his professional classroom assistant "breathing down his neck". He said he was tired and summed things up as follows: "Last year, I wasn't that disabled but now I really am."

Followed, as he is, by a home social work service and integrated individually, Marc has never been extensively in contact with children who, like him, encounter similar difficulties. This individual integration with a brother who created a link with school pals actually created a false sense of security (adhered to by all) but that turned out to bear a heavy price for Marc to pay psychologically. To tell adults and children alike and have them acknowledge the reality of his situation (that he can no longer ignore), all that was left to him were behavioural disorders that further compounded his difficulties.

That false sense of security already mentioned also, in part, prevented other children from exchanging directly with him and making bonds other than those remotely controlled or pre-formatted by adults and his brother.

For the disabled child, the opportunity to be chosen as a friend by others is a major issue. The way in which services to be asked of others are gauged represents a kind of alchemy that calls on all the subject's intelligence and vigilance. This vigilance and the calculations it involves demand of them considerable psychic energy and the child does not always wish to seek help from parents or teachers. Thus, many children with disabilities suffer from being unable to create bonds on level terms with their peers who, at best, help them just as adults could be expected to do or, at worst, mistreat them or ignore them.

This situation can hardly remain tolerable for very long as the disabled child, like all other children, has an overriding need to build his or her own personality through creating bonds on relatively equal terms, real bonds and not just relations or interactions.

To do so, there is a need to choose, and be chosen by one's peers, to create pacts and alliances with them as mentioned at the start of the present section.

When the adult is attentive to the child, it is relatively easy finally to identify the moment when "just social" relations are no longer enough, when the child ceases to put up with the idea of "just" being the one who is always different, never like the others, never able to jointly choose those with whom they will establish the most intimate and reciprocal bonds.

Shame and guilt

Shame and guilt are often involved in the process of subjectivation of the disability in children. Such feelings are of intrapsychic and intersubjective origin and derive from movements of identification with guilt and shame that they apprehend in other members of the family and the special and changing relation that each child in the family maintains with the condition of disability (Scelles, 1998).

While theoretically making a distinction between guilt and shame is a matter of heuristics, in discourse from children, these two senti-ments are often associated. While guilt relates to a threat of imaginary castration and the superego, shame, meanwhile, relates to a threat of loss of love and the ideal of the ego and affects the subjects' narcis-sism. These are affects, associated with representations rejected by the ego, repressed and displaced, that give rise to a sense of guilt. The more the subject manages to repress his emotions, renouncing or post-poning the realisation of his libidinal satisfactions, the more he engages on the path of guilt. When the child does something "bad", he is not so much afraid of being punished as of losing the love and esteem of those he loves. The child also adheres to the family, social, and cultural values of those close to him so as not to risk being rejected, devalued, or, worst of all, being divested of interest. This observance is accompanied by a narcissistic satisfaction and a boost in self-esteem (Ciccone, 1997; Tisseron, 1992)

Guilt, aggression, and reparation

Children imagine that their parents are responsible for the disease or for being unable to find a cure for it. They then sometimes go on to accuse themselves of having "done wrong" but, most often, they think they have "had bad thoughts" or "not loved enough". This pervasive power of thought that can hurt "in reality" might lead them subse-quently to become extremely wary in seeking to control a thought that seems to have the capability of acting out their desires (and even the most secretly held ones) in reality "without them doing anything".

Seventeen-year-old Alain, suffering from myopathy, speaks slight-ingly of his younger, fifteen-year-old, brother. He does this preferably in front of people his brother appreciates and, more specifically still, when this involves his girlfriends. He also suffers from time to time from a state of collapse that leads to everyone panicking when he feels that too much attention is being given to his younger brother. The entire family is aware that Alain is jealous of his brother's normalcy and is seeking revenge. Nobody really dares to punish him as this violence is interpreted as being the sign of his own revolt against his disability. From a very early age, his brother has got used to putting up with it, keeping quiet, and not seeking help as his parents will inevitably say that "It's not his fault".

These unpremeditated, non-elaborated acts of aggression that remain uncontained by protective adults can generate feelings of guilt with devastating effects on each of the children and the bonds that exist between them.

The disabled child feels guilty for not being the ideal child and, while he may enjoy the benefits of occupying parental psychic time and space, he might also harbour anger against himself for, as one adolescent put it, "having deprived my brothers and sisters of parents" or "having chased away my father". Thus expressed, this sense of guilt can be a way of resisting non-sense and fatal passivity and calling on the other. This can then open out to passing from the status of "object" to that of "subject".

Obviously, the adult remains guarantor of the existence of a framework, a capacity for containment, ensuring that the process of learning about how to live together between children endangers none of them and that the feelings at stake in such bonds do not too painfully overwhelm one or more of the children involved.

Shame: ashamed of . . . and ashamed for . . .

Shame emerges whenever one's behaviour is contrary to the image one would have wished to have projected. According to Tisseron (1992), "the greater the distress, that is, the more serious is narcissistic collapse, the more resorting to a superlative form of guilt will be seen to be an alternative" (p. 27, translated for this edition).

The sense of shame felt by children arises without warning when faced with a scene, a situation that involves a pattern of behaviour, more generally an attitude, a being "out there in the world", "in the world", and "for the world" that attracts the mocking and disapproving gaze of all bystanders. Those bystanders as a whole do not feel shame, but together take part in that feeling bursting forth. Finally, each person expresses in his own special way the same discomfort: the spectator laughs, looks on, asks questions, while the shamed person blushes, becomes angry, runs away, has jelly legs, and feels devastated . . . In all events, such reactions "show" and "make apparent" a feeling of embarrassment when confronted by the disability and no mediation by thinking through matters can provide a salving effect here.

The person who mocks and laughs might have the feeling of having fun, but such laughter, thought on again, reconsidered in other circumstances, can, subsequently, take on another meaning. The feelings and emotions that emerge within the scope of confronting the pathology have consequences that are all the more complex in so far as it is impossible to consider the *agent provocateur* as being "guilty". Certainly, the disabled child is at the origin of the shame, but he or she cannot be punished or condemned to repair the moral prejudice suffered.

Clearly, the disabled person can always be accused of playing on his disability to provoke rejection, but everyone knows that, in the long run, while he can "use" hia weaknesses in various ways, in reality, his difficulties, deficiencies, and incapacity are "uncontrolled". "It's not his fault if he's like that, but it's still tough for everyone," as a ten-year-old sister put it.

In individual and clinical interviews, it often arises that the unease shown by children takes root in a feeling of shame. Once expressed, this feeling almost systematically triggers avoidance of eye contact (the child looks at his shoes or the ceiling), followed, once things have been said, by a glance towards the parents when they are present and, more furtively, towards the psychologist when the parents are not present.

This way of cutting oneself off from others, then "checking" the effect produced on the adults, or again looking for their support, their recognition, shows to what extent the child's feeling of shame closely depends on the way they are looked on by the adults.

Living with the shame of adults . . .

Children identify with the shame they know inhabits their parents. Thus, they notice that even if the parents do not say so explicitly, they go out from home as little as possible so as not to have to confront various situations that might give rise to a feeling of shame.

So, they understand that the parents are ashamed of their child, of themselves, and, finally, of their family. They also know that they feel guilty and shameful.

They interpret the fact that their parents ostensibly make it their business to "show" their children and impose them everywhere, refusing to go out without them, as a way of denying their shame.

A twenty-year-old young woman affirms that her father made her sister sing at all family meals, although she sang off-key. This was, for him, a way of fighting back against a feeling in favour of rejection and an expression of the ambivalence that marked his feelings. This young woman thought that her disabled sister suffered considerably from the way in which her father thrust her to the fore, sometimes violently. But she had nothing to say about it before adolescence, as she would have feared increasing his suffering.

Deciphering the embarrassment lurking in other people's looks can sometimes lead to a real traumatism in children. It is as if seeing in the other's gaze the feeling that they were seeking to ignore forced them to relinquish any dishonesty towards themselves:

"When I saw the lady behind the counter grimace as she saw my brother dribbling, I understood that I, too, would have liked to pull a face but that, because it was my brother, not only did I not have the right to do so, but that I would be ashamed of my shame for the rest of my life."

There is a close link between the confidence that children have in themselves, their ability to talk about disability, and the way they take a stance on the social scene. The more unhappy and uneasy they are, the less they have the feeling that others can help them, the more they withdraw into themselves and the more they suffer from the words, looks, and attitudes of contempt or aggression met from others (Scelles, 2010).

When a disabled brother behaves embarrassingly, this places his brothers and sisters face to face with the conundrum as to whether to give pride of place to the bonds that exist between them on the matter of shame and, in that case, by "contagion", become ashamed themselves, or distance themselves from their disabled sibling and then risk judging or even rejecting them as "strangers" do and, in that instance, suffer from having broken family solidarity.

Sometimes, even before a third party has done anything, the brothers and sisters expect them to react inappropriately to the presence of their disabled sibling. Indeed, they fear first that past history repeats itself and, second, they project on others their own unease.

The disabled subject

For the disabled persons themselves, this question arises in its own special terms. Indeed, they will act as if their pathology did not affect them and the looks and remarks of others no longer hurt them, failed to hit their target. But, here again, nothing can shield them from a look or a comment that will get through to them by surprise at a moment when, unprepared, they have not had time to protect themselves.

Over time, some end up finding procedures of subjectivation of the pathology and negotiation on the bonds they have with others, enabling them to attenuate the traumatic effects of shame. Such strategies bring with them a higher or lower price tag in the psychological stakes involved.

Thus, pretending to understand, or not speaking to avoid stuttering, can have a temporary utility but might become alienating over the longer term. Moreover, some forms of impairment cannot be concealed. Other strategies will then have to be resorted to, sometimes in a highly creative manner. They may then bring in people considered benevolent (as are most brothers and sisters).

Seeking to resolve the enigma and experiment the power of release that combined thinking between children can unleash

Within the family, there can be an unconscious defensive alliance that Kaës (1988) calls a denegative pact. This hinges less on the name of the pathology than on the emotions and affects it triggers in everyone.

The less adults talk, the more they seek to mask their feelings and their emotions and the more children become expert in deciphering the meaning of what is verbally forbidden. They then over-interpret all the clues, enabling them to better understand the meaning of this strange reality of deficiencies and incapacity (Scelles, 1998).

When faced with what is strange or disturbing, children resort to the thought thinking apparatus (Bion, 1963) so as to think out the situation and overcome sideration. They then change into budding scientists, seekers of clues, and become expert in deciphering non-verbal language.

Cunningly, such children will persevere and alone pursue their path to solve the enigma facing them, seeking in Knowledge (with a capital "K") how to find a solution. Like the sister of the young schizophrenic who decides to become a psychiatrist, such a child will eavesdrop, read other people's mail and reports surreptitiously, and, when implicitly, or even better, explicitly authorised so to do by

adults, talk with his or her peers and, more especially, with his brothers and sisters. This quest has positive effects if it can be deployed
without the child feeling too stricken by guilt through infringing a
family taboo.

Why children do not talk

Parents rarely explicitly forbid children from talking about disability
but, relying on clues garnered here or there, the children quickly
learn, without discussing the issue or arguing about it, whether it is
appropriate or not to raise the matter between brothers and sisters,
with comrades, or with their best friends.

When the individual no longer has confidence in the ability of
others to help him, he loses every possibility of being able one day to
be listened to, consoled, or even mothered (Burlingham et al., 1949).

Sometimes, to reduce suffering, to protect the other, each person
will take care not to talk about things and just carry on regardless. The
child hides away to shed tears and sometimes, unfortunately, manages
to almost believe that he does not even want to cry. He then cuts
himself off from his own feelings, his emotions, and seizes on those of
others, in this instance, those of the parents.

Sometimes, too, the child does not look for the adult to speak to
him as he knows that those matters not talked about in the family
relate to taboos with which they are all so familiar: death, sex, and
parental guilt. He even also refuses to be talked to and to speak out,
so as to protect the adult, so as not to be a "bad child" and not trigger
suffering in others or have to suffer their refusal to talk to him. Such
a refusal would even further affect the parental image.

The child also does not speak because he tells himself that if things
are not stated then they do not exist either for himself and/or for
the other. A ten-year-old child declared (while avoiding any eye contact with me) "Really I know I'm disabled forever, but don't tell
my mother I know it 'cos she thinks I believe I'm just like everyone
else."

All children are subjected to a tension whose intensity varies over
time between the desire to know and not to know. But even where
there is a desire not to know, there is the idea in the end that there is
something to know about. This not-knowing then becomes a temporary point whose vocation, if all goes well, would be to gradually open

out to the possibility of putting images and words to the discovery of the enigma that the disability's existence poses to being human.

Why adults do not talk to children

There are many reasons why adults, parents, and professionals do not to talk to children, including the difficulty of formulating what they want and what they wish to say; the fear of not being understood; imagining, without believing, that the child does not know and that you must not worry them . . . admit to them that you don't know . . . Now, for the work of thought to be possible between children, the parents must first have granted its authorisation (Raimbault & Zygouris, 1991).

At school, the teacher is reading some literature on disability to her class the very day the disabled child is absent. She says to the children in an indirect manner that it is forbidden to raise the issue of disability in the said disabled child's presence but only discuss it between "us".

This leads to wondering what the adult fears and that would be so serious if she expressed verbally and through her attitude her approval for the pupils to talk with the disabled child about who she is, what she wishes for, the difficulties she encounters, and also those they themselves create.

Talking

The child who feels the adult is ready to listen, who does not fear hurting them, who has the feeling that his or her affects will be contained, can take part actively in constructing the process of narrativity about the pathology.

During family consultations, it is not rare for a child who has started to speak to help their parents in turn to express what they feel; in return, the child feels authorised and legitimised in continuing.

In the dynamic of the process of identification fostered by the proximity of age and shared emotions, a child may put things into words, speak of the shame that another person cannot express by themselves. For example, the brothers and sisters, more than adults, know that their disabled brother or sister is sometimes ashamed of dribbling, failing to understand, making strange movements.

It can arise, especially with adolescence, that children develop (sometimes highly creative) strategies to oblige adults to speak out.

A ten-year-old child had developed a sort of "phobia" of cakes; he did not want to touch them and doing so would trigger major anxiety.

This child's small brother had a serious metabolic disease. Due to the said illness, he ran the risk of dying if he ate certain foods, including cakes. The parents had been determined to see their son lead a "life like everyone else" despite his condition and for that food ban not to disturb family life in any way, either in general and, more particularly, at meal times.

They had not talked about this pathology to their children, and the child concerned was supposed to know about his disease, that while it was forbidden to eat certain foods, other questions as to the origin and prognosis were taboo. During a consultation, the mother said to him, "You're not allowed that, but it's just a detail, just a little thing that you can't have. It's not worth going on about it. Other kids have much worse things than you."

As far as a "little thing" being concerned, it actually involved a metabolic pathology that was accompanied by a slight linguistic and cognitive deficiency that nobody mentioned within the family. The parents had been informed of this during a consultation where the child was present. Following a remark relating to their son's supposed "not-knowing", the father explained things as follows in his presence:

"He was very young when the consultation took place where we were told and he can't have understood. And then after all there's no point him knowing about it, it'll just worry him. We need to carry on as if he was normal, just that he mustn't eat some things—it's like electrical sockets, touching them is out for all kids, except here it's just him who mustn't eat cakes."

It transpires that his brother, by developing his "symptom", had really launched an appeal to the adult to allow him to know what he already knew but also that he authorise his brother to acknowledge it, too, and that they be able to talk about it between the two of them.

Both brothers attended the same school and, in the recreation yard, the elder brother had often heard the other children refer to his younger sibling as "Mongol". He just answered that he was ill, but he knew that these insults merely put into words, brutally, a truth that the adults were unable to admit but that he had clearly understood.

At that time, this child was not seeking to unearth the truth about the disease, but he needed to be able to say what he thought he had understood and formulate the questions he had on his mind.

A boy who came into consultation alongside his brother with cognitive deficiency said that he could no longer put up with the latter throwing his exercise books in his face as soon as he was frustrated in any way. As he said these words, he met his mother's look of sadness and told her, "You see, you're completely fed up with it all, he gets on your nerves, too."

The disabled brother was present and began to shout, which immediately triggered a reaction from the boy who looked at him straight in the eyes and said, "We can't even talk to you."

The child was taken aback by this comment, shut up, and gazed back at his brother (I noted this attention paid to the words that had just been uttered) and, at that instant, the mother started in turn to talk about her exhaustion. This was followed by an exchange in which the disabled child, in his way, took part. The end of the interview was to see the two children play together, sometimes making noise to drown out the words of the mother who told of her inability to see how the family atmosphere was going to develop, disrupted as it was on a daily basis by her son's tantrums.

At that moment, the thinking shared between adults and children opened out to the creation of a reassuring and structuring bridge between the world of "grown-ups" and that of the "kids", and allowed the children, too, to come together, leaving the adults to themselves.

The resonance effect between what the adult experiences and what is expressed by the child enables the former to play on a dynamic tension between identification and essential differentiation, so that the adult, letting themselves be surprised by what is said to them, allows the child to feel safe to talk. In other words, the adult must be familiar enough with his or her own emotions to create within them a sufficient psychic space for the child to find support in their listening, in the parent's thoughts, so the child can, in turn, develop his or her own thoughts.

Bion (1963) talks about the adult's "negative capacity" that enables him or her to tolerate not knowing, not understanding, so as to open out to the child a space where co-construction of thought becomes possible. To do so, one needs to take the risk of accepting feeling jointly and thinking jointly with the child.

The meaning the child gives to his pathology, the place and function it takes in his intrapsychic and intersubjective life, is always, to a certain extent, jointly built with those in whom they invest emotionally. Now, parents, brothers, and sisters may find themselves unable to give meaning to what the disabled child experiences and, failing the ability to identify with the way they function, he or she is not thought of as a "subject-child", being seen, rather, according to the case, as "a failed robot", "a frail plant" . . . A child said, during an interview, "My brother's a bit like a car with a breakdown, but there's no mechanic to get him going again."

As matters evolve, all psychic life might be denied him; this involves a form of defence aimed at managing the impossibility of supporting this over-strange child in his process of humanisation. André-Fustier (2002) writes in this respect about an "adhesive identification with the psychologically moribund child".

While the disabled child fails to understand the meaning of what is said by adults about her pathology, she perfectly grasps the emotions relating thereto.

Deligny and Joseph (1998) invite adults to "let children get on with things" and advise that to do so we need to remain open to the singularity of responses the child has to offer. "Letting them get on", for children among themselves, does not mean not wanting things or imagining things for them, but simply accepting the idea of giving free rein to their unpredictability and the wealth of potential they have in their capacity to create and learn mutually. Being able to ensure exchanges between children helps each person, gradually, to better know themselves and build their own way of "being with" while simultaneously getting to know others. This does not just revolve around how to talk to children, but also how to leave them to talk among themselves of the disability and foster opportunities that they will jointly build together to determine how they will live with the disability.

Children talking among themselves

Only true idealists still think that children are "naturally kind" and that a peer's disability does not pose a problem to them or that they fail to see it. Indeed, even when highly protected, it remains impossible to raise a disabled child in a bubble where he or she is not called on to meet other children who will say unpleasant or nasty things to them. The only thing that can then help them is to afford them the possibility of mentioning such hostility in an atmosphere of kindness, without them feeling guilty of hurting the person listening to them.

When it comes to settling into school, brothers and sisters are often there to speak out on behalf of the disabled child.

An eleven-year-old girl became angry during a consultation and said, "I'm mad with the teacher. She tells mummy she looks after Mathieu really well. But at recreation I can see he's all by himself with the others ragging him and she says nothing."

I then ask Mathieu why he does not complain and he answers that there is no point to it. The father, who is also present, is astonished by this and, getting angry in turn, says that he will go and see about the matter at school. Mathieu then begs him not to and adds, quite rightly, that he did not bring the matter up and is not complaining, he just wants to avoid it all. He then looks at his sister and bluntly reproaches her for having brought the matter up at home.

Mathieu remains quiet because he knows that his parents are happy for him to "go to school like everyone else"; by letting them believe that all is well it was as if, in his own way, he was taking part in making amends. Moreover, were he to denounce those who harass him, Mathieu would fear even greater isolation and, finally, he does not feel protected by the adults, and is not sure they are able to help him without compounding his problems.

More profoundly (and individual interviews will show this), he feels hurt in being unable, without outside assistance, to live life with others. It becomes, for him, a kind of challenge to manage to do so while failing therein provides confirmation of his "uselessness". His sister's intervention hurts him as, once again, she took on the role of protector. This is something he can no longer put up with. But at the same time, he recognises that if she were not with him at school, it would be even harder. The disabled child can neither escape from the questions of his peers, nor from the sense of guilt felt when he makes those other children's lives more complicated or instils in them a sense of unease.

Ms B. is the mother of a five-year-old daughter who had an arm amputated at the age of three. She recounts the following story that took place at the swimming pool where, after much hesitation, she had taken her child.

> A small boy of about five years of age approached her daughter, stared intensely at her stump, and said to her, "Who was it cut it off you?"
>
> According to the mother, her distraught little daughter looked back at her as she answered, "Nobody."
>
> The mother said she felt faint and wanted to take her daughter away, but the two children seemed to be mutually fascinated as the boy asks, "But how do you manage to swim?"
>
> "I can't swim."
>
> "Well, I can't swim either."
>
> "So, you see?"
>
> "Yes, but it's not much good having just one arm."
>
> Just then, the little boy's mother burst in to drag her son away. She proffered apologies but still pulled the boy (who failed to see what he had done wrong) away.

It is easy to imagine how that mother justified her behaviour to her son. She probably said things like: "You shouldn't pass comment. She's unhappy and you make her sad talking about all that . . ." Talking to another adult rather than directly to the child (who would nevertheless have heard it) this might well have been expressed as: "All the same, she should have a false arm. Seeing that is shocking . . .". Another take might well have been "Nowadays, they would have seen what was wrong with the ultrasound and her parents could have seen to the abortion . . ."

It was the attitude of the child's mother that most deeply hurt Ms B. She had the feeling that this woman had accused her of having dared take her daughter to the swimming pool and had sought to protect her son from possible contamination: "My daughter's not got the plague or something—she didn't have to stop her son being with my daughter like that."

I note that apologies were made to the mother and ask what her daughter said. "Nothing" was her reply.

This is a fairly common scene where, as so often, the story of what happened and what she experienced is recounted in front of the child (while she remains silent) and, in the background, her mother is there crying. I intervened to ask her what she thought about it all. At first, she did not reply, but then, a little later, she came out with the following: "First, to tell the truth; it wasn't nobody. The doctor cut it off."

Then she asked if it was true that you cannot swim with just one arm.

This scene reminded her painfully to what extent adults are embarrassed by that missing arm and also that it would appear to be forbidden, or even dangerous, to talk about the matter even among children. However, the small boy's questions were on the same wavelength as her own thoughts and could finally have allowed for a true exchange to take place between children without representing too much of a hazard for her. Indeed, the small boy realised, just like the little girl (though clearly from another perspective), the full significance of that missing arm, and the sharing of emotions, with the accompanying questions it raises, could have made of the trauma that isolates a bridge between human beings, thus rendering it more tolerable.

The little girl finished off, as if to comfort her mother, by saying, "You know, at school, people often tell me that. You get used to it."

Conclusion

Whether they have a disease or not, the child's confrontation with disability raises questions, emotions, and affects that (where putting words to things remains forbidden) can generate suffering that the child sometimes successfully manages to hide in order to protect his or her parents.

In the family and at school, the child learns what he or she is supposed to know, what it is "good" and "useful" to know, and what must not be known, must not be said, or even "thought". When children come to notice that the adult reckoned it was "bad" or "dangerous" to talk of or think about certain things, they most often refrain in turn from doing so.

In this context, the opportunity offered the child to fall back on his or her peers or siblings in order to attempt to resolve the enigma that the disability poses to both children and adults has a soothing effect and benefits both the subject (a feeling of greater self-esteem and relief) and perceived reality (that becomes less strange and threatening). Whenever the child seeks to find meaning, to resolve the enigma and manages so to do, he or she will feel recognised as being a player in the production of knowledge, and whoever takes part with him or her in that quest also achieves esteem. Thus, in sharing with another person such questions and one's answers, the subject feels the desire to achieve recognition narcissistically. In this process of exchange, the question of the one (the unique being) can become that of the other, which presupposes a certain structuring of thoughts and a process of subjective appropriation of reality.

If the child remains unable to give meaning to what he feels or if his emotions fail to be recognised, not corroborated by the adults who enjoy his trust, he might work towards forgetting them. He will "draw into himself" the other's emotions to fill the void left by those emotions he cannot succeed in working up himself. He will experience the feeling of having his own existence while being invested or invaded from outside (by others with their emotions).

Often, when seeking to protect the child, adults are actually protecting themselves. There is, thus, a need to encourage, in so far as possible, the means whereby children, confronted as they are by disability, try out the advantages of being part of a group, thinking as part of the group. It might then become possible for those children to feel free to enjoy speaking out. The adult will only see the effects and will only know what the child is willing to tell them. The cold and stark nature of the disability, that brings adults to tears, might then become an object that can be transformed by thought, and, thus, more readily subjectivated.

References

André-Fustier, F. (2002). Les adaptations familiales défensives face au handicap. *Le divan familial, 8*: 14–24.

Bion, W. R. (Ed.) (1963). *Elements of Psychoanalysis*. London: Karnac, 1984.

Blos, P. (Ed.) (1967). *Les adolescents*. Paris: Stock.

Burlingham, D., Freud, A., & Berman, A. (Eds.) (1949). *Enfants sans famille*. Paris: Presses Universitaires de France.

Ciccone, A. (1997). L'éclosion de la vie psychique. In: *Naissance et développement de la vie psychique* (pp. 12–37). Ramonville-Saint-Agne: Erès.

Deligny, F., & Joseph, I. (Eds.) (1998). *Graine de crapule*. Paris: Dunod.

Kaës, R. (Ed.) (1988). *Différence culturelle et souffrances de l'identité*. Paris: Dunod.

Raimbault, G., & Zygouris, R. (Eds.) (1991). *L'enfant et sa maladie*. Toulouse: Privat.

Scelles, R. (1998). Les frères et soeurs et la non-annonce du handicap. *Pratiques psychologiques, 2*: 83–91.

Scelles, R. (Ed.) (2010). *Liens fraternels et handicap. De l'enfance à l'âge adulte.* Toulouse: Erès.

Tisseron, S. (Ed.) (1992). *La honte: psychanalyse d'un lien social.* Paris: Dunod.

CHAPTER EIGHT

Bodies lost and bodies gained: the major periods in the history of disability

Henri-Jacques Stiker

Introduction

History sidles forward crab-like and we can never step into the same river twice. These two images argue that a linear presentation (suggesting that there is a rectilinear progression) might be misleading and forewarn against what are too loosely called the lessons of history. In each period, there are tensions and counter-currents. Each era reorganises things in its own manner, meaning that talk of progress or regression remains largely meaningless. The terms mutations and metamorphoses strike me as being more apposite. This view renders its full significance to history as the current patterns can only be understood if we look back over the path that led us to where we stand today. The historian, though, loves chronological order, as making time's sequence of events easier to understand and no one in their right mind would try to put the pharaohs after the French Revolution.

My second preliminary remark is in terms of anthropology. Infirmity is the broken mirror of one's positive self-image. Facing infirmity, individual and group alike feel ill at ease, afraid, tend to shy away from misery and deviance, and are confronted by the finitude and fragility of their condition. From this disturbed psyche may arise fantastic mythologies, archaic or highly elaborated symbolisms, and more or less random ways of tackling the issues. Each society or culture constructs its universe of the disabled body.

The symbolism of infirmity

The greatest divide in the history of the Western world came, as we all know (Stiker, 1999), at the time of the Renaissance, when the world became secularised as it sought release from its heteronymous conception of things, meaning its fundamental link with divine power. Four phenomena were to radically change the conception that I shall call religious and that, under very different forms, was shared by all societies: Galilean science, that gave autonomy to reason; a new political philosophy (with the theoreticians of the social contract), that endowed society with free will; the Reform, that afforded the believer independence in relation to the Scriptures; and social disorganisation, due mainly to constant warfare and major epidemics (the plague, cholera, and other scourges), that called on absolute monarchy to order matters in accordance with rational standards.

Under the divine gaze

Deformed birth, a message from the gods

In Antiquity, birth defects were considered to be a curse. Deformed birth was a warning sign from the gods addressed to a guilty social group at risk of deviance. The meaning carried by the malformed new-born baby was to be returned to its senders to show that the message had been received.

The practice that followed is what the Greeks called exposure of such children, for which they reserved a quite special word: *apothesis* (as opposed to another form of exposure known as *ekthesis* that concerned children born from forbidden, or simply undesirable, unions). On decision of the leaders of the city, children showing anomalies (palmed fingers, incomplete or deformed limbs, etc.) were taken out of the social space into the wilderness where they were to die, not being killed directly, but left to the will of the gods. Those who survived, at least in the social imagination, became charged with meaning, unless they fell into the hands of slave traders or traffickers in prostitution.

The case of Oedipus is symbolically exemplary. According to a historian of Ancient Greece, Marie Delcourt (1944), Oedipus represents the fate of those who, by their abnormal birth, embody misfortune, bear it, and carry it along with them. He symbolises an extreme form of "difference" that haunted the Greek mind-set, condemned as he was to repetition and *mimesis*, since he was to marry his mother, kill his father, and see his children tear each other apart. The deformed birth is an evil but, at the same time, it hints towards the (impossible) acceptance of those others. Repetition of the species must be maintained identically and the anger of the gods must be warded off.

Aristotle called for a law to forbid anyone from taking care of children born crippled and Plato sought to rationalise customs of exposure by eugenic considerations.

Under various forms, the evil figure of the child born with a birth defect is to be found over and over again in different cultures over time.

Being whole to approach Yahweh

Looking now to Hebrew culture (*La Bible*, 2010), infirmity appears as an impurity. It always involves a transcendent meaning of infirmity. Any cripple shares with other beings (impure animals, unworthy to serve as offerings) and other human situations (menstrual periods, afterbirth, traces of sperm, etc.) the function of underscoring what separates the divine and the human. Indeed, in the Book of Leviticus, telling the story of the priestly tribe, the sons of "priests" born infirm are forbidden from taking part in rites. They may not make offerings. When you approach the places of the presence of the All-Other, you have to be unblemished, untainted. Hebrew thought imposes conditions on the encounter with the One, the Unnameable (the Tetragrammaton). Religious prohibition was strong but limited, and led to no expeditive solution. In contrast, Hebrew ethics unrelentingly urged that the poor and the infirm be treated with compassion and kindness, although no particular institution was assigned to them.

Infirmity takes part in marking the sacred, without exclusion from society. Infirmity is an otherness opposed to that of God, but, like that otherness, it remains immeasurable; in social life, however, it is a mere difference, very much secondary to the fact that all men are sons of God.

Infirmity as divine manifestation (the evangelical shift)

In the Gospel narratives, Jesus Christ comes into contact more than twenty times with cripples. He transgresses his Jewish tradition on a number of matters: he rejects any connection between infirmity and sin (example of the person born blind in Chapter 9 of the Gospel according to John), he heals the sick on the day of the Sabbath (Luke 6: 6–12) and newly defines the relation between purity and impurity that both became interior. He lets himself be touched by the infirm and the sick although claiming to represent God's presence in our world. Infirmity may no longer be radically excluded as in so-called pagan antiquity, and no more may it continue to feature in the category of impurity. Rather, Christ gives full force to the ethical tradition of the Jewish people: considering the poor and infirm to be the countenance of the sons of God, and, therefore, to be respected and loved. As for Mohammed, he was to make the same demand: "No crime shall it be in the blind, or in the lame, or in the sick, to eat at your tables" (Sura XXIV, 60).

Relieving affliction and attaining salvation (the medieval outlook)

During the medieval period, two great figures of infirmity are to be encountered: the poor cripple, the object of "works of charity", and the crippled buffoon.

The perspective of salvation also informed the charity one owed to the disabled person considered as resourceless. Hospitality and alms were, therefore, due to them. This was quite a different instance to that of the buffoon. The poor were to be granted hospitality through the multitude of foundations set up by rich laymen, princes, bishops, or monastic orders: hospitality and alms to win one salvation. Such charity, in the noble sense of the term, left the poor and the beggars, among whom most of the infirm were to be found, in the same condition. For just as alms giving was a duty in one's quest for salvation, so the prevailing theological outlook led to a passive attitude when faced with suffering, inequality, and disadvantage. Indeed, the world, fully fashioned by the hand of God, was the work of divine wisdom. Rather, it is we mere humans who remain unable to comprehend God's design. So, medieval society devised no discrimination process towards the infirm and neither did it seek a means to eradicate or reduce infirmity in general. There remained a conceptual integration of the infirm and a concrete form of tolerance that were commensurate with the impenetrable ways of God to which one was to submit in order to gain Paradise.

The jester is in relation with another world

Buffoonery represents a whole system of thinking. This term can be taken to encompass both mystical over-evaluation and over-evaluation of the court jester. In this latter instance, the infirm (the dwarf, the lame, the deformed person, and, above all, the fool) were assigned a function of derision. Infirmity was a constant reminder of the fragility, the human arbitrariness of the established scheme of things and the powers that be. It hinted at the existence of a world upside down and granted the privilege of speaking out and saying what no other person may tell the powerful. In the case I refer to as mystical, the infirm were considered to be the very "locus" of contemplation of the divine and as the extended incarnation of Christ. As an image of transcendence closing in, it was to lead us to what is beyond, in the same way as the fool points to the topsy-turvy other side. The court jester, or fool, of the princes and the leper whose hand St Francis of Assisi kissed have in common that they tore apart the veil of appearances, of our netherworld, and showed us the unspeakable, the "meta-worldly". The buffoonery of infirmity played a mediating role between two worlds and questioned the foundations of society. And even when the infirm, above all in the fourteenth and fifteenth centuries, were considered to be the expression of a form of devilry (the case of certain forms of "madness", although one cannot say that madness and possession can be seen as one), here again this is because it represented the sign of another world to be rejected (Lever, 1983; Stiker et al., 2013).

The infirm buffoons spoke from "elsewhere", a place that could judge the "here and now". They took part in another world that was also a world of otherness. The same construction applies for the infirm and the poor when, for some seekers of the spiritual, they provided the vehicle for identification with Christ the Saviour.

Towards a secularised vision

The demonised infirm: vagrants, the possessed, and bandits (centuries prior to the Renaissance)

When, from the mid-fourteenth century onwards, the great plagues took their toll on the populations throughout Europe, leading to an unprecedented demographic upheaval, and when unending war lay waste to the countryside and made insecurity the rule, the infirm were reduced to vagrancy. They then lost their Christ-like personas to become threatening figures. Moreover, real and fake cripples were to be found side by side in errant bands of uncontrolled vagrants, the sound of mind and body imitating the infirm. From vagrant to bandit, it was easy to cross the line, both in real life and in social perceptions. This, too, was the time when the Inquisition was in full swing and madness, or simply a form of deviance, could lead to the stake. We have witness accounts of women declared to be mad and massacred or burnt alive under the pretext that they were possessed by the devil. These centuries where fear prevailed should not cast a shadow over the preceding thousand years of the Middle Ages, but they were to lead to the classical revival (Delumeau, 1978).

Correcting infirmity: the first technological approaches (Ambroise Paré)

As infirmity lost its spiritual aura (harsh though society was towards it—the Middle Ages not being renowned for gentleness), society moved towards a purely political form of consideration and modernity began to emerge, too, in the first technologically inspired undertakings.

True to say, people have never stopped dreaming of being able to repair the human body with its failings, although they continued to nurture fantastic or religious representations (and often both at the same time) of infirmity. The threshold to modernity in the matter was first crossed by Ambroise Paré (1573) as the prostheses he invented started to be articulated and adapted to the amputated individual's body. Such prostheses were no longer just props but, rather, extensions to the body and functional substitutes. Ambroise Paré also wanted to spread the use of these devices (de Bissy & Guerrand, 1983). Alongside prostheses made from heavy body armour, he designed ones made of boiled leather for the poor. Thus, he opened the way to reduce their weight and investigate different materials. Ambroise Paré (1509–1590), surgeon to French Kings Henry II, Francis II, Charles IX, and Henry III, and the father of modern surgery, was lucky enough not to have attended university but, rather, to have gained his experi- ence on the battlefield, which enabled him, like other scholars of the Renaissance, to see the infirm body differently.

Imprisonment in the name of reason and order (absolute monarchy)

Then came centuries when the entire mental universe—relation to Nature and relations between people—and the social world—political theories and governance—shifted. The emergence of modern rationality, which radically distinguished between reason and insanity, was to imply the question of tackling the issue of unreason through the new reason so defined. Meanwhile, the political autonomy of society asserted itself. As from the emergence of absolute monarchy, the idea of thinking of political power and the organisation of society as being based on, and dependent on, something outside was abandoned. The source of power was now immanent. So, as society found its underlying justification within itself (as best expressed in the idea of the social contract), it no longer sought what it signified outside of itself. It was within society that reasons and solutions were to be sought. Infirmity now became the object of a social treatment and no longer a projection of meaning in relation to an elsewhere. Finally, the human being was to become an object for science and investigation and also, as a result, an object for social practice and social treatments.

Infirmity found itself on the side of the irrational. It represented what you cannot integrate without running the risk of destabilisation. Everything belonging to social marginality, as with poor wretches, criminals, beggars, madmen, and those suffering from physical deformity, constituted a negative that had to be circumscribed and, thus, relegated to areas specially designated for them. This is what informed the famous "Edict of the King bearing on the establishment of a General Hospital to confine poor mendicants of the City and Suburbs of Paris" of April 1657, dealing with the disabled as much as with the poor and the mad. Deprived of the rights associated with misery and stripped of its glory, madness (like poverty) entered into the hard logic of the State.

Modernity did not start under favourable conditions for the disabled.

Gaining citizenship

Empowering the disabled

What is known as the Age of Enlightenment marks the start of the process of normalisation, not as the nineteenth century was to do with the idea of a "social mean", but through promoting the demand for equality between citizens.

The infirm individual became a person to be educated, with the idea that any citizen, under an egalitarian scheme of things, has the right to education. Such equality by law was accompanied by extreme diversity in reality. This led to actions being organised to reduce such shortcomings so that social equality could emerge.

As a general rule, the encyclopaedists and philanthropists were all to share that common enthusiasm for education, as with Rousseau and Pestalozzi.

Diderot was to write his much celebrated *Essay on Blindness in a Letter to a Person of Distinction* in 1749 (Diderot, 2001). One of the effects of the essay was to show that all minds are equally worthy once nurtured by the necessary instruction and education.

The disabled found themselves released from their specific condition that led them to be considered as inferior beings.

From then on, those who found themselves held back by their deficiency or confined for the crime of non-reason were capable, if the appropriate moral fervour and technical knowledge were brought to bear, of returning to society when they could play a part.

Diderot's ideas help us to understand the dynamic initiated by (1) Valentin Haüy taking on the education of the blind (with other schools across Europe following suit), which led to the invention of braille by a pupil, Louis Braille, in the 1820s; (2) the education of the deaf and the invention of a language of their own, sign language, by the Abbé de l'Epée in the years 1770–1780; (3) care for those suffering from mental disorders, henceforth considered as being curable, and the invention of psychiatry by Philippe Pinel (1801).

Following on from this, the nineteenth century saw attempts to educate those referred to as "idiots", "retarded", and "imbeciles" with

Jean-Marc Itard (1774–1838) who strove, unsuccessfully, to educate the wild child, Victor of Aveyron, and Edouard Seguin (1812–1880) taking up where Itard left off to create special education (1846).

Hard-grained prejudices: how to move on from monstrousness?

In pursuit of philosophical coherence, John Locke (1689) had no hesitation in assigning "idiots" (those who we would nowadays consider to be severely mentally disabled people or those with multiple disabilities) to belong to an intermediate species between the animal and Man, while Leibnitz (1900) hesitated and was prepared to consider they belonged to humanity.[1] Reckoned to be monsters (of a non-human kind), they were only to emerge from this confusion at the same time as monstrousness was to egress from the intermediate position assigned to it, after acrimonious discussions that were to come to an end with Etienne Geoffroy Saint Hilaire (1772–1844) and his son Isidore Geoffroy Saint Hilaire (E. Geoffroy Saint-Hilaire, 1826; I. Geoffroy Saint-Hilaire, 1837). As Georges Canguilhem (1904–1995) was to explain (Canguilhem, 1966), at the end of the nineteenth century, in the context of what is described as social Darwinism, the concept of degeneracy had conquered the world of the learned. The degenerate (who could just as well be from other than the white race, along with those on the margins and, above all, the mad) were to be found on the lower echelons of a scale measuring different degrees of humanity.

The fight that Dr Treves (1853–1923) took up on behalf of John Merrick ("Elephant Man"), that of Jean-Marc Itard for the wild child, Victor of the Aveyron, and the great educators of "idiots", Edouard Seguin and Désiré Magloire Bourneville (1840–1909), played vital roles in breaking away from prejudices and false ideas.

Prospects for integration

From infirmity to handicap

At the end of the nineteenth century, the matter of injured workers became a major problem in all industrialised countries. Industry, unbridled by regulations and intensely exploitative, maimed a great number of citizens. The idea of social responsibility was something that had to be fought for. Henceforth, there was an obligation to repair and, later, to compensate for the harm induced by the hazards of work, this being something that not only bosses had to address as individuals, but also was demanding a response from the nation as a whole. Efforts were gradually made to restore an economic and social place to those injured at work.

François Ewald (1986) mentions this quiet but thoroughgoing revolution of a society that managed to inaugurate a new social deal around ideas of collective responsibility, social insurance, of applying standards as the general rule, of reparation and compensation. These ideas were to lead to the great ambition of "social security" (or "welfare"), no doubt one of the sturdiest foundations of our modern democracies. But what should be stressed here is that this change was brought about, as a major reference, with that new wave of infirmities. Infirmity played a major role in a growing awareness and consideration of the overriding need for social solidarity. In other words, it appears that social issues always arise from central mechanisms that drive the whole system, and that are accepted by (almost) everyone, but one can see how a social issue can mutate from the initiative of a group posing a vital question. What I can also construe, through the emergence of recognition for injured workers, is the start of a new way of looking at infirmity that, in its entirety, will be seen through the prism of such victims of workplace accidents. Any infirmity, gradually, will appear as relating to collective responsibility and solidarity, as part of an "accidentology", if I may resort to such a crude term, meaning that it loses its natural condition to become socialised. It will be seen as a scourge on society as much as a health issue. The State now found itself involved. The revolutionaries had already put forward these ideas but they failed to be enacted (Charoy, 1905). The disabled person was no longer seen as an unlucky individual whose lot was sealed by fate, to subsist mainly on public hand-outs if not on private charity, but began, rather, to be someone entitled to collective solidarity, having fallen victim to society's very progress.

A second event came in to reinforce this anthropological emergence with the carnage of the 1914–1918 war. Once again, countries found themselves confronted by a host of former soldiers crippled, maimed, or disfigured for their "fatherland". Social welfare found expression through a form of collective guilt accompanied by an economic imperative not to let so many agents—who also made claim to resuming their place in society and their right to reparation and compensation—fall by the wayside of production. As from the first years of the war, legislation came into effect so as to open institutions and businesses to vocational rehabilitation. The return to work became an imperative and a strong social demand. In addition to the quiet revolution of social insurance systems, the wounded from the First World War added the determination to get back into the economic and social race; a return to the world as it was, or simply a return to life with their fellow men.

The third event that can be evinced relates to the condition and the claims made by those suffering from tuberculosis. It is accepted that tuberculosis is not just considered to be contagious, but also related, at least in most cases, to certain social conditions in terms of income and hygiene. It is referred to as a social scourge and not just a health problem. Numbers here, too, are crucial; moreover, those coming back from the sanatoria demanded the opportunity to return to their studies or to the employment they had been forced to abandon.

Schools, too, finally opened up more to disabled children. It has been a long road from compulsory schooling through to new generations of parents who wish their disabled child to remain in normal day school or have the choice of a specialised institution; the contagious effect of initiatives taken in some countries, such as Italy, the general wave of de-institutionalisation, and the pressure exerted by disabled people's movements have gradually forced the legislators to pass laws on integration.

To name situations where bodily or functional injury is produced by social phenomena independent of nature (work, war, and living conditions) and that brings on the urgent need to return to the economic field and work as part of society, deficiency-related terms (incapable, crippled, invalid, helpless, etc.) were no longer adequate. Borrowings from the sports world have offered specially tailored semantics: the load weighing down on certain candidates is exogenous, arbitrary, and relative; the handicap race is one that imposes parity between competitors, equality of opportunities; the testing ground of a sports competition implies training sessions within certain structures and particular techniques. Over the period of economic growth that was perhaps not altogether appropriately known as the thirty-year post-war boom period (the French "Trente Glorieuses"), adoption of the word "handicap" was a welcome move to signify the determination to ensure integration. Thus it was that the mid-twentieth century introduced a new perspective.

The handicapped person, the handicap situation, and inclusion

A new period opened out internationally

As from the 1970s, there came, in turn, publication of the first *International Classification of Impairments, Disabilities and Handicaps* (1980), then adoption of the social model as opposed to the medical model, followed by the second *International Classification of Functioning, Handicap and Health* (2001).

In this movement, Quebec played a central role, with the document entitled the *Disability Creation Process* (as early as 1983).

The notion of inclusion became a central issue. These perspectives are now so widely shared by researchers, professionals, and the parents themselves for me to feel relieved from having to give anything more than a broad outline.

This change is mainly based, in my view, on disabled people speaking out for themselves in movements in which they themselves organised. Around the rejection of any discrimination came the claim for independence with the major accompanying idea of *empowerment*; not only full civic rights were demanded, but, more than that, the transformation of everything which, for want of a better term, we can call social spaces came to the fore.

Knocking down barriers of all kinds, in terms of people's perceptions and in architectural, legislative, educational, and communicational matters became the priority and called on society to ensure complete accessibility, so that all citizens could come together in an overall context of *mainstreaming* (Albrecht et al., 2001).

The concept of disability is, henceforth, construed as a form of interactivity between various factors, and evolutive and dynamic forms of interactiveness. The model for disability can only be regarded as systemic (to use what has become a fashionable term). To round things off and give the rights of people said to be disabled their full efficacy, the international community has signed the *International Convention on the Rights of Persons with Disabilities*. The application of its orientations harnesses considerable energy from the people and groups concerned in all those countries that ratified it, thereby making it a legal obligation. This text, which is quite remarkable in many respects, drawn up and discussed with the participation of people themselves in situations of disability, is not an adding on of new rights, but an encouragement to make all existing rights effective for the country's citizens. It comes in to stimulate, amplify, and support the movement that will enable the disabled to play a key role in today's society. I would like to finish by considering the contribution disabled people make to social life.

Towards the future

One of the great fantasies that haunts us is that of omnipotence, including the illusion of immortality. Disabled people, in my view, constitute one of the regulators, both philosophically and socially, of our excesses, of our *hubris*. That we should thus be reminded of the reality of our condition is a good thing, tempted as we are to throw ourselves headlong into the pursuit of greater efficiency in terms of technological and sentimental well-being, and material wealth, etc. Should not wisdom, that so many philosophers, as also certain texts from the Bible, exalt, be honoured and rewarded, every bit as much as performance and strength? The condition of disability is a condition of wisdom, as it is limiting (although this does not mean that all disabled people are models of sagacity in the everyday acceptance of the term!). The crux of my argument should now be clear. Without wisdom, without awareness of our limits, we can so easily get carried away, individually and collectively, by the unreason of omnipotence. That we need to rein in our excesses in believing we can control everything seems to be incontrovertible.

Recognising the value of boundaries avails us of the means to shift the frontiers in our favour. Payrolling deficiency is all about planning for its extinction. This is at least as good, and even better than, merely sticking to relieving it and compensating. Who now will take up the challenge of organising things so that disabled people can get on with making their full contribution, in return for the salary they rightly deserve?

We can easily list many sectors where the presence and participation of disabled people in debates and experiments would contribute towards that regulation that we so need: in the workplace, to reform often arduous and ineffectual working conditions, and obliging managers to devise and organise matters differently (Stiker et al., 2013); in social policies by instilling the need to accompany people facing difficulties and injecting a policy of *care* into justice and solidarity. By that same logic, the question of disability can be a major element in fine-tuning social policies to cater for both collective needs and also to ensure the well-being of the individual. Nowadays, where forms of individualism are often exacerbated, disabled people are in a position to remind us of the necessity of such forms, without neglecting general well-being.

In such a manner, if disabled people were called on to take part in the debate on each of the major social issues, society would become increasingly accessible to a greater number of citizens, whether disabled *stricto sensu* or not. That would be the path towards that inclusive society that, from so many quarters, we yearn for (Gardou, 2012). The inclusive society is indeed that where social barriers are thrown over for all. Disabled people can be the spearhead for the emergence of such a society.

Note

1.   Locke was also sensitive to the question of blindness, providing him with a focus to elaborate on the sources of knowledge, with Molyneux's famous question, meaning that at each moment in history contrasts, or even contradictions, are encountered between different perspectives.

References

Albrecht, G. L., Ravaud, J. F., & Stiker, H. J. (2001). L'émergence des disability studies: état des lieux et perspectives. *Sciences sociales et santé*, 19(4): 43–73.

Canguilhem, G. (Ed.) (1966). *Le normal et le pathologique*. Paris: PUF.

Charoy, F. (1905). *L'assistance aux vieillards, infirmes et incurables en France de 1789 à 1905*. Paris: Université de Paris.

De Bissy, F., & Guerrand, R. (Eds.) (1983). *Œuvres complètes remises en ordre et en français moderne d'Ambroise Paré*. Paris: Union latine d'édition.

Delcourt, M. (Ed.) (1944). *Oedipe ou la légende du conquérant. (Bibliothèque de la Faculté de Philosophie et Lettres de l'Université de Liège, Band 104)*. Paris: Belles Lettres, Édition: Confluents psychanalytiques, 1981.

Delumeau, J. (Ed.) (1978). *La peur en Occident*. Paris: Fayard.

Diderot, D. (2001). Letter on the blind for the use of those who see. In: M. Jourdain (Ed. & Trans.), *Thoughts on the Interpretation of Nature and Other Philosophical Works*. Manchester: Clinamen Press, 1932.

Ewald, F. (Ed.) (1986). *L'Etat providence*. Paris: Grasset.

Gardou, C. (Ed.) (2012). *La société inclusive, parlons-en !* Toulouse: Erès.

Geoffroy Saint-Hilaire, E. (Ed.) (1826). *Considérations générales sur les monstres, comprenant une théorie des phénomènes de la monstruosité*. Paris: Tastu.

Geoffroy Saint-Hilaire, I. (Ed.) (1837). *Histoire générale et particulière des anomalies de l'organisation chez l'homme et les animaux . . . ou, Traité de tératologie*. Bruxelles: Société belge de librairie, Hauman Cattoir.

La Bible. Traduction oecuménique (2010). Paris: Le Cerf.

Leibnitz, G. W. (1900). Nouveaux essais sur l'entendement humain. In: P. Janet (Ed.), *Oeuvres philosophiques I* (pp. 243–257). Paris: Editions Lacan.

Lever, M. (Ed.) (1983). *Le sceptre et la marotte: histoire des fous de cour*. Paris: Fayard.

Locke, J. (1689). Idea of solidity. Book IV, Chapter IV. In: J. Locke (Ed.), *An Essay Concerning Humane Understanding* (pp. 62–67). London: Holt.

Pinel, P. (Ed.) (1801). *Traité médico-philosophique sur l'aliénation mentale ou la manie*. Paris: chez Richard, Caille et Ravier.

Seguin, E. (Ed.) (1846). *Traitement moral, hygiène et éducation des idiots et des autres enfants arriérés ou retardés dans leur développement, agités de mouvements involontaires, débiles, muets non-sourds, bègues, etc.* Paris: J.-B. Baillière.

Stiker, H. J. (Ed.) (1999). *A History of Disability*, W. Sayers (Trans.). Ann Arbor, MI: University of Michigan Press.

Stiker, H. J. (2010). Locke et Leibniz. Présentation. *ALTER-European Journal of Disability Research/Revue Européenne de Recherche sur le Handicap*, 4(2): 138–140.

Stiker, H. J., Ribes, J. L., Théobald-Segalen, C., Flamant, N., Ihl, O., Azuar, C., Heilbrunn, B., Weber, F., Barruel, F., & Hunyadi, M. (Eds.) (2013). *Réfléchir le management au miroir du handicap*. Lormont: Le bord de l'eau.

CHAPTER NINE

Prenatal diagnosis and handicap

Sylvain Missonnier

On the basis of my clinical experience in a French maternity ward and in an institution for early medico-social action (CAMSP, *Centre d'Action Médico-Sociale Précoce*), prenatal diagnosis (PD) seems to me to deserve our full attention for at least two reasons.

The first is that PD today has shaped the process of parenthood and the prenatal genesis of the identity of the child to be born in a singular manner. It now has an essential role in what I have called the "first chapter" in the biography of every individual, whether afflicted with a disability or not. This first pre-birth chapter is all too often forgotten, and PD is in indeed an essential component.

It seems to me that PD is at once a set of technical procedures used to screen for foetal anomalies, and, at the same time, a window on to the complexity of becoming a parent, on to the human birth process and on to the essence of caring in perinatal settings. Any attempt to separate these two facets, technical and psychological, is a denial of the singleness of the entity involved.

One important point is that this duality applies to any pregnancy, whether "normal" or not, confronting parents with PD.

The second reason why the issue seems to me important is that I had occasion to approach PD when I was a consultant in a CAMSP and in charge of a parent support group (Missonnier, 2005). This gave me the opportunity to realise the imprint of PD when it involves a pregnancy giving cause for suspicion, or the revelation of a foetal abnormality, or, conversely, when it has failed to detect an anomaly in the antenatal period that is diagnosed after the birth. Thus, clinical practice has shown me that the inadequacy of PD as practised today, for the disabled individual and for the family members, is central to the debate on relations with parents, medical care, and, more widely, the ethical and societal dimension of disability.

To go further along these lines, I successively summarise the history and the techniques of PD to provide adequate contextualisation. I then approach the psychological aspects of "all-comer" PD, mainly focusing on its much-dreaded uncertainty, and each individual's anticipatory response. Finally, the theme of worries about impairments bridges the gap between obstetrically "normal" pregnancies and those in which PD means suspicion, or disclosure, of a foetal anomaly. The clinical and legal contexts of my arguments are French but I am betting here that the issues go beyond this limit and retain the attention of English-speaking professionals.

Prenatal diagnosis (PD)

The legal definition of PD involves "in utero detection of a condition that is particularly serious in an embryo or foetus" (French law, 29 July 1994). The term PD is used to refer to any technique enabling this detection.

History

It was at the start of the 1970s that what we now call foetal medicine, or prenatal medicine, appeared. The foetus became a patient in his own right, for whom ultrasound scans and biological tests can provide increasingly complex investigations for the purpose of diagnosing anomalies, diseases, or malformations.

Chromosome analyses (the determining of the foetal caryotype) following amniocentesis was one of the first biological methods used.

It has been, and will continue to be, the most widely used biological exploratory technique on the foetus, on account of the large number of chromosomal anomalies occurring (one birth in 175).

The 1980s saw the development of molecular biology techniques and the cloning of numerous genes responsible for relatively frequent genetic diseases (such as Duchenne's muscular dystrophy, or cystic fibrosis), which have considerably improved reliability and the scope for early diagnosis, enabling the detection of healthy carriers (hetero-zygote) in families. DNA amplification using polymerase chain reaction (PCR) has increased the power of genetic tests, enabling results to be obtained faster, and tests to be performed on very small quantities of DNA, as in the case of foetal samples. This progress is considerable, since the different advances enable parents in families with the painful previous experience of genetic diseases to know if they risk giving birth to a child with the condition, and, should this be the case, to have access to an early, reliable prenatal diagnosis enabling the pregnancy to be terminated in the best possible conditions if the foetus is affected.

In this third millennium, new techniques will undoubtedly revo-lutionise foetal diagnosis techniques. DNA chips result from an indus-trial procedure that enables DNA testing via a single reaction for an adult, a child, or a foetus, applicable to an extraordinarily large num-ber of different mutations. The study of foetal DNA in maternal blood could fundamentally alter screening for Down's syndrome, enabling all pregnant women to know if the child is affected from a simple blood test.

The past twenty years have seen a considerable improvement in ultrasound scan techniques. The publications in the literature in the 1980s focused on the semiological description of the main morpho-logical anomalies. The generalisation of morphological studies in the second trimester has led to the establishment of ultrasound-detected syndromes based on the increasing refinement of warning signs.

While the efficacy of caryotyping on the basis of ultrasound signs is evident when indicated from examination of a foetus with one or several severe malformations, the efficacy of very small signs for this purpose, that is to say, of anatomical variants in the foetus that do not amount to a malformation, has never been scientifically established.

The 1990s were revolutionised by ultrasound scans in the first trimester of pregnancy, and by the nuchal scan[1] which has become routine and has proved to be a reliable alternative to screen for Down's syndrome, certainly preferable to the serum markers of the second trimester. These first trimester scans also enable screening for morphological anomalies, in particular cardiac, and for genetic syndromes.

Thus, today specialised multi-disciplinary teams can diagnose very rare conditions, using a combination of ultrasound scans and genetic explorations. Molecular biology increasingly provides firm diagnosis, which is only really possible from ultrasound scans for the most obvious malformations.

Finally, pre-implantation genetic diagnosis (PIGD or PGD)[2] is undoubtedly the main innovation in prenatal diagnosis in recent years. It was initiated at the start of the 1990s in the UK, and the technique developed fast in France after authorisation in the law of 29 July, 1994.

This mass screening for foetal malformations, chromosomal or morphological anomalies, went hand in hand with funding efforts by public authorities to back up the drive in the medical sphere:

- reimbursement of three ultrasound scans in the course of pregnancy;
- compulsory offer of screening for Down's syndrome using serum markers for all pregnant women, and amniocentesis solely for pregnant women of thirty-eight or older;
- budget provision for pluri-disciplinary centres for prenatal diagnosis.

The magistrate and prenatal diagnosis (PD).
The paradigm of the Perruche affair

The *Cour de Cassation* on 17 November 2000 issued the following ruling:

> Given that the errors committed by the physician and the laboratory in their compliance with the contracts formed with Mme X prevented this person from exercising her choice as to whether or not to terminate her pregnancy so as to avoid the birth of a disabled child, the child can apply for reparation of the damage sustained as a result of the said disability, and caused by the errors evidenced.

This ruling terminated the proceedings initiated by Mme Perruche for the birth of her child Nicolas, born with a severe disability following the undetected contraction of rubella in the course of the pregnancy, while she had explicitly expressed the desire to terminate the pregnancy should the diagnosis of rubella be confirmed.

By allowing for compensation for the harm sustained by the child as well as the parents, the court implicitly recognised that there are lives that are damaging, and that are not worth living.

To put this even more bluntly: it is better not to live than to live with certain disabilities. The elimination of a potentially disabled foetus is a better solution for the foetus, and for the family, than survival of doubtful quality. Going even further, the idea of a disability is so intolerable that a prognostic or diagnostic uncertainty is sufficient to justify termination of the pregnancy.

The mobilisation of professionals

Professor Israel Nisand (2001), one of the figures heading this mobilisation, is worth quoting:

> In a society valuing solidarity, the occurrence of disability, in the name of a form of solidarity, specific to human beings, leads to the instatement of care and assistance required to ensure that decent living conditions are provided. Yet it is the reverse that we can see. When Social Security (the very expression of collective solidarity) supports court action to obtain the compensation for costs, incurred and expected, in relation to the birth of a disabled individual, this equates with considering that the child should not have been born. If the courts confirm this, we find ourselves in a system that, far from allocating a normal place to the disabled child in our society, treats that child as an abnormal burden that should never have existed.

> The Perruche ruling was catastrophic in that it validated the representation of disability as an abnormal accident, for which the person responsible must be found to obtain compensation, in an area where what would be expected is that care institutions and national solidarity should be called upon. But it is also catastrophic because it catches the medical world without philosophical arguments concerning the meaning of the medicine it delivers, signalling that it has the obligation of producing results, and that the only way to protect itself is to resort to active euthanasia. There is an evolution in society behind all

these events where technical and scientific progress, from which we expect reassurance and well-being, is liable to bring with it a form of reification of the human being. (Translated for this edition)

The nullification of the Perruche jurisprudence

Adopting the main ideas of this opposition, article 1 of the law passed on 4 March 2002, relating to the rights of patients and the quality of the healthcare system, entitled "Solidarity towards disabled individuals", put an end to this jurisprudence:

I.   No-one can claim prejudice from the mere fact of his or her birth.

A person born with a disability as a result of a medical error can obtain compensation when the act in question directly caused or aggravated the disability, or prevented measures liable to reduce the disability from being taken.

When the responsibility of a professional or a healthcare facility is established towards the parents of a child born with a disability that was not detected during pregnancy as a result of a characterised error, the parents can demand compensation for the harm sustained by themselves only. This damage cannot include the particular burden resulting from the disability throughout the life of the child. Compensation for this belongs to national solidarity.

The provisions of the present article 1 are applicable to on-going cases, with the exception of those where the decision to compensate is the subject of an irrevocable ruling.

II.   Any disabled person, whatever the cause of his or her deficit, has the right to the solidarity of the whole national community.

III.   The national consultative council for disabled persons, in the conditions fixed by the decree, is in charge of assessing the financial, material and moral situation of disabled persons in France, and disabled persons of French nationality residing outside France, to whom care provision is ensured on the grounds of national solidarity; it is also in charge of presenting the Parliament and the Government with any proposals deemed necessary for the purpose of ensuring care provision of these persons, via an on-going pluri-annual programme. (Translated for this edition)

It is left to the legislators to determine what is to be covered by this "national solidarity". This is, of course, a vast subject, that I will not embark upon here.

The reaction to this nullification of the "Collectif contre l'handiphobie"

"The National Assembly has just put an end to the deleterious trend seen in the Perruche jurisprudence", rejoiced X. Mirabel, spokesman for the *Collectif contre l'Handphobie* (literally the collective against handicap-phobia) on 12 February 2002. "I want to congratulate the legislator for the intervention. In the face of the vast upheaval generated by the Perruche jurisprudence, a strong signal was needed for families. The damaging decisions of the *Cour de Cassation* needed to be halted. The National Assembly has recalled the law, and restated that every life is worth living. Families and disabled individuals are rejoicing. This vote is a victory for right and dignity. In the Parliament, members recalled the determining role of the families of disabled individuals, and their great distress.

"This evening's amendment—no one can claim prejudice from the mere fact of his or her birth—is a wording that we proposed a year and a half ago. It is a great satisfaction for the Collective and disabled individuals to see that they have at last been heard."

Scientism and extremism in prenatal diagnosis

It is now time to turn to the psychological aspects of PD. I would like to start the debate by underlining two major obstacles:

- the frequent "scientism" of a high-tech brand of medicine, purported to shelter the user from illness, death, and castration.
- PD extremism. PD is, indeed, what I will call "extreme" clinical practice, in the manner of a highly interesting seminar organised in Jussieu by Simone Korff Sausse under the title "Les Cliniques de l'Extrême" (19 November 2005).

The extremism of PD can mainly be summed up as follows: despite deceptively ordinary outward appearances, it forces users (parents and professionals) to question themselves about the boundaries of humanness. More exactly, it leads us to explore what it is that is virtually human in the foetus, which can indeed "be born" at the end of the pregnancy but which can, at any time, end in death (voluntary abortion or medical termination), or in unrecognisable deformity, or in freakishness.

This uncertainty is one of the main psychological and ethical components of PD. It is synonymous with "ontological precariousness" (Saulus, 2007). Nevertheless, is this uncertainty attributable solely to PD, which is a historically recent entity? Certainly not. It is the process of becoming a parent (sometimes renewing the experience) during pregnancy itself that has been accompanied since humans have been humans by a thousand and one questionings that are all linked to uncertainty.

"Do I want, do we want, to give life? What does it mean to shift from being a son or a daughter to being a father or a mother, from being a couple to being a family, from being a trio to being a quartet? How will I/we cope with the perinatal bodily and mental changes? Is the foetus/baby developing normally? What is its genetic inheritance? Is it really contained in the perinatal nest? What will I do, what will we do, if the baby dies? What will happen at the birth? And what happens if at birth we discover an impairment or a disability? What about the postpartum period, feeding, care, life, and sexuality in our couple within a new family, what about returning to work, and baby-minders? What will be the baby's temperament and relational style? How will siblings adapt? Is it wise to trust the medical environment with its numerous agents, sometimes not well co-ordinated, its obscure language, its technicalities, and its complex practices?"

PD does not actually create uncertainty during pregnancy, but it amplifies it by anticipating the questioning on the medical normality of the child. Thus, PD provides valuable medical information in real time, while previously there was a blind spot, but this does not remove the uncertainty, and it can sometimes considerably exacerbate it.

In the perinatal sphere, as in life generally, human beings faced with this many-faceted, omnipresent uncertainty tend to have a single response: anticipation—behavioural, affective, and fantasised.

It should, in fact, be emphasised that, with regard to the symbolic adoption of the foetus, the psychological variable of anticipation is crucial, since, provided it is creative, it is the element that provides, on the one hand, a degree of flexibility in the conflict that is inherent in parental and carer desires, and, on the other, a confrontation with the vagaries of biological reality.

In this area, it must be conceded that medical procedures during the follow-up of pregnancy have considerably increased the complexity of managing this anticipation.

On the one hand, the foetus has become a "patient" in prenatal diagnosis, "he" is also a member of a family from the very first ultrasound scan image placed in the photo album; he is also, in some cases, the "subject" of a possible ritualisation of grieving in case of death, or, if he is severely premature, a "survivor" in an artificial uterus from the age of twenty-four weeks; finally, the foetus is at permanent risk of over-hasty humanisation by the family and professional entourage.

On the other hand, medical termination of pregnancy, which is allowed in France up to the end of pregnancy, cynically recalls the status of the foetus, at worst human debris, and at best potential humanity, but, fundamentally, not legally fully human.

This present-day extreme paradoxical tension between humanisation and eugenics increases the complexity of the symbolic adoption of the foetus, a path on a razor edge between nothingness, the nameless and shapeless, the freak, and the virtually human.

In fact, this uncertainty inherent in PD is always potentially traumatic. To cope with this uncertainty surrounding PD, humans nevertheless possess scope for anticipation, an individual, family, institutional, and societal variable which I think needs analysing within this debate, so as to understand the resolutely singular positions of parents and carers.

The uncertainty–anticipation dyad: an essential component in prenatal diagnosis

One misunderstanding needs to be cleared up from the outset. Tempered, adaptive anticipation is not the (illusory) exact forecast of the future, but, rather, entry into a process of symbolisation of the diversity and complexity of the possible scenarios. One of the strengths of the contemporary systemic approach is to stress the recursiveness of human processes: the means to reach an end alter that end, and, thereby, irreversibly suggest new means of some sort. Any undertaking will generate unexpected effects. "We need to be prepared, not to anticipate everything, but to encounter the unexpected" (Favez, 1958, translated for this edition). Healthy anticipation is, therefore, openness towards the unforeseen. But anticipation, even in normal circumstances, is a source of anxiety. This should again be underlined: this (signal) anxiety is the manifestation of an anticipation that is adapted. Automatic or traumatic anxiety, according to Freud (1926d), is the pathological version of the same thing, but, in contrast, it hinders adaptation.

Defined in this manner, anticipation can be seen as a very promising template for understanding "tempered" and "pathological" variations in the manner in which parenthood and the child itself develop in the setting of PD. When the parental project is undermined by the intrusion of a handicap or a mental disorder in the child, the in-depth analysis of the anticipation of each of the protagonists can prove to be clinically relevant. When family expectations are overturned, the quality of anticipation by the carer and the institution is decisive in the healing, containing function of the setting. Thus, damaged expectations and caring anticipation are two inseparable facets in the therapeutic encounter.

It follows, therefore, that to approach the complex interactions occurring in perinatal care, it appears worthwhile viewing this exchange as a negotiation between the anticipation patterns of parents and carers towards the foetus/baby. In this melting pot, clinical assessment of modes of anticipation seems to me to be liable to cast light.

Ideally, in perinatal care, the anticipation of carers will be "tailored", and never systematic. It will back up parental anticipation without trespassing or controlling, which would lead to dependency and the emergence of what prevention sets out precisely to avoid.

An example of anticipation: worries about malformations

"Is he likely to have a handicap, or Down's syndrome?" In our experience this questioning about the child to be born is familiar, in particular in the setting of PD. So as to obtain an accurate idea of the frequency of this distress during pregnancy, it is no doubt useful to analyse the mental imprint in the light of what Freud (1919h) termed "the uncanny" (familiar yet strange). Before the birth, maternal fears of an impairment do indeed belong to this category of affects. According to Freud, there is nothing new or foreign about this, but, rather, something that is and always has been familiar in the psyche, something that should have remained hidden but which has reappeared. Freud views this as a return to certain phases in the evolutionary history of the perception of self, a regression towards a period when the self was not clearly outlined with respect to the outside world and others. The disquieting feeling of strangeness is produced by identical repetition and derives from the psychic life of childhood .

For a future mother, the conscious emergence of, and, *a fortiori*, the ability to put words on, this "imaginary anticipation" of a possible impairment will depend, on the one hand, on the nature and content of her "psychic transparency", and, on the other, on the way in which these manifestations of the uncanny are received by the various people she encounters.

The maternal psychic permeability to unconscious representations that are specific to pregnancy can express itself, among other things, by way of fears of having a freak child. These anxieties are classically interpreted as punishment for the guilt relating to the unconscious desire for incestuous transgression. My professional experience also suggests the extent to which these affects can, at the same time, have resonances of pre-oedipal avatars. It is in this founding melting pot that archaic collapse may be played out, amounting to a break in the continuity of the baby's existence.

Anxieties about malformations find their place in this structural complexity. They are sometimes pervasive and devastating, or, conversely, furtive and discreet, but they are in all events generally present, even if they are not often shared with others. In the area of prevention of parenthood conflict (Cramer & Palacio-Espasa, 1993), and also in the setting of perinatal disclosure of an actual impairment, it seems to me worthwhile exploring the structuring or destructive potential of these anxieties during pregnancy.

Yet, in the literature, there are few accounts from clinical settings of the pervasive presence of these representations of freakishness among pregnant women (Lebovici & Stoleru, 1983; Matarazzo, 1986). There is, indeed, a marked contrast between informal remarks by clinicians on the frequency of this phenomenon and the virtual absence of any mention in the literature.

In the most thorough study of maternal representations during pregnancy, Ammaniti and colleagues (1999) refer to maternal fears about foetal malformations as being the essential characteristic of a sub-group in the category of representations said to be "narrow and non-integrated".

In contrast to "integrated/balanced" representations, which reflect a rich, flexible, and coherent experience of pregnancy, pregnant women with "narrow and non-integrated" representations cope with pregnancy as a necessary phase in life. The crisis of pregnancy is controlled, rationalised, and leaves little room for dreaming about the child and his integration.

For her part, Myra Leifer (1977) considers that an exacerbation of maternal anxiety about herself and the foetus is characteristic of pregnancy. Leifer supports the notion that anxieties about the foetus can be a significant positive sign of the maternal attachment link, and absence of anxieties a negative sign.

These anxieties are interpreted by Olimpia Matarazzo (1986) as, on the one hand, punishment for guilt at an unconscious desire for incestuous transgression, and, on the other, as projections on the baby to be born, seen as a danger, of an aggressiveness originally aimed at the maternal grandmother, and reorientated in this manner.

If there is no detectable or detected foetal anomaly, are these psychic effects the sign of distress in the face of a process of motherhood which, in itself, generates aversion and catalyses, or are they the sign of a creative anticipation that protects from the shock of trauma?

A clinical hypothesis can be suggested: these representations, contained between the dialectic poles of anxiety as a "psychological signal" and "automatic psychopathological" anxiety, are excellent markers of the structural nature and the object maturity of maternal anticipation within the process of "becoming a mother".

In "signal" anxiety, fears of malformation are not invasive. They reflect the potentially creative desire for psychic transparency that revisits tempered separation conflicts, and effective intergenerational containment. Here, one major characteristic is that anxiety is a dynamic vector for symbolisation, which favours the elaboration of the process of parenthood. In this respect, "signal" anxiety can be seen as demonstrating a prenatal anticipation that organises empathetic projective identifications. It is also, at the same time, a preventative anticipation of possible realities: a foetal anomaly, an obstetrical complication, the birth of a child with a disability. These are possibilities that no reasonable professional can presume to exclude on the basis of antenatal investigations.

When anxiety about deformities, on the other hand, assimilates to "automatic" anxiety, this could be a form of revival of muted traumatic fixations on which focus is brought to bear by a disorganising reminiscence that hampers adaptive parental anticipation. The rigid, lasting fear of a malformation could be the expression of an existential frailty recalling the notion of "primitive agony" (Winnicott, 1975), with a "fundamental violence" (Bergeret, 1984) that has remained in the raw state. Taking this unconscious logic to the extreme, the mother and her child cannot both live, because the survival of "him or me" is the rule, with no scope for negotiation. In this case, fears of an impairment in the child could reflect the invasion of "pathological projective identifications" (Cramer & Palacio-Espasa, 1993) in the prenatal period, signalling an alarming parenthood conflict. Behavioural, emotional, and fantastical foeto–maternal disharmony could be the common sign. It would be valuable to be able to recognise this, so that carers can use it as a possible warning light for "ill-treatment of the foetus" (Robineau & Missonnier, 2004).

Of course, this contrasting of "automatic" and "signal" anxieties should be kept distinct from any semiological temptation leading to a dualistic, artificial, simplistic cleavage. In clinical practice, detection of this phenomenon involves two poles between which the dialectic relationship is constant. This complementariness is essential, because it is precisely in a revival of the supporting function of "signal" anxiety over "automatic" anxiety that preventative action can be envisaged.

This perspective on prenatal psychic functioning in relation to the question of the disclosure of a foetal anomaly or a disability at birth has wide clinical potential, and we can make the following hypothesis: the intensity and the metabolism of the shock of disclosure to parents of a genuine abnormality, from the most minor to the most serious, will depend in part on the nature and the outcome of the parents' psychic revivals in the antenatal period, where fears concerning malformations are one of the most significant instances.

Thus, it seems essential to ensure that parents during the pregnancy have access to a venue suited to receiving them and to the preventative elaboration of their anxiety, in particular anxiety of the "automatic" type. The responsibility of all carers in the prenatal period—consultants, preparation group personnel[3]—is clear. However, we can also extend this aim to awareness-raising among ultrasound scan technicians on the subject of this two-faced anxiety about impairment. Balint group experiences among ultrasound scan operators seem to me to be one of the most promising lines of action here (Soulé et al., 2011).

Conclusion

To conclude and "tidy up the ends", I would like suggest that prenatal diagnosis today is a ritual that is in the middle of the river, hesitating between structuring and de-structuring symbolic functions, hovering between cultural propping and iatrogenic obstruction.

The creative ritual is that which is described by anthropologists. The morbid ritual is that of psychiatric semiology.

The former is driven by an organising transition and linking function; it offers scope for the elaboration of archaic anxieties, conflicts, or traumatic excitation, and helps to construct the subject in interaction with the environment.

As a mixture of affect and intellect, a symbolically efficacious ritual has power to generate individual and social links. Its huge paradox is that it is based on a passage through a fertile, transitional disorganisation, between inside and outside. Baptism rites, for instance, prototypes of the rite of passage, have been described as immersion in non-differentiation, in order to emerge better differentiated. Arnold Van Gennep (1909) called this transitory non-differentiation the "margin". It is the epicentre of the ritual sequence: separation, margin, integration.

In its psychopathological form, the individual and social ritual is a symptomatic profile that shows the existence of a serious crisis. Obsessional neurosis is, indeed, clearly an individual, pathological version of rituals that have been turned away from their organising function. Used as ramparts against invading anxiety, the rituals encroach on daily living and can paralyse social life. They take on the meaning of systematic prevention that is pathological, and divorced from reasoned anticipatory perceptiveness towards the environment.

It seems to me that prenatal diagnosis today is in a hesitation waltz between opting for an anthropological ritual and a psychiatric ritual.

And, fundamentally, this individual and societal disquiet towards PD is crucial for our debate, because it should be interpreted as belonging to the first, prenatal chapter in the book of positions to be adopted towards impairment, disability, and handicap in all subsequent periods in life.

For prenatal diagnosis to become a rite of passage, and draw away from the obsessive ritualisation of closure, there are at least three necessary conditions:

- the meaning of the ritual as it is experienced and shared should be the subject of a shared symbolisation by parents and professionals, a *sine qua non* condition for a shared "symbolic efficacy". Today, in maternity wards, the ethical quality of the negotiation of a genuine "enlightened consent" (Séguret, 2004) for PD procedures and investment in individual, couple, and group strategies for preparing for the birth, precisely dedicated to this subject, are two of the most reliable markers of quality;
- professional operators of the ritual should have space for reflection (Balint groups) where expectations and the defensive dynamic of each protagonist can be narrated and discussed;
- the violence of the passage through the "margin" in the transitory psychic transparency of pregnancy, and its amplification with prenatal diagnosis, must be recognised and contained. Here, again, individual, couple, and group proposals for preparing for the birth and parenthood are essential.

In the absence of a favourable setting of this sort, the diagnostic encounter cannot hope to respond positively to the structuring requirement of the ritual, favouring an individual and societal elaboration of the ontological uncertainty of the conceptional margin hovering between death, deformity, and monstrosity in its approach to handicap.

As such, this status as a secular ritual constructing the prenatal diagnosis should, therefore, be viewed as a collective objective to be reached. The aim of this chapter is, ultimately, to submit to the professional arena, and to the community at large, the idea that the answers provided by prenatal diagnosis to clinical, ethical, and political questions are a faithful mirror of the family, institutional, and societal responses that will be delivered later in life to the handicapped individual.

Notes

1. This technique for measuring nuchal translucency aims to estimate the risk of Down's syndrome. The nape of the neck is scanned for accumulation of fluid between the skin and the rachis, corresponding to a zone known as anechogenic (i.e., returning no echo during the scan). Any foetus presents nuchal translucency in the first trimester, but it disappears later.
2. PIGD consists in screening for certain genetic anomalies in embryos obtained from in vitro fertilisation (IVF). Embryos not carrying the anomaly are transferred to the uterus, and the embryos affected are destroyed. PIGD is used for couples who have a high risk for transmission of a serious genetic disease (muscular dystrophy, cystic fibrosis, etc.) assuming genetic diagnosis is available.
3. The French health authority recommendations (HAS) on preparation for birth and parenthood, starting with an early prenatal interview, are along similar lines, in as much as no ethically iatrogenic obligation invalidates a cautious, caring preventative strategy

References

Ammaniti, M., Candelori, C., & Pola, M. (Eds.) (1999). *Maternité et grossesse: étude des représentations maternelles.* Paris: PUF.
Bergeret, J. (Ed.) (1984). *La violence fondamentale.* Paris: Dunod.
Cramer, B., & Palacio-Espasa, F. (Eds.) (1993). *La pratique des psychothérapies mères-bébés: études cliniques et techniques.* Paris: PUF.
Favez, G. (1958). De la contestation. Paper presented to the La Psychanalyse, perspectives structurales, Colloque international de Royaumont, France.
Freud, S. (1919h). The 'uncanny'. *S. E.,* 17: 217–256. London: Hogarth.
Freud, S. (1926d). *Inhibitions, Symptoms and Anxiety. S. E.,* 20: 77–174. London: Hogarth.
Lebovici, S., & Stoleru, S. (1983). *Le nourrisson, la mère et le psychanalyste. Les interactions précoces.* Paris: Le Centurion.
Leifer, M. (1977). Psychological changes accompanying pregnancy and motherhood. *Genetic Psychology Monographs,* 95: 55–96.
Matarazzo, O. (1986). Le fantasmes d'engendrer un enfant anormal. In: J. Clerget (Ed.), *Fantasmes et masques de grossesse.* Paris: PUL.
Nisand, I. (2001). Le foetus et le droit. Le diagnostic prénatal pourrait succomber d'une crise de croissance. Paper presented to the 6ème

journée de médecine foetale. Diagnostic et prise en charge pré et post-natale des affections foetales (cf http://toupet.michel.free.fr/droit04. html), Morzine, France.

Robineau, C., & Missonnier, S. (2004). Une prévention psychanalytique de la maltraitance est-elle possible? ou à quoi rêvent les saumons? In: S. Missonnier, B. Golse, & M. Soulé (Eds.), *La grossesse, l'enfant virtuel et la parentalité. éléments de psycho(patho)logie périnatale* (pp. 399–437). Paris: PUF.

Saulus, G. (2007). Votre enfant est un légume! Des conditions éthiques nécessaires à toute pratique clinique en situation de handicap extrême. In: R. Scelles, A. Ciccone, S. Korff Sausse, & S. Missonnier (Eds.), *Cliniques du sujet handicapé. Actualités des pratiques et des recherches* (pp. 209–2018). Toulouse: Erès.

Séguret, S. (Ed.) (2004). *Le consentement éclairé en périnatalité et en pédiatrie.* Toulouse: Erès.

Soulé, M., Gourand, L., Missonnier, S., & Soubieux, M. J. (Eds.) (2011). *Ecoute voir . . . L'échographie de la grossesse: les enjeux de la relation.* Toulouse: Erès.

Van Gennep, A. (Ed.) (1909). *Les rites de passage.* Paris: Editions Picard, 1981.

Winnicott, D. W. (1975). La crainte de l'effondrement. *Nouvelle revue de psychanalyse, 11*: 35–44.

CHAPTER TEN

Your child is a vegetable! Ethical requirements for all clinical practices in dealing with severe disability

Georges Saulus

> "It is impossible!"
> "Impossible, yes, but do it"
>
> (Dostoyevsky, 2012)

The principles which, as a general rule, inform our notion of clinical practice are proving inadequate in cases of severe disability.

Indeed, with respect to severe disability, the only consideration given to subjectivity in the sense in which it is generally understood (that is to say, taken to mean the status of the subject as the limitation of a psychological maturation process) cannot provide an effective enough framework for our response as clinicians. For we are called on to respond not only to a *psychological* deficiency (as implied by the notion of defective development), but also primarily and of necessity to address the *ontological* deficiency compounded by the circumstances of severe disability. Concern for psychological subjectivity, a familiar subject, should, therefore, coincide with concern for ontological subjectivity, which is less often discussed. In other words: concern for an intersubjective psychological dynamic should be expanded to embrace concern for its necessary circumstance: the instilling of what can be referred to as an ontological intersubjectivity.

The same applies clinically as politically: with severe disability, the granting of the status of citizen (which is the political equivalent of the subject in psychological terms) cannot adequately address the deficiency (itself a political one) that is created by severe disability. In this respect, the need for a concept to supplement or replace the concept of citizenship still remains. That is not the purpose of this discussion. However, there is no question that a collective approach granting a more appropriate political status to severely disabled persons cannot fail to have an impact, similar to a framework effect, on our clinical work providing support for these persons.

However, let us begin with what is meant by severe disability. Severe disability is understood to mean a disability that places the disabled person and those in his family and professional circle in an extreme situation.

Extreme situations

Extreme situations are essentially onto-ethical (Saulus, 1989).

Technically speaking, ethics refer to the aspect of philosophy that deals with the fundamental principles of moral obligation, that is, the fundamentals of action understood as the basis for acting and thinking which makes us participants. That said, as we all know, we spend a large part of our daily lives acting without necessarily thinking in advance about the reasons for our actions. This means that, in most cases, we spontaneously become what is commonly referred to as ethical agents, meaning players having basic ethical values which are reflected in our actions. And these basic ethical values are vaguely considered by some, and clearly so by others, to be founded on reason and to be justifiable. It must be noted that most of the time there is a prevailing degree of harmony and congruence between our basic value system and our actions. This is not to say that we act most of the time in a manner consistent with our values; it means that if we were to think about it, we would mostly be able to find a justifiable reference—previously implied—to an ethical judgement, whether positive or negative, which is likely to be applied to our action.

Mostly, we would say . . .

Since, in exceptional cases, we find ourselves in situations where doubt arises; situations where not only do we no longer know what to do, but, more so, we no longer know the reason or the underlying basis for taking one action instead of another, or no action at all. These situations create genuine states of ethical crisis where the ultimate and often implicit fundamental principles of our ethical position are called into question, as well as our fundamental ethical values. It is these borderline situations, these exceptional situations that are commonly referred to as extreme situations; situations where the human being's fundamentally authentic mode of existence, both personal and inter-personal, is threatened, questioned, denied, and even hindered.

There are two types of extreme situations:

1. The first type are those where our own status as persons is called into question. Numerous accounts of this type of situation have been given by, for example, former concentration camp prisoners, who have related how, in this type of situation, some detainees were capable of doubting their own status as persons (Antelme, 1947; Blanchot, 1969). Perhaps if some persons with extreme disabilities were to give testimonials, they would be in a similar vein.

2. The second type are those situations where, rather than our own status as persons being called into question, it is the status of person of the individual before us. In this type of situation, doubt arises and causes us to question our evaluation of the other person's humanness.

Evaluating the humanness of the other person: fast forward . . .

"Is this severely disabled person before me, this being, really a human person? Does this being deserve, like me, to be called a person? Does he fully share with me the dignity of a human person?"

It is evident nowadays that, although removed from its origins, the concept of the person not only retains its original dignity, but is, more-over, universally claimed as a fundamental value of human society: is not the dignity of the human person the basis of the Universal Declaration of Human Rights? The fact that human rights might not be universally respected is not an issue here: most people who violate these rights are no less demanding that they be fully respected as fundamental values in the way they are treated.

What happened then?

We cannot fail to notice one apparently paradoxical fact: while the affirmation of a person's dignity became an arbitrary matter through the forfeiture of all theological or philosophical justification, it became, at the same time, a matter of consensus, as if, by virtue of remaining consensual at all costs, this affirmation could not have become merely arbitrary.

Consensual affirmation of personal dignity has become what we know as a free creation of value, which is the name we give to an ethical choice lacking a philosophical or theological basis; a choice which, in some way, refuses to account to anyone, be they God or Socrates . . .

Thus, a person is nowadays defined as a being who, by free choice and through consensus, is eminently endued with dignity.

Under such conditions, how do we deal with the question of evaluating the humanness of the Other Person?

Evaluating the humanness of the other person: . . . and back

Every disabled person will have the dignity of personhood attributed to them as from the moment we decide, whether arbitrarily or consensually, that this should be so.

No apparent difficulties are met, therefore, with respect to the general idea of recognising the personal dignity of any disabled person, irrespective of the degree of their disability.

However, a problem arises when the manner in which we make unfounded ethical choices is examined.

In fact, it is proved that these choices, though not based on belief or reason, are not always unsupported: in exercising our ethical choices, whenever we are no longer bound by the logical requirements of theological or philosophical arguments, we hold, more or less, to our own experience.

With regard to the support we provide for severely disabled persons, this experience is the experience we have of their skills (few though they might be) and which we tirelessly strive to improve on, usually with success, and often (contrary to all appearances) which we prefer to think of as misleading. This has been duly noted.

However, what if perchance—and who has not experienced this— our minds were no longer able to find a basis in experience? This could produce, as we all know, the famous "Your child is a vegetable", an illustration of what we would do well to refer to as the ontological vulnerability of the human being, since we are aware that, in the case of certain severe disabilities, our patients demonstrate very little evidence of skills that can serve as a point of reference in support of our evaluation of humanness.

Thus, if we consistently and consensually wish to affirm the dignity of the personhood of any severely disabled person, irrespective of the degree of this disability, our ethical choice must not only be unfounded but also unsupported: the absolute freedom of our ethical choice becomes an absolute necessity. We call this absolute necessity for the absolute freedom of an ethical choice a maximum ethical requirement.

Risk of ontological aplasia

By restricting ourselves at times to a dangerous evaluation of humanness, severe disability opens the way for the ontological vulnerability of the human being and the attendant risks.

Indeed, under such circumstances, ontological vulnerability that is specific to the general human condition, when it becomes extreme, is transformed into ontological precariousness, and even ontological withdrawal at times: a thing which can be withdrawn at any time is precarious; ontological withdrawal, which, following upon actual ontological transformation, can result in what we may refer to metaphorically as ontological aplasia.

In the case of severe, early childhood disability, an appeal for the ontological precariousness of human offspring is made at a very early stage, sometimes even extremely prematurely, as suggested by the virtual-object relation, in the form of the uterus (Missonnier, 2006). This extremely early appeal is centred around an extreme situation which can almost, in this case, be referred to as ontological. It is a situation where appeals are made to professionals and relatives, as indicated by the word extreme, "with the greatest of intensity", "excessively", "to the greatest extent possible" not only in an ethical capacity, but also in a relational and technical capacity; whereas the child places extreme ontological precariousness within his grasp in an extremely asymmetrical way.

The early establishment of such a situation runs the risk of ontological aplasia becoming a risk of ontological agenesis, where it would no longer be a matter of a deficiency but an ontological void.

Conclusion: conditions necessary for
application in extreme situations

Ontological aplasia, that is, the risk of an extreme situation in a clinical setting; a clinical setting for an encounter in an extremely asymmetrical situation, that is, a clinical setting where the encounter takes place within an asymmetry tending towards the removal of any trace of bipolarity, to the point of a borderline proposal in the form of an ontological withdrawal: "I alone possess the ability to think", which is a negation of any possible encounter.

The clinical setting of an extreme situation that, as such, is highly likely to be one of a missed encounter, a pseudo-encounter.

It is for this reason that a somewhat ontological, and not merely psychological, vigilance on our part is sought after as a necessary prerequisite to our psychological work. Vigilance with respect to bringing about an actual encounter, that is, experiencing the presence of a person other than myself, different yet similar; an actual encounter where the pronouncement of ontological withdrawal becomes a pronouncement of ontological substantiation: "I believe that he thinks, therefore he is", as a reflection of "he thinks that I am, therefore I am".

We must be vigilant, therefore, in creating the ethical conditions for an actual encounter; conditions making up an ethical position that, by establishing ontological intersubjectivity, will allow for clinical practice on the basis of an actual encounter in the case of severe disability. There are three of these conditions:

- giving up those privileges which directly contribute to creating actual asymmetry, thereby rendering a true encounter impossible. In our practice in extreme clinical situations, this means taking particular care to better adapt to the relational style and sensory, motor, and cognitive capacity of our patients;
- match our attention span to the other person, who, though different, is very similar; this means paying attention to the particular ontological otherness of the other person, and not merely to the "differences" in their language or behaviour. Radical otherness means seeing past all similarities and all differences;
- finally, developing our capacity for selflessness. In our practice, this means developing impartial attentiveness to the person in an

extreme situation, an attentiveness as unaffected as possible by concern for our professional image: there are no "undignified" jobs in a high-quality clinic, no more than our clinical practice in working with severe disability confers on us a special kind of dignity. Such attentiveness would also be as unaffected as possible by preoccupation with social and/or professional legitimacy, increasingly beset as we are by the weighty inefficacy of certain decrees issued from some quarters in relation to our actions.

Under such conditions, it will become possible to reduce the initial extreme asymmetry of clinics dealing with severe disability and the tendency towards dispelling bipolarity which they automatically create; a reduction establishing ontological intersubjectivity will make it possible to institute an actual intersubjective psychological dynamic.

Once the professionals have worked for themselves under such conditions, clinical practice in severe disability will become possible. Such practice can then, as demanded by the extreme situation, address not only psychological deficiency, but also the ontological deficiency aggravated by severe disability.

References

Antelme, R. (Ed.) (1947). *L'espèce humaine*. Paris: Gallimard, 1957.

Blanchot, M. (Ed.) (1969). *L'entretien infini*. Paris: Gallimard.

Dostoyevsky, F. (2012). *The Brothers Karamazov*. London: Penguin.

Missonnier, S. (2006). Nidification foetale, nidation parentale. In: J. Bergeret, G. Soulé, & B. Golse (Eds.), *Anthropologie du foetus* (pp. 83–98). Paris: Dunod.

Saulus, G. (1989). Approche philosophique et épistémologique du poly-handicap. In: *Les enfants, les adultes polyhandicapés qui sont-ils?* (pp. 21–34). Paris: APF, Bulletin des Etablissements médico-éducatifs, HS.

CHAPTER ELEVEN

Adolescence: psychic process or a mere stage in biology?

Denis Vaginay

W hat exactly are we talking about when we associate adolescence and mental deficiency?

Do we accept the idea of seeing anything other than the evocation of a given age, meaning a real orientation towards a subjectivity defined by an oedipal affect, or do we rather yield to the overtly well-meaning attitude that, having first recognised the difference, involves denying it without further ado, assimilating it within the norm, to the common and unique measure of things?

To answer this question, we first need to come to an agreement as to the meaning of the terms used and also on the social context in which we deploy them, a context that determines the adolescent's fate in our society.

A few definitions as markers

Puberty is easy enough to understand for a consensual definition of it to be accepted. It corresponds to a physiological phenomenon that makes the child able to procreate. It emerges suddenly and evolves rapidly.

Adolescence proves much more complex to discern, even though we have got into the habit of using this concept as being self-evidently tangible and universal. We shall define it as a set of psychic phenomena initiated or accelerated by puberty that enable a child to change status and acquire that of an adult by re-mobilising oedipal positions. It represents a period of change that is often disturbing due to the transformations undergone, especially bodily, but also through the lack of visibility as to the places, roles, and functions to be occupied. This passage is more or less facilitated by the surrounding group of adults. Its duration may coincide with that of puberty or, conversely, be pursued over many years.

In traditional societies, certain strictly encoded rites offer initiatory and accompanied routes that provide the markers needed to help young people make their way through this stage rapidly. Meanwhile, in our industrialised societies, the choice of possible pathways seems to be very much open, depending essentially on the young person's personal resources.

The adolescent phenomenon then appears as a form of cultural creation, to the extent that some, such as Huerre (2007), affirm, "No, adolescence does not exist, unless it be taken as a term defining our inability to get from the state of being a child to that of adult".

Adolescence would then be a sort of waiting stage, of cultural origin, during which the subject concerned occupies an intermediate status.

Here, we shall retain as triggering elements for the modern notion of adolescence the supervision of young people's sexuality in sixteenth century France, especially by the "internment of some of them in college boarding accommodation" (Muchembled, 2008) and, in parallel with this, adults' reluctance to accept seeing their offspring occupy a place equivalent to their own in sharing and practising such sexuality, or even their veto to their taking part in the festival of the flesh.

> Not only do adolescents now have very restricted access to pleasures of the flesh, but they may also feel considerable, serious anxiety as to their future in an active and moving world, or even doubt as to the validity of the tacit contract of substitution imposed at such a high cost by the fathers. (Muchembled, 2008, p. 53)

At the time when sidelining of youth in this manner was invented, the arguments put forward to justify doing so were more of an economic nature. Despite this argument, we may also note that this reserve felt by adults with regard to their juniors illustrates aggressive tendencies on their behalf, deriving from a reversed oedipal complex.

Aggressiveness dissimulated and a distancing strategy

Currently, direct arguments, so valued in an authoritarian patriarchal society, are no longer possible, especially as they would reveal the violence and the arbitrariness that are present in any educational act whenever that coercive dimension is denied or, at least, disowned.

Distancing of sexual practice is, thus, indirect and is dissimulated behind reasons of protection considered all the more useful in that children are increasingly being understood and treated as fragile beings that need above all to be protected against any danger or traumatism.

This no doubt explains why sexuality is described as dangerous for children: they must be wary of adults (including their parents) with perversion lurking everywhere. The notion of paedophilia,[1] so prevalent in the media, extends so far as to include among its victims adolescents, or even young adults. Meanwhile, the age of sexual majority, even though set at fifteen years in France, is completely disregarded (Schneider, 2007), even though it is clearly defined legally; it is the age from which a civil minor may engage in a sexual relation with an adult without that adult committing a criminal act, but it is also the age at which our society considers that a young person is capable of discerning what is good for them in sexual matters, without having to account to the adults in their entourage. The very idea of a sexual initiation (and, thus, a form of transmission) by an older partner, still fashionable just a few decades ago (Juliet, 1991), is considered to be obscene, harmful, and unacceptable.

Sexual practice is also dangerous, since it can pass on mortal diseases.[2] It imposes suspicion that is harboured against the partner in whom one is persuaded never to have trust, at least until tests have been conducted proving the absence of contamination, and to ensure systematic protection.

Pregnancy can only be disastrous for a young girl who, if she is healthy in body and in mind, cannot be thought to wish for such an outcome.

Maternity in the adolescent girl brings with it two orders of difficulties, almost always involving accidental pregnancy, not desired to start with, experienced in considerable isolation, with difficulty in communicating with friends and family. Pregnancy occurs for a physically and above all psychologically incomplete being, and may reveal relational problems, a much disturbed and highly conflictual family situation. The maturing process under way during adolescence—uncertainties, reworking of one's identity, bodily changes, search for one's femininity—risk becoming frozen. Plans for the future—the wish to study or train professionally—are suspended, or even postponed *sine die*. (Guettier, 2001, translated for this edition)

What is more, that young girl (with the age at which she is so considered steadily moving upwards[3]) is reckoned to be incapable of taking care of a child who can only be considered to have spoilt its mother's future.

I had my first child when I was 17 years old and it's hardly worth telling the black looks and the lack of respect you meet with. I just don't understand, whether you're a mother at 17 or 30, what's the difference in the end? As long as there is love between the couple and you have the means to look after the child? We're probably better able to change a nappy than some others. I could tell you about all the nastiness I got but that never stopped me getting on with my life and being proud to be pregnant: the proof is I've just had my second child at 19 and I'm now awaiting my third at 22. So please, have as much respect for those young girls and for 30-year old women! (Account published on the Doctissimo website)

Faced with an adolescent who has just revealed her pregnancy, a nurse or social worker at the upper or lower secondary school, just like a marriage counsellor in maternal and child welfare, often have, as a first reflex, to inform the juvenile court judge. As if that pregnancy could only reveal precariousness and a fraught situation, without stemming from a genuine desire, whether of an ambiguous, or even uncertain, nature. However, without overlooking individual situations that might well be dramatic, it might be that the increase in pregnancies among adolescents (or young women) could signify something other than distress. For example, let us remember that a young person can make a place for herself in society at an early stage, taking responsibilities and playing a part in its generational renewal. Yet again, behind what might be considered to be a certain naïve idea that the natural resort would be to entrust one's child to one's grandparents or a child minder, we could posit the notion that a child does not belong just to its mother or its parents, but to a whole community that should show signs of solidarity and responsibility for the child from the outset.

The following incident, as reported by the American weekly *Time*, gives an insight into the issue when it reported that Joseph Sullivan, the principal of Gloucester High School (Massachussets), had stated that seventeen schoolgirls had started pregnancies at the same time after having made a pact to do so and bring up their children together. All the girls concerned were less than sixteen years of age (*Le Parisien*, 20 June 2008).

The young fathers are set aside, out of the picture, as if they, too, as men, could not possibly wish to have a child.

Informed and shared consent is claimed to provide the basis for any sexual engagement, which denies the share of unconsciousness and ambivalence at play in any relation, especially when it seeks resolution in the sexual dimension.

Alongside this, infantile sexuality, while accepted in theory, is rejected as soon as it emerges, as perfectly illustrated when we talk about perversion for practices identified in five-year-old children, this being, to my mind, nosographic.[4]

However, during adolescence and young adulthood, a hygienist practice is recommended, or even fostered within the well-meaning proximity of the surrounding adults, in what increasingly appears to be a form of behavioural management. Its criteria resolutely direct it towards partial objects, as with over-valuation of visually stimulated pleasure, the explosive development of oral sex (Bezançon, 2008), and the banalisation of sodomy. Everything appears possible as long as the young people revolve around the genitalia while avoiding procreation.

It is as if the sexuality of adolescents (who are considered to be fragile) was only acceptable for adults when thought of as a game. This implies that they must practise it without responsibility (outside the domain of contamination that conjures up drama and mortality) and with no real issues at stake. A sort of playful sexuality—for a laugh.

The corollary of this is a de-erotisation of the bond with (or, at the very least, a sense of perplexity when confronted by) the body of the other. Maybe, too, this new orientation can be seen to be behind the sexual abstinence that ever more young people say they adhere to (12.7% of men of eighteen to twenty-four years of age and 18.5% of those of twenty-five to thirty-four state that they are sexually inactive) (Bajos & Bozon, 2008).

In parallel with this sort of watering down of their sexual practices, young people's social isolation is exacerbated by the way adults impose on them the logic of systematically being grouped together by (narrow) age bands that here, too, limits the effects of direct transmission and the process of initiation, much as the greater length of time devoted to studies keeps young people outside the system of production and the field of social responsibilities: "A classification by age range can still be surmised".

Adolescence, thus, corresponds to an age group that is suspended, as if put on hold by a society that seems not to need it and that, above all, remains wary of it and keeps it away from serious projects and commitments. "Adolescence, a modern (not to say capitalist) phenomenon, is the result of being ejected from society, the effect of exclusion from the city" (Mendel, 1971, translated for this edition).

This uncomfortable position adolescents find themselves in has started to be highlighted by researchers like Fize (2007) who have also denounced the negative stigmatisation to which young people were subjected: "Intimidation is a strategy commonly used against youth, as is well known. Many disturbing things are also said about adolescents" (p. 76). From this have emerged a host of studies, press and media reports, and various articles covering the sufferings of adolescence, anorexia, high risk or suicidal behaviour patterns, explosive revolts, or the increase in forms of violence. Adolescence became something frightening, a kind of space where independence was to be sought, as an egression from humanity, both for the children and for the adults.[5] When the evidence of a form of rejection became obvious and too flagrant, social discourse turned around and more and more studies started to be published demonstrating that, in their overwhelming majority, adolescents were contented with their lot and were living out their changes and transformation happy and satisfied.[6]

What, then, to think if the protagonists themselves find nothing to say as to the lot we assign to them? Finally, adolescents are doing just fine! Which amounts to an almost perfect crime. And the adults, innocence restored, their consciences salved, can continue to set aside those wishing to take their share, especially in sexuality.

Adolescence and cognitive deficiency

Not so long ago, nobody would have entertained the idea of talking about adolescence as a process in people with an intellectual disability. Indeed, few of them showed typical manifestations of such a process and they represented too small a contingent to bring into question the idea that the intellectually disabled were children and would remain so. This meant they were considered incapable of overcoming their condition of dependence (often of a quite dramatic nature) that could only find a viable outcome in a strong dual relation.

For adolescence to exist, there has to be, if not a resolution, at least an oedipal problematic, and, thus, a triangulated relation leading on to a subjectivation with strong indices of generational and sexual identity. The radical commitment of one of the parents for the cause of the disabled seemed to forbid such a development, crushing rather the parent–child dyad thus formed in an indistinct entity. The child might well grow, but he or she would nevertheless remain dependent on another person taking on a tutelary role who absolutely had to offer themselves as an anaclitic support, failing which collapse would be inevitable (often enough of both one and the other). While the bond was strong and essential, support remained fairly readily interchangeable in so far as it was barely differentiated and even less individualised. The presence and availability of the "tutor" counted more than his or her individuality as a subject. We can find a masterly illustration of this dependence on the other available, but not necessarily identified, in M. L. Eberschweiler's work (1981). Her son, so deeply attached to his father as to seem unable to do without him, reacted strongly to his death, regressing and suggesting that he would never recover. However, all he needed to do was find another available adult with whom he was to establish a relation similar to the previous one in order to resume the life he had led previously, without giving the impression of having suffered any great loss.

No doubt due to the combined effects of early education, removing guilt from the parents, and the real policy of social integration, the way in which people with cognitive disabilities evolve really does seem to have changed.

In particular, in all places catering for young people, you can see manifestations that ever more clearly evoke adolescent attitudes that we need to understand and analyse, as with the presence of aggression working itself out, a changing form of opposition, a trial and error experimentation in sexual relations.

It is worth noting that puberty and its effects of maturation generally appear in people with an intellectual disability at the same age as in the population as a whole. It is, thus, surprising to observe that hormonal upheavals, objectivable phenomena, have had such little effect on a number of generations. We can deduce from this long-lasting absence, appearing as a form of effacement, the quite considerable role that conditioning plays in the development of sexual behaviour, as also confirmation of the dual origin of the drive, which is both biological and psychic, the latter readily taking on greater significance than the former.

The role of the environment and resorting to rites of passage

Parental and social attitudes have changed towards adolescents with cognitive disabilities, who are in greater contact with other young people of their age, especially through integration at school or activities of all types. This friendlier and more familiar atmosphere is felt directly and stems from positive policy measures as enshrined in the legislation.

There are also many more discreet clues that seem to us to be highly significant of this change. We shall just mention one of them that belongs to the pseudo-rites of passage that our society regularly tries to produce, that of wearing a dental brace.

First, let us recall that rites of passage, which, as Van Gennep (1909) taught us, imply exclusion, waiting, and aggregation and which take place in an often dramatised staging, are intended to facilitate radical access to a new status, especially that of being an adult. While traditional societies are highly ritualised, our present day societies are less so, as, among other things, the statuses to be conquered are hard to identify clearly, are poorly defined, where they even exist in the immediate environment.

With the development of individualism, we could even imagine that each and everybody's path is deeply original, having to be invented at each and every turn, with minimal support being afforded by the group (in the form of general culture, for example). Now, the clearly growing interest our industrialised societies show for rites demonstrates a certain nostalgia for them. This is no doubt because they correspond to the only group responses that can provide a (partial) solution to the individual anxiety caused by change and as the violence they contain finally proves to be less than that which circulates freely in young people's minds.

Many researchers even seek to show that these rites still exist, hidden under the camouflage of modernised forms.

This is what Lardellier (2005) seeks to show by analysing many current practices that bring into play group identities, often in strongly symbolic moments (weddings, induction ceremonies, funerals, etc.). Now, this author appears to us rather to recall the obsessional tendencies, expressed in the form of frozen and repetitive rituals, of any secret group faced with the unknown, but also notes the current failure of such defensive attempts. Indeed, what he describes as a rite is merely an ersatz whose nature is revealed by a continuous renewal of occurrences and by the variability and even the personalisation of the forms used. The ceremonial embryos he writes about affirm, in our view, the failure of modern ritualisation faced with the shifts in life. Indeed, in parallel with these pathetic attempts, increasingly severe laws both frame and thwart the only residues of rites of passage that some forms of ragging or hazing, for example, may represent. Such rituals are seen as too laden with a content of violence and even sadism for them to be acceptable.

In a rite that was for a long time widely accepted, but that has now disappeared, we could mention the hazing surrounding call-up for military service in France. Such violence was evinced in the widely heard rumour that where losses (meaning quite explicitly the deaths of conscripts) were below 7%, the authorities were not to be held to account by anyone.

The price to be paid was in blood, even if that threat served in reality rather as a reminder of an archaic situation, sending a shiver down the spines of members of parliament who felt somehow aggrandised, sharing vicariously in a form of heroism.

Nowadays, we are happy to have rites, as long as they push symbolisation to the point of the whole thing being watered down out of all recognition. We are prepared to live alongside phantoms, as long as they are of the operatic variety.

But coming back to the idea of our rite, it is interesting here to decipher in the burgeoning development of orthodontics something other than a public health issue. Indeed, without bringing this form of therapeutic treatment's efficacy into question, it is curious to note that it is not in any accessible way backed up by explicit works that could demonstrate its prophylactic value, or even, much more simply, that would show its incidence in the population's health and well-being. The lability of the criteria it retains, especially the age of the children it targets for care, could even lead to the validity of its bases being brought into doubt, as with the absence of a long-term statistical evaluation.

There is also the fact that others roundly criticise it, at least in its generalisation, including osteopaths, who consider that it leads to more problems than it can resolve. Its adoption by a large number of patients could, thus, be due to other reasons than its effectiveness in health terms.

It might seem surprising to consider wearing a brace to be a rite of passage. However, historically, this practice concerns adolescents (it was even concomitant with puberty before more recently concerning younger children as they came to be regarded—and certainly not by accident—as pre-adolescents). Its real function is hard to discern. It is long-lastingly painful and even includes recognised risks of injury (headgear bows that release and can pierce the cheek or even damage the eye), suggesting a dose of sadism in those prescribing the treatment (protected by the scientific nature of their procedure and by health service coverage of their medical acts).

It confronts the subject with loss and symbolic castration as applied by his or her elders in the form of frequent tooth extraction, with the premolars and, later, the wisdom teeth. It lasts a clearly defined and quite considerable length of time (about eighteen months) during which the "followers" can recognise each other. It is also very much a part of growing up, with children often not so much asking whether they will have to wear a brace but at what age it will happen to them. It has an integrating effect, as so patently evinced in class photos of young Americans all smiling the same smile before the objective that will immortalise the uniformity. The strong aesthetic dimension is undeniable.

Here, we could risk positing a parallel with the practices of certain African ethnic groups (Gaye, et al., 1995) who file down their youngsters' incisors or who practise the avulsion of their canine teeth. Note that this "mutilation" is not compulsory, but young people who refuse it would have practically no chance of finding a partner as they would appear both cowardly and also ugly, or merely unattractive. Obviously, such practices horrify us and we consider them barbaric, so remote are they from our own mores. But is that really so very true? Are we, too, not seeking, finally, the same objective as these societies that thus define criteria for belonging and physical traits to facilitate seduction?

It is also noteworthy that this form of ritualisation makes no distinction between the sexes, since it applies to both girls and boys, while most rites of passage are strictly sexuated, precisely to help further differentiation. Similarly, as soon as this practice was confirmed in adolescents, it was "recovered" by adults, who are to be seen in ever growing numbers steeling up their smiles, as if, yet again, the idea of leaving the former alone to occupy the terrain (of seduction) could not be contemplated. There is, too, what can be construed as a fudging of the differences between the sexes and generations.

Now, returning to our initial purpose: some fifteen years ago, very little dental care was dispensed to people with an intellectual disability and, where it proved indispensable, one often had to resort to general anaesthesia to practise it. Nowadays, very many young people with an intellectual disability actually look forward to wearing a brace and then proudly display it with as much ease as other adolescents. To give an idea of the scale of the phenomenon, we observed that in a medico-educational institute in the Lyon region (no doubt representative of what happens elsewhere in France), more than half the seventy-five young people consulting (between twelve and twenty years of age) were orthodontic care patients and were provided with an appliance.[7] The notion of aesthetics, so evident for all of us, is not foreign to them and they play on their image, their way of presenting themselves to others in a relationship of seduction, accepting the constraints, the passing ugliness, and the pains that go with the process. They count on an aesthetic improvement as the result of the efforts they make and seek to get closer to a form of uniformity of their appearance with that of their peers.

As a corollary, what also appears fundamental here is the position society adopts in accepting, by rendering it banal, this integration by aesthetics, meaning, in all likelihood, that it better tolerates this confrontation with the facial deformation, this encounter with a disturbing otherness.

Adolescence as a means of access to a subjective position of the person with an intellectual disability

The most flagrant aspect of this undeniable trend is the subjective mobilisation of the young people involved who perform true psychic work whose roots, coherence, and effects can be readily distinguished and that all seem to mobilise, to a greater or lesser extent, elements deriving from oedipal issues.

Clearly, it would be appropriate to determine whether we are indeed in the presence of a process based on an appropriation, rather than a mere imitation that would be a more sophisticated mode of expression deriving from a structuring of a false self aiming, yet again, to match the desire of the tutelary other, on whom the person with an intellectual disability remains dependent.

For our approach to be evidence-based, we shall seek to establish our observations on young people who show major deficiency and who are, *a priori*, furthest away from a usual form of psychic development. The brief clinical vignettes that follow show that puberty does indeed provoke identity related disturbances, and behavioural changes as well as a psychic mobilisation in young people with an intellectual disability.

The pseudo-delirium as a means of liberation

Merick is seventeen years old and was born in Turkey, but his parents are fully integrated socially in France. He has always been seen to be a normal child whose development and relational capabilities were a source of pride to those close to him. His good learning abilities enabled him to achieve good reading skills to secondary school certificate level. He was also widely recognised for his kindness. Then, shortly after puberty, he suddenly suffered an emotional collapse when holidaying with his family in his country of birth. Adolescence then became hugely problematic. He literally abstained from any relationship, continually resorted to dialogue with imaginary interlocutors and, above all, became aggressive when people tried to coach him out of his withdrawal, especially towards his mother, who became unable to ask anything of him without the risk of being struck by him. Here we were faced with something bordering on the pathological, with a form of behaviour that recalls common "pubertal madness", faced with the phantasmatic return of a "primordial mother–baby incest bringing forth the Archaic" (Richard,

2005, translated for this edition). The stay in Turkey, during which Merick lived in a free and easy manner, spending time outside with young people of his own age, eating, like the others, when he felt the need, sleeping, too, when he wanted, must surely have worked as a detonator by revealing, on his return to France, how far he had become subject to constraints and conventions that he had not managed to fully accept and that, therefore, he had to sustain artificially. His state of delirium can then be interpreted as an attempt to break free from a dangerous bond, dominated by the risk of incest. The game, with its multiple doubles, was used to seek protection from a persecutory reality while holding it at a distance. Mild neuroleptic treatment (that was well tolerated) allowed for a partial return to reality that, in turn, facilitated therapeutic work during which it became possible to address with Merick the reality of his situation and the issues that seemed to imprison him. Normal speech was recovered, corresponding to a new stance adopted in relations, being more respectful of the identity of each of the protagonists. Merick can now start to look to his future, independently of his family, and describe a relation with a young girl, imagined for the time being, but not imaginary.

Overcoming a delusional position

Françoise is twenty-one years old. For some time now, she has shown psychotic tendencies that hide behind highly affected attitudes and strong anxiety. Despite this, through respecting ritualised approaches, she has shown an ability to adapt and can work regularly. She is highly dependent on her parents and can do little without asking for their advice. One day, she developed a strange relation with a female special education teacher accompanied by ambivalent feelings towards her, being extremely protective at times, applying charm, even to the extent of bodily contact, and at other times being almost sadistic. Following a relational problem between them (although this was not the deciding factor), this special education teacher resigned. Françoise wants her back, worried at the idea that her complaints in her direction could have undermined her. She would like to invite her home, that is, to her parents', even though the lady in question adopted the position of a rival to them. She contributes elements that help identify the existence of an ambivalent relationship towards her, where love and hatred, envy and anger intertwine. Through having explored the foundations of this relation, after an interview where her contradictory and changing feelings found expression, she finished by asking herself how she could have been angry with her mother (without being destroyed in return). In parallel with the emergence of this questioning and investigation of the varied (less and less threatening) feelings accompanying it, the psychotic manifestations became milder.

Rivalry and love

Jules is seventeen years of age. He enthuses about devising and putting on scenarios where, after a tough fight, a father figure is beaten and destroyed (always against an appropriate background, with psychodrama and time of expression). The victor (himself) obtains the favours of the beauty (a princess, the man's wife). In these stories, the first part, that of the battles, is more consistent, while the second seems a little contrived, added on perhaps by conformity. During a game in playing out a psychodrama, Jules proposes to kill the father (who works at night, occupied in what more precisely recalls trading in sex rather than a conventional job). Playing out his role, he goes through with the murder, knifing his victim. During discussion, the game organiser comments to him that he did not strike the blow just anywhere. Right, he answers, in the genitals; I love it! Following which, confrontations emerge in real life, always with figures of authority, with the idea of taking their place once having reached adulthood. He even projects himself into a future professional activity, developing perceptions of ever more precise and faithfully drawn positions of responsibility. His behaviour improves, the insults in which he was such a specialist become considerably less frequent, and he begins an intimate relationship with a young girl of his own age. At least that's how the two of them portray things.

Rivalry, aggression, and identification

Joëlle is seventeen, is extremely inhibited, and hardly expresses herself verbally at all. She has a tendency to cling to some female special education teachers, manifesting towards them a form of declared homosexual love. She maintains a very strong relation, tinged with aggression, with her mother.

She noticed that one teacher, her favourite, loves tortoises as she has a tattoo of one on her ankle. She even brings a live one in to the medico-educational institute to raise it there.

One day, Joëlle steals a bunch of keys from her (representing both a work tool and a sign of power and responsibility) attached to a key ring with an effigy of the animal on it. It proves impossible to find them again. One day, having been chastised by this teacher after she had been especially unpleasant towards one of her female classmates, she quietly places the live tortoise on its back at the bottom of a bucket, leading to its certain death. Undeniably, this behaviour results from a complex strategy that required real anticipation. The teacher was clearly targeted, on a radically aggressive mode, through her "totemic" animal.

To confirm her ambivalent relation, she regularly sends her teacher short messages (she gets her mother to write some of them, who in turn takes advantage to stage her own ambivalence) where the themes involve loving kisses, an assassin, and a prince. Love and death combine in fairly unsophisticated scenarios that, nevertheless, begin to reach a greater level of organisation.

The work of mourning

The process of subjectivation that is perceptible in the vignettes described above is confirmed by the attitude of the subjects in relation to death and by the emergence of a real work of mourning in the event of loss of a loved one that is no longer a tearing away. No more situations resembling that of Meb are to be seen.

Marie has always had a tendency to make things up, with a preference for erotic themes, having attained adulthood. This even goes as far as putting care professionals in difficulty when she accuses them of having predatory attitudes. She has a very strong relationship with her father, tinged with an incestuous dimension, at least on her side. After her father suddenly died, over the following year she was overwhelmed by the image she retained of him, crying out the sense of loss she felt. She also discovered her own mortality and expressed fear of her own death. Gradually, she managed to remember the man for what he was, asking herself questions as to the reality of his personality, especially in revealing the not so bright side to his nature, with his fits of anger and a certain intolerance, for example. She abandoned her erotic fables and invested "wisely" in the romantic relationship her best friend was pursuing with a man, imagining that she would be able to experience something similar later on.

Dynamics in play

In all of these situations (that appear somewhat child-like due to the mental deficiency involved) we may discover attempts, albeit some of them tragic, to be released from the two-way deadly relationship. In this dynamic, the imprint of a third party becomes fairly clearly apparent. Thanks to their presence, aggressiveness develops, beyond hatred, to allow for detachment, the first stage on the path to subjectivation.

The object of love that emerges under the aegis of a triangulated relation seems still preferentially feminine in both sexes, underlining maternal prevalence. This also seems to be corroborated by the frequent hesitations in the choice of objects of love in young people of the same age of either sex, indicating the (momentary?) persistence of infantile bisexuality and maintaining the mother in a status of the inaccessible adult. But we would appear to be in the presence of a particular stage rather than an insurmountable condition, as would seem to be suggested by the evolution of some of the slightly older subjects who achieve some stability in their choice of object and who develop love affairs (with the affirmation of clearly identified projects and desires capable of embracing parenthood). The same applies to an even greater extent (although this is hardly so surprising) in how young people with lesser deficiencies develop.

Social resistance

What is striking is that this psychic work of young people with an intellectual disability, concomitant with the social declaration that recognises their right to a sex life, becomes possible right at the time when all adolescents are being confined to a play-orientated practice of their sexuality.

It is almost as if, socially, we had accepted the idea of welcoming them in just at the time we found we could keep them out by camouflaging such a rejection beneath that (already largely disguised) applied to modern adolescents. It remains possible that the provisions made in favour of their prolonged and systematic schooling reinforce that association, just as they are set aside from systems where they may assume responsibilities.

In social terms, the intellectually challenged would then quit their eternal state of childhood to join in with that (hardly more enviable) status of eternal adolescents: the status of the person who, being irresponsible and fragile, cannot be taken seriously. The risk involved is not a slight one and the professionals keep it alive when they persist in considering such people to be eternal victims, or when they put themselves forward, as expiatory and complacent victims, in the role of necessary but clumsy torturers. In both cases, this comes down to reinforcing the invisible barrier that separates us from them and restricting their ability to identify, like us, with sexuated and adult models.

Conclusion

We can identify an ever more frequent and clear identity-orientated dynamic in adolescents with an intellectual disability, suggesting a real process of subjectivation sustained by psychic work whose progress is readily observable.

If aggressiveness prevails to the detriment of sexual identification, we can surmise that the latter will prove accessible once detachment has become sufficient. But then, for this to happen, non-deficient people must not be shocked by this change and be prepared for it to continue.

Notes

1. "The social consensus around paedophilia expresses the projection on a few criminals of a massive trend for contemporary sexuality to regress towards infantile forms (autoerotic, fixed on partial zones and impulses, centred on preservation of the ego)" (Schneider, 2007, pp. 57–58, translated for this edition).
2. It should be recalled that interest in disabled people's sexuality came after a period of ten or so years during which fear prevailed that they may be a major vector in contamination of the general population by the AIDS virus. AIDS has also been a recurring topic in schools with a view to prevention.
3. The average age at which mothers have their first child in France is now thirty. Admittedly, this higher age corresponds to the greater control women have over their own bodies, together with a cultural shift opening out new perspectives for greater independence and opportunities for further eduction.
4. Take the example of three five-year-old boys thrown out of school two or three years ago by an education chief when they were found

in the toilets playing out sexual games with a young girl of their own age.

5.   See the impressive number of works devoted to adolescent malaise, addictions, risk behaviour, violence, etc. For example, Lazar, 2002.

6.   "*Au secours, mon ado va bien!* They are 16 or 17 years old, don't drink alcohol, don't slam doors, don't secretly smoke joints . . . Is it serious, doctor?" (Legrand, 2007).

"Des ados heureux de vivre" (Mallaval, 2008). The article cites a study by Ipsos and Inserm, conducted on behalf of the Wyeth Foundation in March 2008 and taken up by all the French press, concluding that "finally, when you combine all the indicators, that all amounts to 5% of adolescents who feel bad".

7.   Personal contribution, established thanks to the institution's nurse.

References

Bajos, N., & Bozon, M. (Ed.) (2008). *Enquête sur la sexualité en France: Pratiques, Genre et Santé*. Paris: Editions La Découverte.

Bezançon, R. (Ed.) (2008). *Le premier jour du reste de ta vie* (film tous publics). Issy les Moulineaux: StudioCanal.

Eberschweiler, M. L. (Ed.) (1981). *Meb, le peintre joyeux. Histoire d'un trisomique 21*. Paris: Editions Nouvelle Cité.

Fize, M. (Ed.) (2002). *The Black Book of Youth*. Paris: Editions Petite Renaissance, 2007.

Gaye, F., Kane, A. W., Ndoye Diop, A., & Mbaye, M. (1995). Esthétique bucco-dentaire en milieu traditionnel au Sénégal. *Odonto-stomatologie Tropicale—revue dentaire internationale panafricaine* (www.sante tropicale.com/), *69*: 19–22.

Guettier, B. (2001). Grossesse, maternité : circuit court ou court-circuit ? *La lettre de l'enfance et de l'adolescence, 3*(45): 67–71.

Huerre, P. (2007). Condamnés à l'adolescence? In: A. Braconnier (Ed.), *L'adolescence aujourd'hui* (pp. 37–41). Toulouse: Erès

Juliet, C. (Ed.) (1991). *L'année de l'éveil*. Paris: P.O.L. éditeur.

Lardellier, P. (Ed.) (2005). *Les nouveaux rites: du mariage gay aux Oscars*. Paris: Editions Belin.

Lazar, J. (2002). *La violence des jeunes; Comment fabrique-t-on des délinquants?* Paris: Ed. Flammarion.

Legrand, Ch. (2007). Au secours, mon ado va bien! *La Croix*, 14 February, 2007.

Mallaval, C. (2008). Des ados heureux de vivre. *Libération*, 21 May, 2008.

Mendel, G. (Ed.) (1971). *Pour décoloniser l'enfant: sociopsychanalyse de l'autorité*. Paris: Editions Payot.

Muchembled, R. (Ed.) (2008). *Orgasm and the West: A History of Pleasure from the 16th Century to the Present*. Cambridge: Polity Press.

Richard, F. (Ed.) (2005). *Les troubles psychiques à l'adolescence*. Paris: Editions Dunod.

Schneider, M. (Ed.) (2007). *La confusion des sexes*. Paris: Flammarion.

Van Gennep, A. (Ed.) (1909). *Les rites de passage. Etudes systématiques des rites*. Paris: Picard, 1981.

INDEX